WHOSE UNIVERSITY IS IT, ANYWAY?

*W*HOSE UNIVERSITY IS IT, ANYWAY?

POWER AND PRIVILEGE ON GENDERED TERRAIN

EDITED BY

ANNE WAGNER, SANDRA ACKER
& KIMINE MAYUZUMI

SUMACH
PRESS

WOMEN'S ISSUES PUBLISHING PROGRAM

SERIES EDITOR BETH MCAULEY

LIBRARY AND ARCHIVES CANADA CATALOGUING IN PUBLICATION

Whose university is it, anyway?: Power and privilege on gendered
terrain / edited by Anne Wagner, Sandra Acker, Kimine Mayuzumi.

Includes bibliographical references.
ISBN 978-1-894549-75-2

1. Sex discrimination in higher education–Canada. 2. Women–
Education (Higher)–Canada. 3. Women in higher education–Canada.
4. Minority women in higher education–Canada. 5. Discrimination in
higher education–Canada. I. Wagner, Anne, 1966– II. Acker, Sandra
III. Mayuzumi, Kimine

LC1766.W54 2008   378'.00820971   C2008-904321-9

Edited by Beth McAuley
Designed by Liz Martin

*Sumach Press acknowledges the support of the Canada Council
for the Arts and the Ontario Arts Council for our publishing program.
We acknowledge the financial support of the Government of Canada through
the Book Publishing Industry Development Program (BPIDP)
for our publishing activities.*

ONTARIO ARTS COUNCIL
CONSEIL DES ARTS DE L'ONTARIO

Printed and bound in Canada

Published by

SUMACH PRESS
1415 Bathurst Street #202
Toronto ON Canada
M5R 3H8

sumachpress@on.aibn.com
www.sumachpress.com

CONTENTS

PART IV: FINDING SOURCES OF STRENGTH

ACKNOWLEDGEMENTS

This project would not have been possible without the efforts of all the contributors, who remind us by example that many dedicated and courageous people are working for equity and social justice within and beyond academia. Anne would like to express her gratitude to her family for their ongoing encouragement. Sandra notes her appreciation to Dorie, Paul and Chris in Toronto and her sisters Betty and Debi. Kimine wishes to thank her partner Riyad who has supported her throughout this project. In addition, we highlight the importance of the Department of Sociology and Equity Studies in Education at the Ontario Institute for Studies in Education, University of Toronto, where the idea for this collection originated. Finally, we acknowledge the splendid team at Sumach Press and especially Beth McAuley, who generously shared her expertise throughout the development of this book.

INTRODUCTION

Anne Wagner, Sandra Acker

& Kimine Mayuzumi

OVER THE PAST FEW DECADES, THE CANADIAN ACADEMY HAS BECOME AN increasingly contested site, as marginalized populations have challenged the myth of the ivory tower being a haven of meritocracy and equal opportunities. Despite resistance at each stage of challenge, there have also been gains in both practice and scholarship. Students, and to a lesser extent faculty, have become increasingly diverse. At the same time, and perhaps paradoxically, a range of biases has been identified. The academy has been charged with being androcentric and Eurocentric and with discriminating overtly or covertly against those who do not meet the white, male, middle-class, heterosexual and able-bodied norms which have been taken for granted throughout much of its history. Yet the means of achieving greater equity and diversity in the university are far from clear. Blackmore (1997) points out that equity discourses have actually lost ground in higher education in competition with discourses promoting efficiency and excellence.

The contributors to this book engage with these competing discourses from various positions within the academy and often from its margins. Gender takes its place in the foreground as a result of the editors' shared feminist commitment, but we have explicitly sought to acknowledge connections to other social dimensions, thereby avoiding the trap of homogenizing women's experiences and sometimes equating them with those from the mainstream. Hence, each contributor agreed to locate gender as a central organizing theme, while simultaneously working to integrate various additional aspects of identity. This commitment to an intersectional approach, which examines multiple dimensions, thereby highlighting the complexity of identity, is a guiding focus of our work. As the Editors of the journal *Politics and Gender* indicate,

> [V]iewing gender as a stand-alone factor necessarily distorts reality. Gender never really operates independently from other aspects of political life, and so it is misleading to think of gender as an autonomous category of analysis. Instead, gender differences must always be understood within a particular context and in connection with other aspects of identity, both individual and collective. ("Intersectionality": 229)

We now offer a brief review of previous work on (mostly) gender in the Canadian academy, in order to position our book in a context of tradition as well as transition.

GENDER IN THE CANADIAN ACADEMY, THEN AND NOW

We could date interest and concern about gender and the academy from many starting points. The "modern" phase, however, could be said to have originated with 1960s second wave feminism, gaining momentum in the following decades. A key event in Canada was the *Report of the Royal Commission on the Status of Women*, issued in 1970 and republished several times afterwards. The commission was an outcome of intense lobbying by women's groups, including some in universities, and its publication was followed by a sharp increase in numbers of women's organizations and feminist activism (Canada's Rights Movement, 2007; Morris, 2008). The *Report* had a major chapter on education, including sections on women's access and representation in universities. Indeed, access was a serious issue, judging from the statistics provided: in 1966–1967, women earned just over a third of bachelor's degrees, about 20 percent of master's degrees and about 8 percent of doctorates (Royal Commission, 1977/orig. 1970: 169). By the late 1970s, employment equity also became prominent in discussions of Canadian public policy, at the same time that affirmative action was being debated in the United States (Bakan & Kobayashi, 2000).

Not surprisingly in this historical context, feminist education scholars, who were often sociologists, began to problematize and theorize educational sites, occasionally including universities. In the 1970s, Dorothy Smith (1974; 1978) wrote of the monopolization of knowledge creation by men and the exclusion of the standpoint of women, ideas further developed in Smith (1987). From a different perspective, Margrit Eichler (1979) also considered knowledge questions in her analysis of concepts of sex and gender. *But Can You Type? Canadian Universities and the Status of Women,* by Jill Vickers with June Adam, was published in 1977, focusing on opportunity structures for women students and academics. In 1987, Jane Gaskell and Arlene McLaren edited *Women and Education: A Canadian Perspective,* "the first book-length overview of Canadian scholarship on women and education" (5), which contained a few chapters on higher education. Two years later, Gaskell and McLaren were joined by Myra Novogrodsky (1989) in the authorship of a slim but useful volume on women and education that included a chapter on post-secondary education. Issues discussed were typical of the times: equal opportunities and representation, curriculum, sexual harassment, feminist scholarship and employment questions.

The late 1980s and early 1990s also brought book-length critiques of the treatment of women in universities by Anne Dagg (1988), Magda Lewis (1993) and Paula Caplan (1993). Caplan's book, *Lifting a Ton of Feathers,* contained advice for aspiring academics. Summing up the spirit of much of what was appearing at the time, Lewis wrote: "I know by my own experience that for feminist intellectual workers — whether they be students or teachers — the academy is, for the most part, an uncomfortable and unwelcoming home" (52). Concern over curriculum and pedagogy continued, marked by a special issue of the *Canadian Journal of Education* on feminist pedagogy edited by Linda Briskin and Rebecca Coulter (1992) and containing a number of notable articles.

Two key Canadian publications of the 1990s were *Unsettling Relations: The University as a Site of Feminist Struggles,* by Himani Bannerji, Linda Carty, Kari Dehli, Susan Heald and Kate McKenna (1991), and *Breaking Anonymity: The Chilly Climate for Women Faculty,* edited by The Chilly Collective (1995). For Bannerji et al., universities were "sites for the reproduction of power and privilege" (5). Using language not yet familiar to most readers of the day, they argued that "white middle-class, heterosexual feminists who are in 'comfortable' academic positions need to deconstruct the comfort and the power available to them" (8) — in other words (as in our subtitle) to confront their own privilege.

Breaking Anonymity brought together documents related to the "chilly climate" (Prentice, 2000) from several institutions but mainly at the

University of Western Ontario in the late 1980s. The introduction of the 1986 *Employment Equity Act* (later strengthened in 1996), which was federal legislation, gave added prominence to equity issues across Canada in the late 1980s and 1990s (Bakan & Kobayashi, 2000) and activism in the academy around the status of women or the chilly climate became the focus of much feminist writing.

In this period, and continuing for the next decade or so, individual universities often produced reports on the status of women or on climate issues, many of which would not readily reach the reading public. *Breaking Anonymity* was notable not just for collecting together such documents but, like Bannerji et al. several years earlier, for making an effort to tackle issues of diversity among women by adding chapters dealing with racism and homophobia and the experiences of an Aboriginal woman in the academy.

By the late 1990s, "power" and "privilege" were increasingly understood as aspects of the university and it was becoming increasingly commonplace to challenge the previously dominant and taken-for-granted constructions of women, students and faculty as being white. Edited collections such as *Dangerous Territories: Struggles for Difference and Equality in Education* (Roman & Eyre, 1997) and *The Illusion of Inclusion: Women in Post-secondary Education* (Stalker & Prentice, 1998) emphasized heterogeneity among women, and questions of diversity, gender, resistance and backlash featured prominently in this feminist literature. In fact, the diversity of women's higher education experiences in Canada, especially as faculty members, could be pieced together by reading individual narratives that spanned the 1990s. Himani Bannerji (1991) wrote of being a South Asian woman teaching race relations through her body-as-lesson, Vera Chouinard (1995/96) of her battles with the university for accommodation as she became increasingly disabled, Homa Hoodfar (1992) of the challenges of being a visible minority teacher with a critical perspective and Roxana Ng (1993) of resistance in the classroom and lack of support from administration.

As we come to the 2000s, women have achieved a level of prominence in higher education compared with the days of the Royal Commission. In 2003–2004, women made up 58 percent of full-time undergraduates, 48.7 percent of full-time graduate students and 31.7 percent of full-time faculty (Drakich & Stewart, 2007). Drakich and Stewart bemoan the paucity of available statistics that would allow going beyond simple gender categories. Despite apparent improvement, authors continue to document tensions and contestations within the academy. Personal narratives are featured in several collections, including *Women in the Canadian Academic Tundra: Challenging the Chill* (Hannah, Paul & Vethamany-Globus, 2002), *York Stories* (York Stories Collective, 2000) and *The Madwoman in the Academy* (Keahey & Schnitzer, 2003). Detailed personal accounts of diversely situated academic women were offered by scholars such as Vijay Agnew (2003) and Helen Lenskyj (2005). Highlighting specifically the realities of racially minoritized women academics, *Seen but not Heard: Aboriginal Women and Women of Colour in the Academy*, edited by Rashmi Luther, Elizabeth Whitmore and Beatrice Moreau (2003), is an outstanding collection grounded in an anti-racist feminist approach (see also Elabor-Idemudia, 2001; Samuel & Wane, 2005). Njoki Nathani Wane, Katerina Deliovsky and Erica Lawson's 2002 book *Back to the Drawing Board: African-Canadian Feminisms* also marked an important contribution to feminist theorizing. Critiquing mainstream feminist theorizing of the past, the editors asserted the need to articulate a "multiplicative Black feminist standpoint" (13), including various chapters which addressed how such theorizing may be meaningfully integrated into academia. This work was furthered in 2007 with the publication of *Theorizing Empowerment: Canadian Perspectives on Black Feminist Thought,* edited by Notisha Massaquoi and Njoki Nathani Wane. This diverse collection focused on the significance of developing Canadian Black feminist thought and how such theorizing may usefully inform scholarship within sites of higher education as well as beyond. The current decade also brings concerns about globalization, corporatization and the environment into the mix, and with it relevant books such as *Inside Corporate U: Women in the Academy Speak Out,* edited by Merilee Reimer (2004) and *Teaching as Activism: Equity Meets Environmentalism,* edited by Peggy Tripp and Linda Muzzin (2005).

Although only a select sample of several decades of sources on women in the Canadian academy has been reviewed here, several trends are evident. Particular themes such as access, feminist pedagogy, sexual harassment, globalization or environmentalism have come (and sometimes gone) over the decades. Individual experience has been prominent as a means by which to convey the complexity of identity and experience.

Although over time, writers have generally become more sensitive to the need to integrate gender with other dimensions of identity, progress has been uneven. Even recent scholarship has not always fully acknowledged the heterogeneity of gender categories and has used language like "women and minorities," which can serve to suggest that women are necessarily white, thus reinscribing the dominant biases. We also note that not all elements of identity have been equally probed — for example, disability is still missing from most collections; sexuality is sometimes seen, sometimes obscured; white ethnic variation and Jewish issues are muted; gender often translates to women alone; age is barely mentioned — while the emphasis has been on faculty, and to a lesser extent students, with administrative staff or other university workers mostly invisible. Still, we can conclude that the Canadian academy has been powerfully and persistently contested from a number of perspectives. Following the path of these trailblazers, we also seek to generate debate and discussion.

WHY THIS BOOK NOW?

This book developed out of a collective interest in issues related to women, higher education and social justice. Initially undertaken as a panel presentation at the 2006 Congress of the Social Sciences and Humanities conference, this project quickly took on a life of its own and was transformed into the book you are now reading. The journey began when four of the contributors (Kimine Mayuzumi, Tina Martimianakis, Patrice White and Anne Wagner) were inspired by Sandra Acker's class on women and higher education at the Ontario Institute for Studies in Education, University of Toronto, and decided to use our theorizing for that class as a basis for the conference presentation. Engaging with the topic from divergent points of entry and sharing a commitment to social justice, we sought to challenge conventional dominant conceptualizations of the category "women" and to delve into some of the realities for women navigating academic terrain that are less frequently brought to the fore.

The conference further energized us as we considered the ways in which each other's perspectives could usefully inform our own. Sandra's comments as discussant highlighted common themes, tensions and challenges embedded in the set of papers. Further, the audience's obvious engagement with the issues provided further incentive to continue this work. Shortly thereafter, the idea of the three of us collaborating on a book blossomed.

When recruiting additional contributors, the potential enormity of the scope of the subject became apparent and we were faced with many challenging decisions about how to maintain our commitments to gender and inclusivity, yet realistically limit the number of chapters. It was readily apparent that to engage fully with the range of potential topics, we would need to publish not a single tome but a series of books. Consequently, the decision was made to focus on the Canadian academy and choose a selection of authors who would focus on gender while seeking to challenge conventional conceptualizations of gendered experiences in the ivory tower.

This commitment to ensuring a diversity of perspectives is evident not only in the social locations that each of the contributors has chosen as their entry point into their analysis but also through our decision to employ a three-dimensional matrix to theorize the issues.

First, our gaze has been filtered through the perspectives of diversely situated subjects within the academic community: students, teaching assistants (TAs), administrative staff, contingent faculty, tenured/tenure-track faculty and administrators. Each of these groups of stakeholders is critical to the functioning of the ivory tower and their perspectives are integral to the ongoing transformation and integration of social justice in sites of higher education. Although we acknowledge that further differences exist within these groups (for example, students may be pursuing undergraduate, professional or doctoral degrees and be enrolled in various disciplines and programs) and that some categories remain unrepresented, we have greater coverage than most similar books have managed. This approach has also enabled us to more fully to explore the dynamics of power and privilege that pervade the ivory tower (as well as the ivory basement — see Eveline, 2004). We have highlighted some of the perspectives of those within the academic enterprise who, although indispensable to its existence, are often overlooked (Acker & Webber, 2006).

Second, while maintaining gender as a central theme, we have sought to include a wide range of demographic/identity categories (based on gender, race, ethnicity, class, sexuality, disability, Aboriginality, experiences of violence/trauma, commitment to spirituality) into the topics covered and in the process to feature a diverse group of contributors. Again, we could not "cover" the entire spectrum of potential identity markers, but we believe we have achieved a measure of success in balancing intersectionality and gender.

Third, we chose to include two different but complementary methodological approaches: theorized experiences and empirical qualitative studies. The first approach consists of narrative pieces that have a personal meaning to the authors and explicate their experiences in the enterprise of higher education; the second refers to reports of research on a variety of relevant topics. Such different forms of writings complement each other and together enhance our understanding of the contemporary Canadian academy from an equity perspective.

Two more points are relevant as we explain the genesis of this project. One is the "OISE connection." Historically, the Ontario Institute for Studies in Education has been fertile ground for feminist scholarship, going back to the 1970s where we began our review of related writings. The Centre for Women's Studies in Education co-ordinated some of these efforts, many of which were by scholars in the Department of Sociology in Education (where Dorothy Smith, Margrit Eichler and Mary O'Brien were pioneer feminist faculty members, later joined by Roxana Ng, Kari Dehli, Sandra Acker, Helen Lenskyj, Sherene Razack, Njoki Wane and others) and the Department of History and Philosophy (Ruth Pierson, Alison Prentice). All three of the editors are members of the successor to Sociology in Education, now (significantly) renamed the Department of Sociology and Equity Studies in Education (SESE). Almost all of the contributors are faculty, staff, current students or graduates of either SESE or another OISE department. The one exception is Wayne Martino, who happened to be examining a thesis at OISE when we thought of asking for his contribution! Whatever the shortcomings and exclusions of the academy, OISE and University of Toronto included, due tribute must be given to the intellectually exciting atmosphere that has made so much excellent equity and social justice work possible.

The other point still to be made concerns the book's title. Our original choice was "The Academy as a Contested Site," later "The Contested Academy" and eventually the current title, *Whose University Is It, Anyway?* For the subtitle, we turned to the "notion of power as a dynamic relation, which is negotiated continuously in interactional settings" (Ng, 2003: 208), which puts the emphasis on the struggle for identity and agency within the academy. From the accumulated literature of the past we borrowed the idea of a gendered (and dangerous) territory, or terrain, while adding to it broader questions of (who has) privilege and power.

At this historical juncture in which there is an ongoing impact of globalization and neo-liberalism, the issues discussed in the chapters are likely to be relevant to other parts of the world although the collection happens to be on the *Canadian* academy. The bottom line is that equity is embedded in hope for justice regardless of location. These chapters initiate (or in another sense continue) a dialogue about the current constraints and systemic barriers faced by gendered subjects in academia and are offered in the spirit of challenging current hegemonic structures and practices.

OVERVIEW OF CHAPTERS

The collection begins with an exploration of the ways in which diverse groups of women are represented and understood as belonging within institutions of higher education. We open with Cyndy Baskin's inspiring critical analysis of the ways in which Aboriginal perspectives may be meaningfully integrated into the curriculum and used as tools of decolonization and healing. While acknowledging the ongoing marginalization of Indigenous systems of thought, she simultaneously offers hope that shifts are possible. Continuing the theme of contesting curriculum, policy and representation, Tina Martimianakis's chapter explores the ways in which "equity" and "diversity" discourses are embodied in policy, using the University of Toronto as a case study. Through a post-structuralist lens, she argues that "equity" and "diversity" practices are interpreted alongside a discourse of "excellence" and "accountability," thus diffusing the collective challenge to the system. Hence, she questions the extent to which equity has been truly realized through the increased presence of women and those from other designated groups. Susan Ferguson and Tanya Titchkosky complete the section, writing from the perspective of scholars who embody a marginalized identity in the academy. Drawing on similar themes of the negation of diversity and devaluation of difference, they interrogate the ways in which disability is conceptualized as a void within masculinized and colonial systems of knowing.

The second section explores some of the challenges inherent in navigating the ivory tower for those who do not easily fit with mainstream dominant conceptualizations of the normative group. Writing from the perspective of an educator and graduate student, Patrice White offers a glimpse into how she has been "chilled" by attention that fixates on difference and seeks to thrust her onto the "hot seat," representing the perspective of *all* Black women. Reflecting on her position as being doubly minoritized, she explores "the personal and academic tensions of a system that rewards and credits my lived experiences" while simultaneously seeking to constrain her intellectual curiosity by circumscribing the topics that she is expected to address. In the following chapter, Anne Wagner takes up a similar theme of constraint, exploring the perspectives of women students who have encountered violence in their lives. Acknowledging the diversity of women's embodied experiences, this chapter interrogates the extent to which women's lived realities are acknowledged within sites of higher education and specifically within feminist classrooms. Next, Donna Murray presents a thoughtful reflection of her personal journey as a woman who was kept unaware of her Aboriginal heritage and how this struggle to define her cultural identity came to figure prominently in her undergraduate and graduate studies. Completing this section is Wayne Martino's provocative reflection on his experiences as someone who is read as "both non-Canadian and queer." Problematizing the significance of how he is perceived by students, he interrogates the ways in which heterosexism leads him to carefully manage the presentation of the various facets of his identity in ways which those in more privileged positions may never need to consider.

In the third section, we turn our attention to those people within academic institutions whose contributions are less often the focus when considering the academic project. Ann Kristine Pearson pulls back the proverbial curtain to offer a glimpse of the reality of those whose work is often rendered invisible — administrative support staff. Challenging simplistic notions of these feminized professionals as interchangeable cogs in the giant machine, she questions the ways in which these skilled workers have been cast into the shadows of their feminist sisters who climbed the academic career ladder. In the following chapter, Michelle Webber explores the realities of teaching assistants (TAs). Occupying a fraught position between students and faculty, TAs must navigate often unsteady terrain, especially as they seek to introduce feminist theorizing to students without evoking insurmountable resistance. Continuing with the theme of invisibility, Linda Muzzin and Jacqueline Limoges explore the situation of contingent faculty. Reporting on a national research project of faculty and academic administrators across various professional fields, here focusing on nursing, the authors discover that pervasive structural gendered inequities perpetuate the marginalization of women in traditionally feminized disciplines. Reflecting on claims that the use of contingent faculty was a short-term solution, the authors wonder whether we are instead witnessing a strategy of ongoing oppression of women. In the next chapter, Sandra Acker offers a compelling reflection on her experiences as a departmental chair, revealing some of the tensions associated with a woman moving into a supposed position of power. By bringing into focus the emotional component of the chair's role, the chapter questions how these dynamics can negatively affect women who aspire to leadership roles and ironically perpetuate the status quo of white male domination in sites of higher education.

Shifting our focus to yet another aspect of academic experience that has received relatively scant attention, the authors in the final section contemplate strategies that enable them to survive, or in some instances thrive, in academe. Kimine Mayuzumi and Riyad Shahjahan begin by exploring the way in which a group of racially minoritized women faculty evoke their spirituality as a means of coping with the often chilly climate of academia, suggesting that spirituality may provide both a means of sustaining one's spirit and an act of resistance. Significantly, they posit the value of such individual actions as an integral step towards transformative change of the dominant social order. In the following chapter, Njoki Wane provides a visceral account of the spirit injury experienced by faculty who do not fit the dominant white male middle-class standards enshrined in academia. Drawing on her experiences as a faculty member in an education department, she describes the emotional and intellectual costs of attempting to unsettle dominant ways of thinking among teacher candidates. Throughout the chapter, she challenges us to grapple with our own complicity in reinforcing the status quo, starkly delineating the ways in which we may invisibly support oppressive practices. The section concludes with Si Transken's provocative, challenging and thoroughly engaging story of attempting to achieve "the impossible" within academia. Using poetry and critical reflection, she conveys both the challenges and the rewards of academic life.

Taken together, these chapters convey the tensions, contradictions and possibilities that circulate in sites of higher education. We hope you enjoy this glimpse behind the scenes, designed to draw these women and men out of the shadows, so that we can more fully begin to explore their contributions to the project of education.

REFERENCES

Acker, S., & Webber, M. (2006). Women working in academe: Approach with care. In C. Skelton, B. Francis, & L. Smulyan (Eds.), *Handbook of gender and education* (483–496). London: Sage.

Agnew, V. (2003). *Where I come from.* Waterloo, ON: Wilfrid Laurier University Press.

Bakan, A.B., & Kobayashi, A. (2000). Employment equity policy in Canada: An interprovincial comparison. Retrieved 10 April 2008 from www.swc-cfc.gc.ca/pubs/pubspr/0662281608/index_e.html.

Bannerji, H. (1991). Re: turning the gaze. *Resources for Feminist Research 20*(3/4), 5–11.

Bannerji, H., Carty, L., Dehli, K., Heald, S., & McKenna, K. (1991). *Unsettling relations: The university as a site of feminist struggles.* Toronto: Women's Press.

Blackmore, J. (1997). Disciplining feminism: A look at gender-equity struggles in Australian higher education. In L. Roman & L. Eyre (Eds.), *Dangerous territories: Struggles for difference and equality in education* (75–96). New York: Routledge.

Canada's Rights Movement: A History. (2007). *The Royal Commission on the Status of Women.* Retrieved 25 April 2008 from www.historyofrights.com/events/rcsw.html.

Caplan, P. (1993). *Lifting a ton of feathers: A woman's guide for surviving in the academic world.* Toronto: University of Toronto Press.

Chilly Collective (Ed.). (1995). *Breaking anonymity: The chilly climate for women faculty.* Waterloo, ON: Wilfrid Laurier University Press.

Chouinard, V. (1995/96). Like Alice through the looking glass: Accommodation in academia. *Resources for Feminist Research 24*(3/4), 3–11.

Dagg, A. (1988). *MisEducation: Women and Canadian universities.* Toronto: Ontario Institute for Studies in Education Press.

Drakich, J., & Stewart, P. (2007, February). Forty years later, how are university women doing? *Academic Matters.* Ontario Confederation of University Faculty

Associations. Retrieved 25 April 2008 from www.ocufa.on.ca/Academic_Matters_February2007/forty_years_later.pdf.

Eichler, M. (1989). *The double standard: A feminist critique of feminist social sciences.* New York: St. Martin's Press.

Elabor-Idemudia, P. (2001). Equity issues in the academy: An Afro-Canadian woman's perspective. *Journal of Negro Education, 70*(3), 192–203.

Eveline, J. (2004). *Ivory basement leadership.* Crawley: University of Western Australia Press.

Gaskell, J., McLaren, A., & Novogrodsky, M. (1989). *Claiming an education: Feminism and Canadian schools.* Toronto: Garamond.

Gaskell, J., & McLaren, A. (Eds.). (1987). *Women and education: A Canadian perspective.* Calgary: Detselig Enterprises.

Hannah, E., Paul, L.J., & Vethamany-Globus, S. (Eds.). (2002). *Women in the Canadian academic tundra: Challenging the chill.* Montreal: McGill-Queen's University Press.

Hoodfar, H. (1992). Feminist anthropology and critical pedagogy: The anthropology of classrooms' excluded voices. *Canadian Journal of Education, 17*(3), 303–320.

"Intersectionality." (2007). *Politics and Gender, 3*(2), 229–232.

Keahey, D., & Schnitzer, D. (Eds.) (2003). *The madwoman in the academy: 43 women boldly take on the ivory tower.* Calgary: University of Calgary Press.

Lenskyj, H.J. (2005). *A lot to learn: Girls, women and education in the twentieth century.* Toronto: Women's Press.

Lewis, M. (1993). *Without a word: Teaching beyond women's silence.* New York: Routledge.

Luther, R., Whitmore, E., & Moreau, B. (Eds.). (2003). *Seen but not heard: Aboriginal women and women of colour in the academy* (2nd ed.). Ottawa: Canadian Research Institute for the Advancement of Women.

Massaquoi, N., & Wane, N.N. (Eds.) (2007). *Theorizing empowerment: Canadian perspectives on black feminist thought.* Toronto: Inanna Publications and Education.

Morris, C. (2008). Royal Commission on the Status of Women in Canada. *The Canadian Encyclopedia.* Historica Foundation of Canada. Retrieved 25 April 2008 from www.thecanadianencyclopedia.can/index.cfm?PgNm=TCE&Params=A1ARTA0007674.

Ng, R. (1993). "A woman out of control": Deconstructing sexism and racism in the university. *Canadian Journal of Education, 18*(3), 189–205.

Ng, R. (2003). Toward an integrative approach to equity in education. In P.P. Trifonas (Ed.), *Pedagogies of difference: Rethinking education for social change* (206–219). New York: RoutledgeFalmer.

Prentice, S. (2000). The conceptual politics of chilly climate controversies. *Gender and Education, 12*(2), 195–207.

Reimer, M. (Ed.). (2004). *Inside corporate U: Women in the academy speak out.* Toronto: Sumach Press.

Roman, L., & Eyre, L. (Eds.). (1997). *Dangerous territories: Struggles for difference and equality in education.* New York: Routledge.

Royal Commission on the Status of Women (1977/orig.1970). *Report.* Ottawa: Minister of Supply and Services Canada. Retrieved 25 April 2008 from www.acsw-cccf.nb.ca/english/documents/Status_of_women_PDF.pdf.

Samuel, E., & Wane, N.N. (2005). Women of colour in academe: Complexities and challenges. *Journal of Negro Education, 74*(1), 76–88.

Smith, D.E. (1987). *The everyday world as problematic.* Boston: Northeastern University Press.

Smith, D.E. (1978). A peculiar eclipsing: Women's exclusion from man's culture. *Women's Studies International Quarterly, 1*, 281–295.

Smith, D.E. (1974). Women's perspective as a radical critique of sociology. *Sociological Inquiry, 44*(1), 7–13.

Stalker, J., & Prentice, S. (Eds.). (1998). *The illusion of inclusion: Women in post-secondary education.* Halifax, NS: Fernwood.

Tripp, P., & Muzzin, L. (Eds.). (2005). *Teaching as activism: Equity meets environmentalism.* Montreal: McGill-Queen's University Press.

Vickers, J., with Adam, J. (1977). *But can you type? Canadian universities and the status of women.* Toronto: Clarke, Irwin.

Wane, N.N., Deliovsky, K., & Lawson, E. (Eds.) (2002). *Back to the drawing board: African-Canadian feminisms.* Toronto: Sumach Press.

York Stories Collective (Ed.). (2000). *York stories: Women in higher education.* Toronto: TSAR Publications.

PART I

CONTESTING CURRICULUM, POLICY AND REPRESENTATION

CHAPTER 1

"I DON'T KNOW WHAT HURTS MORE — TO SHUT UP OR SPEAK UP":

ABORIGINAL FEMALE LEARNERS IN THE ACADEMY

Cyndy Baskin

THIS CHAPTER, FILLED WITH STORIES OF EMOTION, IS BASED ON A research project conducted with twenty-seven Aboriginal women who were attending schools of social work throughout Ontario during the time of the study in 2003–2004. The women who participated ranged in age from twenty-one to fifty-six, came from the Ojibway, Cree, Mohawk, Oneida, Seneca and Kwawutl Nations, worked for their communities, were daughters, aunties and mothers, and a few were even grandmothers. The research was conducted through an anti-colonial framework (Laenui, 2000; Sunseri, 2000; Wilson, 2004), implementing an Aboriginal research methodology — storytelling circles — which followed the cultural protocols and ethics of the women who participated (Baskin, 1997; Lanigan, 1998; Fitznor, 2002).

I, too, am an Aboriginal woman — Mi'kmaq Nation — schooled in social work and now a social work instructor in the academy. I decided for several reasons to conduct a research project with Aboriginal women who were studying social work — first, to determine whether or not their education was as painful as my own had been. Second, I wanted to highlight the fact that social work tends to be a profession dominated by women and that the service users are usually women as well. Third, I intended to examine the changing nature of social work, long a tool used to colonize Aboriginal women, and yet today appearing to be a profession we have taken up in the process of decolonization.

Although several themes emerged out of the data from this research project, I have chosen to focus on those that I believe best reflect how gender and race come together for Aboriginal women in higher education. These themes relate to the reform of social work education, which can be encouraged through the inclusion of Aboriginal world views, an awareness of the history of colonization and the instigation of a process of decolonization that includes healing.

The title of this chapter incorporates a quotation from one of the women who participated in this project. Her name is Billie Allan (she has, of course, given permission to be named here) — a beautiful Anishnawbekwe inside and out, the mother of two daughters, who at the time of her involvement in this research was in a Master of Social Work Program (she has since graduated and has begun a PhD). Her statement reflects both the struggles and the strengths of being an Aboriginal woman studying the profession of social work within the academy. This chapter is dedicated to Billie.

BUNDLE ONE: INCLUSION OF ABORIGINAL WORLD VIEWS

The issue addressed within this section of the research was how to balance competing world views in social work education (Hart, 2002; Hurtle, 2002; Baskin, 2005). Every student who participated in this project was adamant that Aboriginal world views ought to be a component throughout the curriculum for both Aboriginal and non-Aboriginal students. Aside from those who were in programs designed for Aboriginal social work students, all of the women enrolled were critical of the way in which Aboriginal perspectives and Aboriginal ways of helping were marginalized in their social work courses. At best, they described educators who spent one class out of an entire year on content related to Aboriginal peoples. Any discussion on the content was described as general, without any gender analysis, and readings typically consisted of only one article. In addition to this type of dismissal of an Aboriginal perspective, several students referred to hearing not only generalizations about Aboriginal peoples in their classes but also stereotypes, particularly about women. Students' reaction to this type of racism was anger, although they often did not feel they "had a voice to speak out against some of these comments" (all quotations come from the participants).

Educators were implicated as seriously lacking any knowledge about Aboriginal world views and history. Many students stated that they could not trust their professors to accurately present any material in these areas, and that they could only rely on themselves to find the appropriate material and make their own interpretations. These Aboriginal students were all in agreement that their social work education had fallen short in teaching them relevant content and in incorporating their ways of knowing and seeing the world into the work of helping others. For the most part, this neglect angered and disappointed them, but because of their disempowerment in both the classroom and the academy and because of their social status as Aboriginal women, they kept this disquiet to themselves.

The majority of the students who participated in the research circles insisted that both Aboriginal and non-Aboriginal students should learn something about Aboriginal perceptions of the world within their formal education. Of course, the reasons cited for the value of such learning for each population of students — Aboriginal and non-Aboriginal — were different. These students believed it was important for Aboriginal peoples' world views to be represented in their social work education because they wanted to feel like they belonged in the academy and that their ways of helping were respected and valued as useful tools. They also believed that they had much to teach other students and their educators. If this inclusion existed in the academy, then Aboriginal students would be more likely to view their formal education as relevant to the work they are doing or will be doing in their communities. These women are asking for acknowledgement. They want their world views, which currently exist on the margins in social work education, to be brought into the centre, alongside the dominant Eurocentric ones.

The position that some students take on this topic is interesting, because they suggest that formal education could become a vehicle for passing on knowledge of Aboriginal world perceptions to Aboriginal students who may be unsure what those world views are. One student, who is currently enrolled in a social work program specifically for Aboriginal students, explained that, despite the fact that she grew up in a First

Nations community, she did not learn about the world view prevalent there. According to her, Aboriginal world views "definitely should be taught in university or college, because I learned so much just from going into the program and I'm still learning." This statement speaks to the issue of colonization, which will be explored later on, as well as to the possibility of what formal education could be for Aboriginal women.

Another student talked about attending a college that had a high percentage of Aboriginal youth in attendance. At this school, she took a Native Studies course that was taught by a white teacher. Although this student stated that the course was a struggle for her in many ways, it also provided a doorway for her to seek out her own learning. As she explained it, "The teacher was Scottish and he knew a lot about his own origins ... he had a strong background in his own cultural teachings. This kind of helped with the learning process, [plus] we were left to do a lot of research on our own ... [which] sparked the interest to want to look into more of my own identity."

This anecdote may say a great deal about how non-Aboriginal educators can best take up the teachings of Aboriginal world views. In some cases, non-Aboriginal professors may be wary of raising this subject in their classrooms, not only because of their ignorance of the topic but also because of a lack of comfort with the material. Others appropriate Aboriginal cultural ways, thinking that they are actually being inclusive, though such an action is offensive to Aboriginal students. It can be argued that those educators who possess their own identities, who know who they are, who have their own cultural understandings and who are not threatened by the limits of their knowledge are the ones who can be most helpful to Aboriginal students. They can do so by expressing their sense of identity and establishing a dialogue about the similarities and differences of each culture on a platform of equality with their Aboriginal students. Such instructors may be the ones with the capacity to encourage Aboriginal students to explore and learn more about their world views and relevant helping practices.

Several students also discussed the topic of Aboriginal instructors within formal education more generally. Several students who had or have Aboriginal instructors pointed out how their mere presence encouraged them to stay in university. For example, one student said, "Being taught with Native instructors opened up my way of thinking because I can relate to their stories," and another said, "I got so much out of having Native instructors because they were role models."

All of the women participants believed that non-Aboriginal students need to learn about Aboriginal world views in their social work education. They spent more time on this topic than on why they saw it as being important for Aboriginal students. Why did they, as one student put it, "so badly want to educate potential social workers on Aboriginal world views"? Students saw this education as important because they know that when non-Aboriginal students become social workers, many will inevitably work with Aboriginal peoples. All of the women agreed with this student's explanation:

> It is important to have [our world views] integrated into the curriculum because sooner or later they're [non-Aboriginal social workers] gonna be in a situation where they're gonna be helping Native people. If that awareness and that understanding [aren't] there, then a lot of things could be misunderstood as far as family and child rearing [goes].

Certainly history has taught us what can happen when the profession of social work "misunderstands" the child-rearing practices of Aboriginal families and communities (Graveline, 1998; Hart, 2002; Bellefeuille & Ricks, 2003).

Another student emphasized that it was important for all social work students to have some understanding of Aboriginal world views because "we have a lot of Native people all over the place, not just on reserves. [They're] in big cities and they would like to know where they come from, who they are, and what it means to have that world view." This student is correct, for, indeed, today at least half of the Aboriginal population in Canada lives in urban centres (INAC, 2005; Statistics Canada, 2005). If non-Aboriginal social workers have an understanding of Aboriginal world views, they will know why identity is so crucial to Aboriginal peoples, regardless of where they live. The emphasis here is on passing on knowledge to non-Aboriginal peoples to help them better serve the Aboriginal peoples they may work with. What is meaningful, then, for the Aboriginal women students is an emphasis on the greater good — on what will benefit *all* Aboriginal peoples.

A few women raised the point of learning about Aboriginal world views for the purpose of promoting healing for both Aboriginal and non-Aboriginal students. One woman addressed this notion of healing by saying,

> Incorporating Aboriginal world views is important to re-establish and repair relationships, to understand the interconnectedness and how this world [needs to operate in order to] respect cultural beliefs and values. Besides understanding the impact and the effects of colonization, they're also learning [about] our own history and way of life before contact, so it's learning from each other.

If one believes that all the peoples of the world have a great deal to offer one another and that life is a reciprocal process, then the point this woman raises is significant in all areas of education.

Another major issue that emerged from the theme of inclusion was what should be included in curricula, along with who should teach it and how. Many of the students interviewed cited specific course work as a major method of bringing Aboriginal world views into social work education. A common suggestion was a course on this topic that all students would be required to take. This mandatory course would then be followed up and built into all other courses. Several students also spent time discussing reading materials and curriculum development, and emphasized that Aboriginal students "have to have our own writers writing books and curriculum" and, since social work is primarily a woman's profession, the writers of course materials need to be Aboriginal women. They were candid in their belief that since non-Aboriginal peoples come to the work with a "totally different perspective," they cannot write in ways that will be respectfully representative of Aboriginal values and teachings. It may be, then, as cited earlier by one of the research participants, that a non-Aboriginal instructor's pedagogy can be conducive to Aboriginal world views, but this does not mean that he/she can develop curriculum that reflects such world views accurately.

These students also saw elders, clan mothers and grandmothers from Aboriginal communities as having a significant role in curriculum development. One idea was to have the people who are most likely to come into contact with social workers (especially women, as they tend to be the caregivers) assist with curriculum development. The reasoning behind these choices was simple: a curriculum that was grounded in the teachings of elders and based on the needs and preferences of service recipients would build better working relationships between non-Aboriginal social workers and the Aboriginal peoples they will serve. As one student expressed it, such a curriculum would teach social work students to "have a better understanding and to be more sensitive to our issues [while helping] some of our people to be a little more trusting when it comes to working with these [non-Aboriginal] social workers." These ideas show that the student participants were speaking not only about curriculum content but also about issues of pedagogy.

BUNDLE TWO: AWARENESS OF THE HISTORY OF COLONIZATION

This section deals with another significant theme that emerged from the data — the omission and denial of history in social work education, both in terms of pre-contact and colonization (Churchill, 1993; Bruyere, 1998; Shilling, 2002). A particularly relevant example of colonization is the *Indian Act* of 1850, which created the reserve system, devised artificial legal categories of Aboriginal peoples and disenfranchised thousands of women and their children by stripping them of their legal status if they married non-Aboriginal men. This Act, which continues to control every Aboriginal person's life today, is rarely studied in social work curricula.

When I raised the topic of the history of colonization with the participants, they began their responses with stories of colonization within their social work education. As one woman stated, "[So many] wrongs have been done to us and they're continuing today. It's not something that happened five hundred years ago. It's still going on today, just in a different way [in education]." Another added, "Silence is violence and that's what's been going on for generations by our oppression of being excluded and hidden. Not being acknowledged for being oppressed throughout all these hundreds of years continues the abuse of our people."

The majority of participants echoed this notion of omission, and referred to pre-contact times in doing so. As one student said, "The history of our people is very important because there was a country, there were nations, communities, values, government and everything else before the colonizers settled [here]." This statement reflects the earlier discussion of Aboriginal world views — these perceptions existed before colonization and not only have they survived colonization but they are also being lived by thousands of Aboriginal peoples today. However, within education, Aboriginal peoples are presented almost as if they did not exist until they were "discovered" by European peoples.

Participants believed that Aboriginal world views were not being acknowledged as legitimate ways of helping within social work education. As one woman stated, "It is time to change the preconceived notions of white ways being the right ways." In keeping with this view, another student described one of her experiences in a classroom:

> In my mandatory social work practice course, my placement was with an Aboriginal organization. Yet this was never talked about unless I brought it up. And, when I did, the instructor blew me off. One time, I spoke about the problems the mothers at my placement had with C.A.S. [Children's Aid Society] and this instructor said, "Oh yeah, I forgot that happened. Let's move on to something else now."

Other students raised points about miseducation that relate to who teaches Aboriginal content and how this is relevant to the political project of decolonization. Miseducation means that when history is taught in the academy, it is not taught accurately. One student talked about non-Aboriginal students' ignorance, which usually goes unchallenged by instructors. She described how some students in class make comments such as "why should those Native people be getting four billion dollars, free education, free housing and that no taxes stuff" without receiving any responses from educators. In these situations, silence affirms what has been said. Thus, some social work educators are not taking responsibility for the damage that social work has caused, such as its involvement in racist child welfare legislation and practices and its silence at times regarding miseducation when it comes to issues that affect Aboriginal peoples. This lack of responsibility is ironic, since the profession is supposed to help change the systems that oppress people. In reality, perhaps, dominant social institutions such as the education system serve as tools that maintain oppression. One participant had a particularly insightful remark regarding why there is so much denial and omission about colonization in Canada. She said, "Colonization is about them [white people] and they need to educate themselves. Yet that's the most difficult thing to look at right — who you are?" This student is talking about the idea of "white guilt" — something that often happens when white people begin to learn about the history of colonization and its ongoing ramifications. Facing their privilege, which they have received via their ancestors' near-destruction of entire civilizations, is not a comfortable journey, so for many, it feels better to not look at this at all. However, the problem with this avoidance is that there is no way to get to a better place — a place that is right for all — without directly facing the emotions that are an inevitable piece of this journey.

The participants pointed out that education about colonization is crucial for all social work students if they are to understand the marginalization of Aboriginal peoples. As one woman commented, "A lot of times people are blamed for things like their behaviour. Look at alcohol [use] for instance — [someone is] drinking too much, but why are they drinking?"

One participant spoke at length about how learning about colonization changed how she views herself. She said:

> I used to live my life according to Western notions of how I should behave as a woman. It wasn't until I looked at the history of colonization that I began to understand how my traditional roles and responsibilities as [an Aboriginal] woman were dismantled, prohibited and not valued. I recognized that that's where a lot of my low self-esteem came from. I believe that having this awareness could empower our women to start to recognize that it [colonization] was not something we wanted. It's not like we consented to it. I think that [this awareness] makes a big difference on a person's psyche.

Consciousness-raising has had a significant influence on this student's view of herself, and she sees how beneficial such a process can be for all Aboriginal women. This learning process, whereby Aboriginal peoples come to understand that Eurocentric ways were forced upon us, combats the effects of internalized oppression. It is the first step in the healing journey, for it is a freeing experience to realize that one's circumstances are caused by forces outside of the self, rather than by personal deficits.

All of the issues raised by the participants are connected, not only to why social problems exist and where they come from but also to who defines them as problems and how they are defined as such. Hence, some people may say the social problems for Aboriginal peoples today are substance abuse, violence and suicide. Others, including myself, would say that these problems are only symptoms and a means of coping with much larger forces (Hart, 2002; Aboriginal Healing and Wellness Strategy, 2003; Aboriginal Healing Foundation, 2003). These larger forces are sexism, racism, poverty and exploitation, which are the result of colonization in Aboriginal communities. The abuse of alcohol and drugs, for example, is a defence against these forces and, although many die from such abuses, others survive for a time because of them. When such individuals come to consciousness — when they gain an awareness of the history of colonization and start living by Aboriginal world views — they put these substances down.

Along with incorporating Aboriginal world views as a part of the education of social work students, the women in this project supported making the history of colonization mandatory. None had any qualms about mandatory course content, for, as one of the students neatly put it, "we have to learn theirs [history, language, etc.] in school, so therefore they should have to learn ours ... [but] not [about] the feathers and the Pocahontas princess. They need to know the real thing about colonization and assimilation practices."

Another student added that "there needs to be mandatory history courses covering colonization in Canada that include the roles of social workers in this process," because the profession of social work played a part in the colonization of Aboriginal peoples, and students going into the field may not know this. This incorporation ought to be an easy matter, given that the origins and history of social work are taught within the first year of these programs. Of course, like everything else that is being examined in this chapter, schools of social work must be willing to move away from denial and face the Eurocentrism within their curricula.

Sometimes the walls that exist between Aboriginal students and non-Aboriginal educators are broken down. As one student related:

> In my course on anti-oppression, I was a bit uncomfortable [with the lack of Aboriginal content], so I spoke to the instructor about this privately suggesting a good book with sections on the "White Paper" and residential schools. [This didn't go over well] and it was a bad year until we confronted the issue and fortunately, in the end, we became allies. After, she confided to me her uncomfortable feelings with teaching [Aboriginal content] because of colonization ... It's important to talk about colonization. It's healthy [to talk about it].

This student's statement provides an excellent example of what can occur between educators and Aboriginal students when the reality of colonization is ignored. When an individual student takes this omission up with a professor, it may create backlash for the student. Fear of backlash suggests that it may not be safe for individual students to take up these concerns with professors. Rather, these concerns need to be addressed collectively by students, particularly at administrative and policy levels. This student's example also shows how relationships between professors and Aboriginal students can be more beneficial when professors are willing to take the risk of revealing that they do not have knowledge about Aboriginal content or they are uncomfortable with topics related to colonization.

Many women in this research project emphasized how bringing members of the Aboriginal community into the academy is a tangible way of breaking down walls of ignorance and assumptions, while demonstrating alternative teaching practices. As one student explained:

> I read the section in our social work textbook on Aboriginal [peoples]. It was dry and repetitive. Then he [our instructor] presented [an Aboriginal woman teacher] to our class. Maybe that's exactly what needs to be done — participants that identify with the Aboriginal culture showing or teaching [other] people and leading the way. There's nothing that I thought was worthwhile other than when [the Aboriginal teacher] did her presentation because it came from somebody who identifies with the culture, who knows what the problems are and gives accurate information, honest information, saying the positive and the negative.

Pedagogy, then, is clearly an issue that needs attention. Another student took up this topic by adding:

> Aboriginal people don't learn by copying overheads. We learn by the way people speak. In the class [taught by an Aboriginal female educator], I didn't write. My notebook has one or two words in it. Yet I learned so much. I came away with more than anything I've ever come away with in my two previous years [of social work education] before that.

A third student went on to say:

> I'd like to hear from women who have that experience [of residential schools, for example] ... I want to know about the effect for real, not just hearing another story from another page in a book. There are families and stories that we bring to class. We bring our content, our knowledge, our history.

These students are speaking to both content and pedagogy. They are suggesting that their history and their issues be represented in the classroom by Aboriginal women themselves. They want to read articles and books by Aboriginal authors. They want Aboriginal individuals from the community coming into the classroom to speak on issues of concern to Aboriginal peoples.

BUNDLE THREE: DECOLONIZATION

All of the women who participated in this research project believe that a process of decolonization has begun. Because of this attitude, their responses were positive, encouraging and helpful. For these participants, the first steps of decolonization must take place within social work education, Aboriginal communities and amongst both Aboriginal and non-Aboriginal peoples. Some students also mentioned that decolonization includes healing. As one student put it:

> [We] use our voices in unison and say what we need to say. [We] say what we want for ourselves and stand up for our rights. That's currently happening right now ... Everybody here in this [circle] and a lot of our communities are working towards that [decolonization]. The numbers are growing. A lot of people are feeling stronger and [are] healing.

The confidence from which these students make a stand may be more spiritual than anything else. As one woman stated:

> [We have] prophecies that come from way back and talk about seven generations [into the future. Today] I hear talk about how we are in [the time of] the Seventh Fire. This is the time where things are going to start changing.

Since colonialism encompasses our total existence, decolonization must include a holistic framework of mind, body, emotion and spirit. Decolonization means taking back control of our personal lives in these four areas. This process involves learning about our true history, languages, identities and cultures. It is about freeing ourselves from the physical manifestations of living under colonial masters for several centuries, such as alcohol and drug addictions, family violence and poverty. It is about putting what we learn into action. We also need to free ourselves from feelings of fear, depression, hopelessness and inadequacy, which are the emotions that keep us immobile and trapped. We need to tap into the power of rage — even though women are discouraged from doing so — and use it as the emotional motivator that pushes us towards change. We also must heal our spirits through processes of reclaiming and reconnecting to the sacred places, ceremonies and medicines that are specific to women. We need to concentrate on our inner worlds, while at the same time connect to those who have gone before us and who are all around us, offering their guidance and assistance, if only we could quiet ourselves enough to hear them.

Making decolonization successful is about connecting via our minds, bodies, emotions and spirits with other Aboriginal peoples. Especially for women, the process of connecting to one another around our commonalities, both our lived experiences of oppression and our world views, helps us to realize that we are not alone, that many others share our feelings and struggles and that there is comfort and strength in numbers. It is only with others that decolonization will occur in a meaningful and realistic way.

"Decolonizing involves all people and includes issues around class, race and gender," declared one of the participants. Indeed, decolonization is not a process that only affects Aboriginal peoples. Everyone is affected by the impact of colonization in Canada, including the descendants of the settler population and those who immigrate here today. White people are affected because they have been robbed of the opportunity to have what could have been — an environment founded upon Aboriginal values and world views, which have much to offer all of humanity. Racially minoritized peoples — both those who are born in Canada and those who immigrate here — are affected because the way in which they are treated here by the dominant population is similar to the way Aboriginal peoples were treated when Europeans first arrived. In this part of the world, colonization was perfected on Aboriginal peoples. Racially minoritized peoples born in Canada are also affected because they do not have the opportunity to learn how much they have in common with Aboriginal peoples in terms of both Indigenous knowledge and experience of oppression. As a result of the systemic nature of colonization, opportunities to form meaningful relationships and alliances between these groups are not realized. Participants articulated how, through being a part of the research project, they were engaging in a process of decolonization within social work education. As one woman emphasized,

> Decolonization is what we're doing right here, right now, by coming together in this university, sitting in our circle with our medicines, and talking about our educational experiences and what we want to change in these spaces. It's about being together and for the first time being able to speak honestly, with emotion, about what has and continues to happen in our education.

I am especially struck by the descriptor "with emotion" in this response. There has been little room for emotion in educational spaces at any level, which contradicts the holistic approach inherent in Aboriginal world views. An Aboriginal approach to teaching and learning is naturally an emotional experience. In addition, the harm caused to Aboriginal students through education has created a great deal of emotion, including sadness, disappointment and anger. I am not referring to the horrors of residential schools here, but rather to the exclusionary nature of Eurocentric education. I advocate that decolonization must not overlook students' needs and desires to have relatively safe spaces where they can express and let go of the emotions that they have been forced to suppress in classrooms for so long. Having such spaces available is in line with earlier statements about how decolonization not only brings Aboriginal world views into the curriculum but also promotes healing for students.

Most students agreed that teachings on decolonization ought to be infused throughout social work curricula from the first year to the final year of the program. As one student aptly put it, "This kind of education and awareness needs to happen all year round." A second student stated that "there should be core courses offered from first year, so that students start with a good understanding of Aboriginal issues and what they must do in their practice." A third student emphasized that these courses ought to be "mandatory for non-Native social work students." Given what has already been reported on internalized oppression, lack of access to their own teachings on ways of seeing the world and other impacts of colonization, I would assert that these courses need to be mandatory for Aboriginal students as well.

As noted earlier, students were consistent about who ought to teach these courses and how they need to be taught. One student emphatically stated:

> These classes should be taught by Aboriginal leaders and elders in the traditional way. They should be taught by role models [who are] Aboriginal social work educators and PhD students who support Aboriginal [undergraduate] social work students, who speak honestly about colonization and its impacts, who bring Aboriginal teaching methods into the classrooms and who conduct their research according to Aboriginal research methodologies.

Some of the women participants believed that decolonization within social work education was already occurring. One student acknowledged, for example, that an Aboriginal traditional teacher "had recently come into our class and she implemented the medicine wheel, which is more expressive of an Aboriginal world view." Another student stated: "In my program, they use our grandfathers as the social work code of ethics, which are wisdom, love, respect, bravery, honesty, humility and truth."

CONCLUSION

The participants were particularly affected, as was I, by Billie's statement, "I don't know what hurts more — to shut up or speak up." The concern about whether to speak up or not is based on fear, and it is certainly justified. However, fear must not deter us in our work of educating both students and educators in the academy. It does mean, though, that we must be strategic in how we go about this work so that we are not isolated, ostracized or otherwise punished for our words and actions. In addition, as much as it hurts sometimes to speak up, I have no doubt that Aboriginal students have little choice but to do so. We who have the privilege of being in the academy must speak out whenever we can. We are not in the academy only for ourselves. We are here on behalf of our communities.

The stories of these women provide a clear message of hope for the future, which is vital in resistance work. Yet the wounds are deep, they go right to the spirit, the memories of past atrocities are fresh in our memories, and colonization continues. Until colonization practices end, true healing cannot occur. Achieving widespread awareness of colonization is the crucial work of today. What I appreciate about the Aboriginal female learners who took part in this research is that they are up to the challenges of the work that must be done. They are today's warriors.

REFERENCES

Aboriginal Healing and Wellness Strategy. (2003). About AHWS. Retrieved 23 June 2007 from www.ahwsontario.ca/about/familyhealing.html.

Aboriginal Healing Foundation. (2003). *Aboriginal people, resilience and the residential school legacy.* Ottawa: Aboriginal Healing Foundation.

Baskin, C. (1997). Mino-yaa-daa: An urban community based approach. *Native Social Work Journal, 1*(1), 55–67.

Baskin, C. (2005). Centring Aboriginal world views in social work education. *Australian Journal of Indigenous Education, 34*, 96–106.

Bellefeuille, G., & Ricks, F. (2003). A pathway to restoration: From child protection to community wellness. *Native Social Work Journal, 5*, 23–43.

Bruyere, G. (1998). Living in another man's house: Supporting Aboriginal learners in social work education. *Canadian Social Work Review, 15*(2), 169–176.

Churchill, W. (1993). *Struggle for the land.* Monroe, ME: Common Courage Press.

Fitznor, L. (2002). *Aboriginal educators' stories: Rekindling Aboriginal world views.* Unpublished doctoral dissertation, Ontario Institute for Studies in Education/ University of Toronto.

Graveline, F.J. (1998). *Circle works: Transforming Eurocentric consciousness.* Halifax: Fernwood.

Hart, M.A. (2002). *Seeking mino-pimatisiwin: An Aboriginal approach to helping.* Halifax: Fernwood.

Hurtle, D. (2002). Native Hawaiian traditional healing: Culturally based interventions for social work practice. *Social Work, 47*(2), 183–192.

Indian and Northern Affairs Canada (INAC). (2005). Urban Aboriginal strategy. Retrieved 23 June 2007 from www.aincinac.gc.ca/interloc/uas/index_e.htm.

Laenui, P. (2000). Processes of decolonization. In M. Battiste (Ed.), *Reclaiming Indigenous voice and vision* (150–160). Vancouver: University of British Columbia Press.

Lanigan, M.A. (1998). Aboriginal pedagogy: Storytelling. In L.A. Stiffarm (Ed.), *As we see ... Aboriginal pedagogy* (103–120). Saskatoon: University of Saskatchewan Press.

Shilling, R. (2002). Journey of our spirits: Challenges for adult Indigenous learners. In E.V. O'Sullivan, A. Morrell, & M.A. O'Connor (Eds.), *Expanding the boundaries of transformative learning: Essays on theory and practice* (151–158). Toronto: Palgrave Publishers.

Statistics Canada. (2005). National Aboriginal day ... by the numbers. Retrieved 23 June 2007 from www42.statcan/smr08_007_e.htm.

Sunseri, L. (2000). Moving beyond the feminism versus nationalism dichotomy: An anti-colonial feminist perspective on Aboriginal liberation struggles. *Canadian Woman Studies, 20*(2), 143–148.

Wilson, A.C. (2004). Reclaiming our humanity: Decolonization and the recovery of Indigenous knowledge. In D.A. Mihesuah & A.C. Wilson (Eds.), *Indigenizing the academy: Transforming scholarship and empowering communities* (69–87). Lincoln: University of Nebraska Press.

CHAPTER 2

RECONCILING COMPETING DISCOURSES:
THE UNIVERSITY OF TORONTO'S EQUITY AND DIVERSITY FRAMEWORK

Maria Athina (Tina) Martimianakis

"WOMEN TO LEAD TOP U OF T SCHOOLS" READS A *Toronto Star* headline, announcing the recent appointment of Dr. Catharine Whiteside to the position of Dean of Medicine and Professor Mayo Moran to the position of Dean of Law at the University of Toronto (Brown, 2005a). The article describes the significance of the two appointments in the context of the university's commitment to "equity" and "diversity." While the appointments are to be celebrated, the author makes sure the reader is aware that U of T's equity and diversity policy framework is in place to redress the ongoing gender gap in academic leadership positions. We learn that despite gains made by female faculty in the academy, women continue to be under-represented in senior academic, administrative and management positions. The point is made with data from the 2005 report of the Senior Women Academic Administrators of Canada, which demonstrated that while women make up over half of the university student population, and approximately 40 percent of the academic hires, they only make up about one-quarter of deans and about one-fifth of university presidents in Canada (Brown, 2005a).

Neither the Faculty of Medicine nor the Faculty of Law has had a female dean before. To have two women at the helm of two professional faculties at one of the top Canadian universities was significant news because, in the words of Connie Guberman, Status of Women Officer at the U of T, "[t]hey will truly serve as role models" (Brown, 2005a). The article ends with a brief description of the experience the two women bring to their new positions and what they hope to accomplish. Consistent with the "role model" discourse, and lest the reader is left wondering what sacrifices these individuals had to make to rise to such leadership positions given all the barriers they must have faced along the way (e.g., chilly climate, insensitivity to family responsibilities, discrimination), the article makes mention that Catharine Whiteside is soon to be a grandmother and that Mayo Moran has an eight-year-old son. Both women are portrayed as having strong academic careers that did not come at the expense of raising a family or enjoying hobbies such as cooking, opera and skiing. Both women articulate a commitment to enhance teaching as part of their mandate, and both intend to continue to engage in their academic careers while in their new administrative positions. Finally, thanks to the photographs included by the paper, the reader is able to see that both women are white.

A week after the appointment of Deans Whiteside and Moran, the University of Toronto announces that the Faculty of Applied Sciences and Engineering has also appointed a female dean, Professor Cristina Amon, originally from Uruguay, but a graduate of MIT and recruited from the Carnegie Mellon College of Engineering. The next day, predictably, the *Toronto Star* follows with another article by Louise Brown. Amon is described, in the words of David Naylor, the newly appointed president of the university, as a "gifted leader, a brilliant academic and committed teacher." Her appointment arrives, Brown notes, "as engineering schools are battling a decline in female applicants" (2005b: B1.). The author continues with the following paragraph, quoting Professor Amon: "'Role models are important, and it is important for young women to see people in senior positions who have a life and have children,' said the married mother of two university students, one of them a biomedical engineering major" (Brown, 2005b: B1). From these two short articles, we now have a portrait of the female academic leader fit for the modern university. Simply put, she is "wonder woman." She is most likely white, embodying simultaneously and unproblematically the following subject positions, all in the service of others: doctor/lawyer/engineer, teacher, researcher, administrator, mother/grandmother. In the process, she has time left over to enjoy hobbies. To some it may seem ironic that the "competence" of these three women, which fulfills the institution's commitment to excellence, is set against a backdrop of feminist discourse that articulates the marginalization of women in the academy and in the process constructs women as "vulnerable" and "disadvantaged." Are we to conclude that without the equity and diversity policy framework in place, none of these women would have been made dean? Do these women want to celebrate their appointments as gender related? Do they want to have their years of commitment and hard work overshadowed by discussions of their personal life and their hobbies?

This chapter explores the tension between seemingly opposed narratives in policy rationales. A discursive analysis of U of T's current equity and diversity framework is conducted with the following objectives: (a) to explore how current policy reconciles such diametrically opposed phenomena — the excellence and competency of successful women academics such as those in our example, on the one hand, and the marginalization of the majority of women academics, on the other; and (b) to consider what implications follow from these policy tensions for women and members of other designated groups (i.e., members of visible minority groups, Aboriginal peoples, persons with disabilities and members of sexual minority groups).[1] I will argue that while "excellence" and "equity/diversity" are competing discourses, they are currently reconciled in institutional policy through a third discourse, namely, "accountability." The current arrangement has unintended consequences. While in numbers the situation for women and other designated groups may look better than in the past, there seems to be less emphasis on collectively sustaining a positive and productive academic environment.

A brief discussion of how I define discourse is followed by a description of the way equity and diversity discourses are taken up within the University of Toronto community. This section leads us into a reading of U of T policy documents related to equity and diversity, and a consideration of how these discourses are incorporated into accounting processes. Finally, implications for the role and status of women and members of other designated groups within the university are discussed.

USING DISCOURSE ANALYSIS FOR UNDERSTANDING
THE IMPLICATIONS OF POLICY

The starting point for understanding how discourse is involved in the negotiation of social relations is an analysis and description of what is currently "visible" and "sayable." Discourses are popular pronouncements linked to institutionalized processes that we draw upon to justify our actions and negotiate meaning in any given interaction. We invest in world views that give definition to our actions and when these actions become commonplace or are unquestioned they take on the power of "truths"; they become a type of knowledge that is used to rationalize and sustain certain processes at the expense of others. The resulting relationships, referred to as social relations, are the organized processes that govern how we do things (Foucault, 1980).

Dominant or popular discourses are identifiable by their pervasiveness and are often embedded in policy documents. Discourse embedded in policy texts has material effects (Blackmore, 1997). Conducting a discursive reading of policy thus entails exposing how discourse is linked to specific practices and analyzing the intended and unintended effects of these practices.

EQUITY, DIVERSITY AND EXCELLENCE AT U OF T

A literature search was conducted on the university's Internet news browsers using the keywords "equity" and "diversity" for the period 1995–2005, leading up to the appointment of the three female deans in medicine, engineering and law in our case example. A close examination of the articles retrieved revealed that during this period there were clearly articulated pro- and anti-equity/diversity positions within the university community. What distinguished the opposing sides was the way the terms "equity" and "diversity" were related to academic "excellence."

Anti-equity positions argued that the marginalization of certain groups in the faculty has not resulted from discrimination; rather, it is a product of personal choice. The implication is that there is nothing wrong with the way academia is organized, or the way it defines excellence, rigour and other markers of productivity. Some members of the academic community, and women specifically, just choose not to engage in these demanding occupations. According to such arguments, imposing equity and diversity policies on the academic community compromises excellence and the mission of the university. In this narrative, commitment to equity and diversity is in direct opposition to excellence.

In contrast, the pro-equity positions articulated in the articles posited equity and diversity as pre-requisites for academic excellence. An example of the pro-equity position is evident in the statement made by Professor Jim Brown of the Department of Philosophy in the context of a campus forum on employment equity: "Equity and diversity do not devalue scholarship but enrich it. This is not a fight between equity over excellence but equity for the sake of excellence ... equity is not about punishment for men but rather a way of broadening perspectives and bringing about fairness" (Soto, 1995: 1–2). Both positions thus relate their arguments back to the mission of the institution, that is, the pursuit of academic excellence. The existence of a formal policy framework[2] supporting equity and diversity within the university appears to demonstrate that the pro-equity side won the debate, and that there is an overarching commitment to redress the system-wide barriers faced by certain portions of the university community. However, the existence of the equity policy framework can also create the assumption that the "mere presence of such policies ... means that equity exists" (Blackmore, 1997). As the contradictions related to this framework are exposed in the subsequent sections of this chapter, it becomes clear that the way equity and diversity were incorporated into the university's policies may in fact have come at a significant cost.

DISCOURSE AND SYSTEMS OF GOVERNANCE:
THE EQUITY AND DIVERSITY FRAMEWORK

In its statement of institutional purpose, the University of Toronto describes itself as "Canada's most important research institution," boasting the highest enrollment of students, the largest number of faculty members and the greatest range of courses compared to other Canadian institutions of higher education (University of Toronto, Governing Council, 1992). It describes its mission as a commitment "to being an internationally significant research university, with undergraduate and professional programs of excellent quality." In fulfillment of this mission, it also commits to

"… fostering an academic community in which learning and scholarship of every member may flourish, with vigilant protection for individual human rights, and a resolute commitment to principles of equal opportunity, equity and justice" (University of Toronto, Governing Council, 1992). Yet how is it that the University can simultaneously commit to upholding "equal opportunity" and "equity and justice"? Equal opportunity implies that the formalized and organized social relations that make up the system or institution do not impede any one member or group from doing their "best." This assumption strongly supports a merit-based system. Choosing the best candidate on the basis of merit is considered not only judicious but also beneficial; it allows the university to maintain or to improve its current position as one of the "leading institutions of higher learning."

On the other hand, equity and social justice start from the assumption that the system is not an even playing field. As a result, in the process of striving to be a "leader" or the "best," certain members of the community are systematically left behind. In other words, race, gender, sexual orientation, social class, religion and other social constructions linked to self and group identification impact on people's social position and ability to engage in social relations and negotiations. At the same time, describing the impact of marginalized groups often has the effect of depicting members of these groups as vulnerable and disadvantaged. Equity and social justice positions thus strongly support a system that takes into account the unequal starting points of candidates, in which the selection process and the "objectivity" of measures of excellence are regarded as problematic, and proactive corrections to the recruitment and selection process are made in order to overcome systematic marginalization (Sagaria, 2002).

Thus, we return to our original question: How is it that the university is able to reconcile a discourse grounded in rational language and which operates through merit-driven strategies and policies with an ethically driven discourse that at a very fundamental level challenges the underlying assumptions of meritocracy and makes visible the ways in which some portions of faculty[3] are systematically disadvantaged?

A close look at the university's *Statement of Institutional Purpose* (1992) indicates that the coexistence of two conflicting policy discourses is made possible by a third discourse, "accountability," which essentially defines the governance structure for the university in such a way that not only allows for competing discourses to coexist but also, in many respects, requires it. Thus, we see embedded in U of T's *Statement of Institutional Purpose* a number of articulated measures of excellence and success that serve to construct the career expectations of faculty primarily in terms of outcomes. Through these outcome measures, the university demonstrates in tangible ways how it contributes constructively to society in a fiscally accountable manner. The commitment to standards of excellence is linked directly to fiscal accountability. In a similar way, the institution's commitment to equity and diversity is also linked to accountability, but this to social accountability. It is through the discourse of accountability that "excellence," "equity" and "diversity" are reconciled. This rationalization is evident in a number of the university's policy documents.

For example, U of T's current academic five-year plan is officially explained in a white paper entitled *Stepping Up ... 2004–2010* (Newman, 2003). During the development process for this plan, a number of green papers were circulated widely within the university community for feedback. One of the goals was to create a companion paper for the *Stepping Up* document on equity, diversity and inclusion. In presenting this goal, the University of Toronto's Office of the Vice-President and Provost (2003a) made the link between equity/diversity and accountability directly: "In support of the next academic plan we are developing a framework for our activities with respect to equity, diversity and inclusion. At this point we are thinking in terms of student outreach, recruitment and success (e.g., graduation rates and career development)" (1).

In the language of governance, a framework implies that a mechanism will be in place to regulate and direct activities related to equity and diversity. Not surprisingly, a number of reporting activities and initiatives have been created to establish the discourse of equity and diversity within the university. All department chairs are required to report on their activities related to recruiting and hiring members of designated groups. To facilitate this reporting activity, faculty are asked to voluntarily identify themselves as a member of a designated group. Department chairs conduct demographic surveys to keep head counts and to plan strategies for recruitment, retention and promotion. Search committee chairs are also required to report who among those shortlisted for a position are members of a designated group, and what proactive processes the search committee engaged in to ensure that candidates from designated groups were not disadvantaged during the search process. These reports and other data are consolidated and made public in annual employment equity reports issued by the Office of the Vice-President of Human Resources and Equity. As well, both visible minority faculty hiring and female hiring are part of the governance performance indicators (Newman, 2003). By linking "equity" and "diversity" directly to the performance indicators currently used to compare U of T's output against that of other institutions, equity is drawn directly into the discourse of "accountability."

EQUITY AS THE RATIONAL CHOICE

Within *Stepping Up*, the university summarizes the context for its current position on issues related to equity:

> Equity requires equal access to opportunity for all who, by virtue of their qualifications, can benefit from that opportunity. Equity requires us to ... appoint the best faculty ... available on the basis of their qualifications for the job. Equity demands of us especially close self-scrutiny to ensure that we are not applying criteria extraneous to the task of admission or appointment in making our decisions; it asks that we fully and equally weigh the qualifications of all candidates. Equity also requires us to administer the university's policies and procedures consistently for all ... employees fully and fairly on the basis of its merits and only of its merits ... to provide all ... employees with opportunities consistent with the quality of their performance in relation to others in their programs and their jobs ... to make accommodations for persons who have the qualifications and abilities to undertake work ... but who are impeded in that work by physical or learning disabilities. Equity prohibits discrimination on the grounds of race, ethnicity, aboriginal status, gender, religion, sexual orientation, or disability. (Newman, 2003: 29)

The university's commitment to "excellence" structures the search and selection process as objective, where the candidate with the best qualifications will be offered the position. According to this statement, equity will ensure that all individuals with the qualifications to compete for the position are part of the competition. The focus then turns to representation. To ensure due process in the selection and recruitment process, the pool of candidates needs to be representative of the demographics of society at large. Throughout the articulated commitment to equity, processes linked to the discourse of "excellence" such as the merit system are reaffirmed; yet just as the discourse of "excellence" has modified the discourse of "equity," the discourse of "equity" has also modified the discourse of "excellence." As outlined in the university's employment equity reports published in the past four years, excellence is no longer just about competency, it is also about representation:

> Our goal is to recruit and retain faculty and staff who are diverse in their cultural, ethnic and socioeconomic backgrounds, who include women, First Nations, disabled persons, and those of different sexual orientations and who contribute to the intellectual diversity of the University of Toronto. (University of Toronto, Office of the Vice-President of Human Resources and Equity, 2004: 1, quoting Interim Vice-President and Provost Vivek Goel)

The university rationalizes its commitment to equity as an investment that will increase "diversification of ideas and perspectives" and thereby enrich "our scholarship, teaching and other activities" (University of Toronto, Governing Council, 2006: n.p.). By engaging "the best talent from the four corners of the world and from within our own country," the University of Toronto will "assure its place among the world's finest public teaching and research universities" (University of Toronto, Office of the Vice-President, Human Resources and Equity, 2004: n.p.). Equity discourse is thus couched in progressive outward thinking with knowledge production clearly linked to the globalization of expertise.

University leaders, policy documents and mission statements are not calling for critical self-reflection, nor are they calling for an acknowledgement of responsibility in the systematic discrimination against portions of society. Rather, equity has been incorporated into the existing processes and governance schemes. In doing so, its ethical base seems to have become overshadowed by language that reaffirms individualism, competition and meritocracy. By using strategically the tools provided by the accountability discourse, issues of equity have been made an institutional priority, and in the process the recruitment, hiring and advancement of women and other traditionally disadvantaged portions of society may improve. However, equity processes must now comply with the techniques of management and control linked to accountability — reporting, benchmarking and assessment — and this connection has implications for the way women and other designated groups experience their academic life.

EQUITY AND ACCOUNTABILITY: AN UNEASY PARTNERSHIP?

Accountability is a process, a technique of management and governance, which forces institutions to reduce very complex processes into objective measures. As a process, it is often linked to funding formulas that rely on comparisons of the productivity and output of individuals and departments. Much research on the effects of what has come to be known as the audit culture has reached similar conclusions: accountability threatens diversity of ideas, it erodes the equal distribution of power among colleagues, it standardizes processes and it threatens the feminist project (Blackmore, 1997; Baert & Shipman, 2005; Butterwick & Dawson, 2005; Strathern, 2000). And here lies the irony. The very process that has facilitated the adoption of an institutional framework to ensure equity in faculty, student and staff employment practices also threatens to erode its ethical foundation and minimize the degree of cultural shift that can take place as a result.

The social justice tradition, most commonly expressed through feminist, anti-racist and anti-colonial writings, within which equity as a concept and a principle was created and sustained, in some ways loses its connection to this tradition once the accountability framework comes into operation (Blackmore, 1997). Thus, we see in the 2003 *Employment Equity Report* that most new faculty (82.4 percent) have filled out a voluntary employment equity survey, which is analyzed as suggesting

> ... that employment equity surveys have become an expected part of the hiring process ... that it's becoming an accepted mechanism for measurement ... and that those who in the past may have been concerned to self-identify on the questionnaire have likely seen that there are no repercussions from doing so. (University of Toronto, Office of the Vice-President of Human Resources and Equity, 2004: 4)

Consistent with techniques of regulation, transparency is a mode of control, a way to standardize and create conformity in a process. This transparency works in positive ways to "remove any opportunity for feelings of unfairness or mistreatment" (University of Toronto, Office of the Vice-President of Human Resources and Equity, 2004). There is always the danger, however, that processes, such as filling out an equity survey, that are analyzed within the report as markers of "efficiency," "acceptance" or "fairness" can also bring about conformity. When a process is left unquestioned, critical reflection is eroded. The focus is suddenly on numbers and not on experiences, while the aims become achieving benchmarks and not raising consciousness or effecting cultural change.

The employment equity reports do a great job of describing how many women, visible minorities, First Nations and disabled prospective faculty received offers, how many accepted and how many declined. These data are very useful in order to compare the various academic divisions within the university to each other. We are able to discern if members of designated groups are clustered in certain disciplines, if members of designated groups are being interviewed consistently by each department, and so forth. We can also see that the proactive approach embedded in the equity and diversity framework is starting to work,[4] since among full-time faculty, women's representation has reached 34 percent, which is close to the external levels of 36.2 percent of the available applicant pool, while representation of visible minorities slightly exceeds the external availability data (13.3 percent) (University of Toronto, Office of the Vice-President of Human Resources and Equity, 2007). What we do not learn is how faculty members experience the proactive search process or what their first few months or years on the job are like. For candidates who qualify as members of one of the designated groups, we do not know if they feel they received an offer because they were the most competent candidate or in order to fulfill one of the university's benchmarks. We also do not know why they decided either to accept or refuse the position. Unfortunately, this is exactly the type of information that is generally left out of reports used for benchmarking.

Yet, amidst the accounting logic that permeates such reports, the following recommendation was included in the *Employment Equity Report 2003*:

> Throughout the Academic Framework 2004–2010 and its accompanying papers there is a focus on using employment equity as a means to ensure that the University of Toronto hires Faculty and staff of "excellent" quality. A focus on equity may also require a re-definition of "excellence" to more broadly recognize non-traditional routes and experience, as well as varying performance indicators. (University of Toronto, Office of the Vice-President of Human Resources and Equity, 2004: 31)

There is no direct evidence that I came across indicating that this recommendation was tackled head on as a policy initiative in subsequent years, nor was a similar reference to redefining what we mean by excellence made in the subsequent reports published (University of Toronto, Office of the Vice-President of Human Resources and Equity, 2005, 2006, 2007). That is not to say that the equity offices at U of T are not working on realizing this goal. In a presentation prepared by Dr. Sara Jane Finlay, director of the Office of the Vice-President and Provost, developed for the purposes of briefing search committees on how to conduct proactive searches, the following points are made:

- Merit should be seen as socially rather than empirically constructed and contextual.

- [We must] recognize that gender-blind or merit-neutral policies are impossible to implement because there are no gender-blind (or merit neutral) evaluators. (Finlay, 2003: n.p.)

The fact that these challenges to meritocracy are happening under the auspices of the Office of the Vice-President and Provost is a significant achievement. Issues of equity are being tackled on all fronts by the senior administrators of the university. Achieving the integration of equity issues into overall university priorities is the culmination of several decades of work to raise awareness of the systematic discrimination and disadvantage faced by portions of the population on the basis of sex, race, ability or sexual orientation. One of the most recent achievements towards this end is the unanimous approval of an official *Statement on Equity, Diversity and Excellence* by the Governing Council. Within this statement, the university asserts that "the creation of an equitable community ... requires the work of every member of the community ... including students, teaching staff, administrative staff, visitors, alumni and guests" (University of Toronto, Governing Council, 2006). While it is not a statement acknowledging the role the academic community as a whole has played in the systematic marginalization of designated groups, it is a statement that makes everyone responsible for eliminating discriminatory processes. Arguably, one of the things that have helped make this possible at U of T is the discourse of "accountability," a discourse that equity advocates drew upon to make a case for creating a sustainable and regulated equity and diversity policy framework. In turn, this enabled them to engage in the cultural work they have advocated for so long with authority and with the support of the administration. In the process, however, the very nature of equity work is changing; its ethical and ideological foundations are being directly challenged and potentially eroded through techniques of governance justified in the language of "commitment to excellence."

Yet is that a problem? If the demographics of the university faculty become more representative of the social fabric of our city or our country, does it matter that we rationalize the process in accounting terms and not in ethical terms? It does matter, if in the process we entrench a new way of "othering," which essentially continues the systematic discrimination against women and other marginalized groups, albeit in a different way, by using the very "discourse" created by social justice and equity scholars (Eyre, 2000). "Excellence" as merit and "excellence" as diversity are both active discourses, and they intersect and clash at the level of the individual faculty member. For members of a designated group, becoming representatives of their designation could set off a series of processes that will create additional expectations with regard to their performance, because the policy constitutes them as vulnerable with a lot of unrealized potential. The existence of the proactive equity processes can create demands that this unrealized potential must be turned into tangible results, and this expectation in turn can structure the way members of the designated groups organize and conduct their work.

CONCLUSION

As 2005 came to an end, it would seem that U of T went out with a "bang" on issues of equity.[5] Three female deans in three professional schools were appointed; one of whom also scored points on the basis of her ethnic background — to all appearances, a victory for the pro-equity side. Or is it? The appointments in and of themselves are certainly victories. But embodying the role of female leader — or should I say "wonder woman" — at the U of T in the upcoming years may prove otherwise at a personal level. All three deans, along with other female leaders at the university, have quite the agenda to fulfill, one that includes role-modelling for students and junior female faculty (see also Sandra Acker's chapter in this volume). They must demonstrate why women are good choices for academic leadership positions while also showing all the doubters that women not only can do it but also they can do it differently and better. They must do all this and continue to show that they have a fulfilling and active personal life, lest they discourage other women from striving for academic leadership positions.

These are not really new battles. They are the same battles women have been facing in academia for the past one hundred years (Rich, 1979). What has changed, then? Arguably, it is the language used to rationalize the effort it will take to accomplish all these things. It is not an ethical argument that is used to convince the administration and faculty that diversification is a good thing, it is a rational argument made through the discourses of "excellence" and "accountability" and witnessed through numbers and benchmarking.

What the numbers do not do is tell us what all this will mean in terms of the way female and other designated groups will experience the modern university.[6] Given that "equity" and "diversity" have been incorporated into the university's governance performance indicators, we must consider if there will be room for members of designated groups to choose to construct their professional identity without drawing on the discourses of "equity" and "diversity" (see Patrice White's chapter in this volume). Have we simply exchanged one master for another, one which, ironically, is of our own making? While the expectation is that tokenism will go away as the numbers of women and those in other designated groups increase, we need to consider the implications of the evolving discourse of role-modelling. Role-modelling can create a different kind of "othering" by adding even more expectations for members of the designated groups to make things better for themselves and their respective groups. In the current age of accountability, numbers matter, and tangible outcomes score the most points. If "equity" and "diversity" are captured through accounting processes, how will role-modelling be assessed? Or will the appointment of women to leadership positions shift thinking away from outcomes and back onto the quality of experience, as many in the pro-equity ranks hope?

The ethical arguments connected to equity and diversity evolved through an elaborate effort to expose how power was experienced. The current discursive terrain at the U of T revolves around an accounting logic that leaves little room to accommodate how work is experienced; the focus is so much on the product that critical reflection on the process seems to happen at a functional rather than substantive level. Taking advantage of the possibilities and fulfilling the obligations of the new discourse of "equity as excellence" may not be difficult for the three new female deans, who have obviously succeeded in their careers in the current merit-driven system, but that may not be the case for other members of the designated vulnerable groups who now have to strive to emulate their success.

While we may speculate how these three women and other female leaders will allow or resist their subjectivity from being through the "equity as excellence" discourse, we cannot know how they have experienced the related discursive struggles until we actually ask them. Having set the stage with an analysis of how dominant discourses are institutionalized, it is important to move towards an exploration of how individuals experience these discourses. Through such analysis we have the opportunity to reflect on how discourse operates, so that the possibility of new ways of doing things can be imagined and then pursued, even in the shadow of dominant and entrenched processes that discipline and regulate our behaviour.

NOTES

1 The *Canadian Employment Equity Act* recognizes four designated groups: women, Aboriginal peoples, persons with disabilities and visible minorities. The University of Toronto has also extended designation to members of sexual minority groups.

2 Since 1986 the University of Toronto, as per federal government regulations, has maintained an equity program and reported yearly on its progress. The program is constantly evolving and the university's commitment to equity is reflected in a number of policies related to hiring practices, remuneration, promotion and advancement, and so on. A complete list and links to all the policies related to equity and diversity processes at U of T is provided through the Office of the Vice-President (Human Resources and Equity), www.hrandequity.utoronto.ca/equity.htm.

3 The following analysis focuses on the way the policies affect faculty at the University of Toronto. That is not to say that the policies do not also have implications for students and staff.

4 As of the 2006 reporting period, persons with disabilities and Aboriginal peoples continue to be under-represented in all faculty groups when compared to external levels (University of Toronto, Office of the Vice-President of Human Resources and Equity, 2007).

5 The latest available data show that women currently hold a total of 32.3 percent of academic leadership positions, compared with 20 percent in 1998. Currently, women make up 50 percent of the president and vice-presidents' group, 44 percent of the principals and deans and 29 percent of the chairs and associate deans (University of Toronto, Office of the Vice-President of Human Resources and Equity, 2007).

6 In the 2006 performance indicator report, the University of Toronto stated that it was developing a process of exit interviews and surveys as a way to understand the employment experience of members of the designated groups within the university (University of Toronto, Office of the Vice-President and Provost, 2007). This type of process will go a long way in building a more substantive consideration of equity issues in university governance. However, the data currently contained in the governance indicators reports and upon which this process of tapping into experiential aspects of equity will be building rely on self-identification, which as I have argued in this chapter may increase expectations and create an unwanted burden of exceptional performance for members of the designated groups.

REFERENCES

Baert, P., & Shipman, A. (2005). University under siege? Trust and accountability in the contemporary academy. *European Societies, 7*(1), 157–185.

Blackmore, J. (1997). Disciplining feminism: A look at gender-equity struggles in Australian higher education. In L. Roman & L. Eyre (Eds.), *Dangerous territories: Struggles for difference and equality for education* (75–96). New York: Routledge.

Brown, L. (2005a, December 9). Women to lead top U of T schools; First female deans of law, medicine; political scientist also makes history. *Toronto Star,* A1, A4.

Brown, L. (2005b, December 17). Woman named dean of U of T engineers. *Toronto Star,* B1, B3.

Butterwick, S., & Dawson, J. (2005). Undone business: Examining the production of academic labour. *Women's Studies International Forum, 28,* 51–65.

Eyre, L. (2000). The discursive framing of sexual harassment in a university community. *Gender and Education, 12*(3), 293–307.

Finlay, S.J. (2003). Faculty recruitment: The search committee. University of Toronto, Office of the Vice-President and Provost. Retrieved 18 January 2008 from www.provost.utoronto.ca/Assets/assets/facrecuit2.ppt?method=1.

Foucault, M. (1980). Two lectures. In C. Gordon (Ed.), *Power/knowledge: Selected interviews and other writings.* New York: Pantheon Books.

Newman, S. (2003). *Stepping Up: A framework for academic planning at the University of Toronto, 2004–2010.* University of Toronto White Paper. Retrieved 18 January 2008 from www.provost.utoronto.ca/plans/framework.htm.

Rich, A. (1979). *On lies, secrets, and silence.* New York: W.W. Norton.

Sagaria, M.A.D. (2002). An exploratory model of filtering in administrative searches: Toward counter-hegemonic discourses. *Journal of Higher Education, 73*(6), 677–710.

Soto, S. (6 February 1995). Equity sides square off over hiring. *The U of T Bulletin, 48*(12), 1–2.

Strathern, M. (Ed.). (2000). *Audit cultures: Anthropological studies in accountability, ethics and the academy.* London: Routledge.

University of Toronto, Governing Council. (2006). *Statement on Equity, Diversity, and Excellence.* Retrieved 18 January 2008 from www.hrandequity.utoronto.ca/equity. htm.

University of Toronto, Governing Council. (1992). *University of Toronto statement of institutional purpose.* Retrieved 18 January 2008 from www.utoronto.ca/govcncl/ pap/policies/mission.html.

University of Toronto, Office of the Vice-President and Provost. (2003a). *Academic planning for 2003 and beyond. Equity, diversity and inclusion at the University of Toronto.* Retrieved 18 January 2008 from www.utoronto.ca/plan2003/equity.htm.

University of Toronto, Office of the Vice-President and Provost. (2003b). *Performance indicators for governance.* Retrieved 18 January 2008 from www.provost.utoronto. ca/public/reports/performanceindicators/2006pi.htm.

University of Toronto, Office of the Vice-President of Human Resources and Equity. (2007). *Employment equity report: October 1, 2005–September 20, 2006.* Retrieved 18 January 2008 from www.hrandequity.utoronto.ca/news/reports/ee.htm.

University of Toronto, Office of the Vice-President of Human Resources and Equity. (2006). *Employment equity report: 2005.* Retrieved 18 January 2008 from www. hrandequity.utoronto.ca/news/reports/ee.htm.

University of Toronto, Office of the Vice-President of Human Resources and Equity. (2005). *Employment equity report: 2004.* Retrieved 18 January 2008 from www. hrandequity.utoronto.ca/news/reports/ee.htm.

University of Toronto, Office of the Vice-President of Human Resources and Equity. (2004). *Employment equity report 2003.* Retrieved 18 January 2008 from www. hrandequity.utoronto.ca/news/reports/ee.htm.

CHAPTER 3

THE CONTESTED SPACE OF THE BODY IN THE ACADEMY

Susan Ferguson & Tanya Titchkosky

The Truth about stories is that that's all we are.
— Thomas King, *The Truth about Stories*

There is a story in every line of theory.
— Lee Maracle, *Oratory Coming to Theory*

Reading the world precedes reading the word,
and the subsequent reading of the word cannot
dispense with continually reading the world.
— Paulo Freire, "The Importance of the Act of Reading"

LET US BEGIN WITH THE OBVIOUSNESS OF EMBODIED DIFFERENCE —
we all have and are bodies that we relate to in different ways. Thus, embodied difference is always part of the complex range of social relationships, educational practices, as well as political and pedagogical commitments that constitute educational life and the work of academic knowledge production. Yet those differences called "disability" are typically lived and studied only as an individual problem and are not regarded as an integral part of our educational lives. From a feminist disability studies perspective, our chapter explores disability as this kind of absent presence within the academy.

Present as an undesired problem, disability is made meaningful (and paradoxically, quite absent) through the ongoing negation of the diversity of bodily relations in everyday life. Negation of diversity, devaluation of difference and a demand to overcome disability are some of the Western ways that we "do" embodiment, that is, make bodies, mind, senses, emotions and so on meaningful for ourselves and others as an absence. As Avery Gordon (1997) suggests, investigating such absences is productive because it "can lead to that dense site where history and subjectivity make social life" (8). Our chapter aims to reveal *how* disability is done as a way to explore some of the pedagogical consequences of our being bodied beings in educational situations that neither expect nor welcome this diversity.

Our chapter is a personal, political and ethical project, both for ourselves as scholars who attentively live with these issues and for the communities we are a part of, within and outside of the academy. We developed this work through a collaboration that was itself a response to the presence of disability in the academy, and a writing process emerged that was responsive to embodied difference (physical impairment for Susan and dyslexia for Tanya). This collaboration was initiated by Susan's participation in a disability studies class taught by Tanya. Two years earlier, in the middle of her graduate degree program, Susan had acquired a chronic arm impairment and was no longer able to handwrite, type or use a computer. While taking Tanya's class, Susan was still awaiting the assistive technologies[1] required to produce written text and complete course assignments in the usual way. So, we, Susan and Tanya, worked together orally and in dialogue with one another as our chapter developed. This process highlights the ways in which bodies are implicated in our practices of knowledge production despite academic conventions that tend to treat the body as a mere vessel for the work of the mind. The danger of disregarding the body is a lesson found in much feminist scholarship and is dramatically symbolized by Sandra Acker and Carmen Armenti's (2004) article, "Sleepless in Academia," where sleepless, or childless, or sickless, or ageless is the kind of body (or bodylessness) expected of women working in universities.

We make use of a narrative of disability composed from a conversation between Susan and a disability service provider whom we call "Graham." By providing an account of Susan's story of becoming a "person with a disability" through social practices imbued with power differences, we underscore how disability is a relationship achieved through people's negotiations. Beginning with the assumption that education reproduces social inequalities, our chapter goes on to demonstrate how, even in the act of accommodating, inequality is reproduced. Methodologically, we employ an interpretive analysis of this story in which disability makes an appearance (only to again be disappeared) as a way to demonstrate how disability might be done differently. By examining how bodily differences are done in everyday university life, we aim to reveal how disability is given meaning in ways that do not disturb interlocking power relations that ground colonialism and patriarchy. Since our analysis is interpretive, we treat disability (and gender, race, class and any other social difference) as neither a cause nor a variable. Instead, we treat social difference as intimately tied to the scene of its appearance — made through power relations within everyday life, disability is, then, a space of interpretive interaction to examine the everyday.

Examining the appearance of disability can teach us about the wider social relations organizing our experiences in the academy and also reveal embodied relations to knowledge production. This approach serves as a reflection of our commitment to working *through* disability towards modes of teaching, learning and being in the world that imagine embodied difference as something we might all *desire* (McRuer & Wilkerson, 2003). Ultimately, we are suggesting that by critically attending to what the university environment already says and does to disability, there is much to uncover and to learn about how embodiment is an achieved social phenomenon. We turn now to a brief narrative of a telephone conversation between Susan and her case manager, Graham, at an agency responsible for providing assistive technologies to students with disabilities.

NARRATIVE NEGOTIATIONS

The phone rings, and it is Graham. Our conversation begins with Graham explaining the purpose of our telephone meeting and his desired outcomes. He expects that by its conclusion, we will have a Technology Assessment Plan, a "TAP," Graham says, which will outline my needs related to technology and education. The logic is that by identifying the disability-related barriers I experience as a student, we can create a plan to address those barriers.

The conversation continues. I am asked to describe a typical day and the difficulties that my disability poses for me. In the face of days that don't seem typical, his request throws me a little. Although I am by now accustomed to telling this story — describing my symptoms, pain, triggers and problems — each time I do it feels tenuous and difficult. I know that this time, concrete resources are on the line. I want to capture my situation as fully as possible.

Graham sounds shocked to hear that I have been unable to use a computer at all for over a year, and that I rely completely on other people to type for me. He seems to understand how difficult this would be, and I feel heartened. Graham tells me a little more about the assistance program and what I can expect. He informs me that the program uses a grant system, and that I will be provided with adaptive equipment. This is intended to level the playing field, Graham tells me, and eliminate the frustrations that I experience because of the barriers that my disability presents. Graham shares with me that he has a disability himself, and so he understands how these frustrations are a "filter to learning." He is here to help me get what I need, to navigate the system with me. Then he says it: "This conversation is not about *if* you need equipment, it is about *what* equipment ..." (so far so good) "... because you have met most, if not all, of the criteria."

I jolt a little at this last phrase — "most if not all" — and then a familiar feeling of panic flows through my body, settling in my stomach. I am concerned but I try to maintain the amicable tone of the conversation.

Graham proceeds to outline the program criteria, including having a verifiable *permanent* disability. The character of my disability — whether permanent or not — has been the stumbling block in this process from the outset. I sought advice, care and, ultimately, paperwork from several different doctors before receiving a "guarded" diagnosis of having a permanent condition. The problem with my eligibility is this guarded assessment. My doctor, when asked on a standard form if my disability was permanent — "yes" or "no" — ticked "yes." But under "prognosis," my doctor wrote: "Guarded. 2/3 chance of permanency." Graham tells me that this assessment was initially a problem, and it could have been the basis for rejecting my application. Luckily, he says, he was able to convince his superiors that because medical expertise considers my condition more likely permanent than not, it should be regarded as permanent.

I am simultaneously relieved, troubled and intrigued as I consider the implications of all this since it seems that there is little assistance for the temporary resident of disability.

Once we established that my disability has been accepted, we move on to discuss what assistive technologies I need to address my educational barriers. I am told that I will receive voice recognition software and a lightweight laptop computer — part of a predetermined package for students with my type of disability. The conversation draws to a close with administrative details and pleasantries. I am glad to hang up the phone.

THE VOID OF LITERACY

This narrative serves as an opportunity to reflect upon how the uneven terrain of embodiment in academia is navigated. Rather than treating this narrative as information about a pre-given condition or experience, we treat it as representative of the culture from which it springs in order to explore how disability is being done in everyday life. While the official discourses mediating the appearance of disability in the academy characterize it as a clear and certain void, our analysis reveals that disability is in fact a complex body-space that is constantly in dialogue with culture. We now consider in more detail the various depictions that make disability appear in university life as a kind of void.

Recall that "Graham sounds shocked to hear that I have been unable to use a computer …" The conversational achievement of disability as represented in the narrative suggests that the medical and bureaucratic responses to disability rely heavily upon a conception of disability as void, and specifically, the void of literacy. This means that the disabled body is represented through a negation, and that disability is taken as an instance of not being able to do those tasks — ordinary ways of reading and writing — which are treated as essential if one is to be regarded as competent within a university setting. The absence of recognized competency in these areas is not a natural outcome. To be narrated as void is already to ascribe a variety of cultural meanings and values which, if left unexamined, not only privilege the lives of some people over others but also make their way into our epistemologies. It becomes important to ask, then, if there is a way to recognize disability without confining it to its negation. Conversations that position some people as asocial problems are an occasion to address and even transform the ways we talk about disability and live with embodied difference.

Graham says that the provision of assistive technology "… is intended to level the playing field … eliminate the frustrations … because of the barriers that … disability presents." Graham also says that he too has a disability, and so he understands how these "frustrations are a filter to learning." Disability is brought into conversation by Graham insofar as it is imagined as a barrier to participation. This barrier is said to exist in individuals, and while many individuals, including Graham, may experience disability as a disruption or frustration to normal participation, this experience is not regarded as a collective one embedded within the organization of daily university life. Ironically, despite the common experience that to have an impairment is to find oneself outside the terrain of participation, disability remains an individual issue in need of individual assistance as determined by the powers that be.

As feminist disability studies scholars have argued, individualizing disability is done through collective taken-for-granted relations to gender (Smith and Hutchison, 2004; Thomas, 2006). Susan Wendell (1996), for example, has shown that within social arenas that regard women as perpetual newcomers, bodily differences become grounds for suspecting women of malingering, exaggerating or otherwise dismissing the validity of our participation. Indeed, conceptualizing women as the suspect newcomers or strangers — while conceiving of knowing as a distant but masculinized objective authority able to determine the true, the real and the good — helps to make disability into a scene for the reproduction of these gendered power relations (Titchkosky, 2005). Whether accommodated or not, the way of knowing represented by Graham is one that "knows" Susan to have a problem and "knows" this problem to be a void that will need to be filled with accommodative procedures. Thus, disability remains the space for the reproduction of dichotomous gendered and colonial relations between bodies and truth.

Alongside Graham's conception of disability, there are others. Through Susan's story, readers can learn that becoming a student with a disability represents both the void of literacy as well as the dynamic space where disability is brought into conversation with others, such as case managers, oneself and other members of the academy. Ironically, the supposed absence of literacy makes present the need to talk about disability, to make disability something to which we respond. That disability can strike us as a void, as a negation, as the inability to do normal things in the expected ways also means that we have *already responded*, or that we have already brought disability into conversation as fully imbued with meaning.

There are, then, a variety of nuanced meanings to disability as it is represented in the narrative. To be disabled is not only to experience a void, it is also to be one who is void, whose absence is not appreciated, whose presence remains unimagined, except as one who requires individualized accommodative measures. For example, it is not as if technology and thus Susan's writing are missing; instead, it was feared that Susan might not write because she could not write and was void of the literacy necessary for participation. There are other examples that illustrate the void that disability is constituted to be in the academy. It is not as if wheelchair-accessible washrooms in a large urban campus in 2007 were missing; instead, this workplace was void of any need to notice the absent washrooms and thus absent participants (Titchkosky, 2008). As another example, one of us (Tanya) is dyslexic. Full and active participation in university life means making dyslexia disappear; it is, after all, only polite to not notice dyslexia and it is not easy to reconcile productive participation with the identity dyslexic. Ordinarily, any difference that disability might make, positive or otherwise, is made absent, that is, voided, from the social scene, which thus helps constitute disability as a "useless difference" (Michalko, 2002: 93).

What is at stake here is not merely a set of best practices to manage disability in the academic environment. What is at stake is the opportunity to self-reflectively engage the conceptions of disability that we already have narrating our lives. Disability-as-void narrates a way that bodily differences are inhabited by culture. Even those stories that assure us that disability is an empty absence, a place we would not, could not, do not hope to inhabit, these stories nonetheless reveal what culture does with embodied differences. Significantly, however, a dominant Western cultural approach to disability is to regard it as a space void of culture, effectively foreclosing the possibility that there is something to be learned in and through disability.

While the story appears to belong to Susan, and while not all people identify as disabled, the story nonetheless teaches us that everyone has a life with disability. In fact, in the midst of our striking diversity one thing that "we all" share is a life as embodied and thus vulnerable beings; we all live in and through this vulnerability. Ironically, we live in a culture that seems quite surprised, or unprepared, when the vulnerable and diverse bodies that we are "show up" on the terrain of everyday life (Michalko & Titchkosky, 2001). This surprise is grounded in the unexamined expectation of a mythical "normal body," and it is this expectation that can now be understood as helping to produce the uneven terrain of the academy.[2]

A TROUBLING EDUCATION

Let us continue to treat this story of disability as an opportunity to learn something new. It is, of course, *not* a new idea that some individuals have impairments requiring assistance coming in the shape of technical aids, organized and distributed through medicalized bureaucratic structures. From a disability studies perspective, the individualization of disability is the dominant taken-for-granted, non-social approach to disability (Oliver, 1996; Wendell, 1996; Erevelles, 2000; Michalko, 2002). However, by treating the personal, yet common, experience of seeking accommodations as a story that reflects the social life in which it is embedded, we can reveal the complex ways in which disability is socially produced through the intersections of power, knowledge and embodied beings.

In the narrative, there are a number of different depictions of disability at work, pushing up against one another to ensure that the concept of disability itself does its work. Disability is depicted, for example, as an obstacle to full participation in university life, and as a condition to be measured and evaluated by the medical profession. Disability is also depicted as a fate that is either permanent or temporary, present or not, and which can be known and addressed as one or the other. These ways of representing disability treat it as a condition that is found in and troubles the lives of some individuals; however, while imagined as an individual problem, disability is simultaneously depicted as constantly in the midst of others. For example, the body is articulated as a contextualized problem for educational life — "Graham is shocked to hear that I have been unable to use a computer." At the same time, and in the same story, the body appears through the evaluative mechanisms of doctors, caseworkers, instructors and the agencies they represent. Clearly, disability is made into a demand in need of response by both self and others situated in particular institutional settings.

Although this narrative represents an imagined entry point into disability as signified by the acquisition of physical impairment, Susan, like everyone, has been living with disability all of her life. As the different depictions demonstrate, disability can never be located in the body alone since we all live with various conceptions of disability all the time. A personal relation to disability then involves a process of simultaneously *being* and *becoming* a person with a disability. Becoming disabled requires more than the acquisition of an impairment, since it also requires that a person come into particular sorts of relations with those institutionalized processes that define what a disability is, what can be done about it and how such definitions and doings are to be appropriately achieved. In the context of the university, it is through engagement with institutional discourses of access and accommodation that some people come to be understood as disabled; it is through these same medicalized discourses that the consequences of, and solutions to living with, disability are determined.

That disability is both an individual condition *and* something to which many people, events and structures must respond is not "caused" by impairment. These depictions reflect cultural conceptions of disability already at work in our lives. Education conceptualizes disability as a kind of natural need found in individuals. Still, people interact with disability in complicated ways, structured, in part, by the taken-for-granted orders of "normal" educational life. The gendered structures of the academy, for example, assume that bodies are things best not to worry about in the workplace — we are to go on maternity leave, or go on disability leave. It is part of normal educational life to *go ahead and remove* the body from our daily concerns. Ascribing the status "disabled" is thus one way Western(ized) societies individualize social inequality and organize the uneven distribution of resources while leaving the normative orders of education unexamined. Even if we were unable to imagine a more equitable or effective process to organize how educational possibilities are meted out, the fact remains that narratives of disability are a way to examine how the social organization of academic life is put together, and put together with uneven results.

Ironically, institutionally organized conversations make disability appear as if it is detached from the demands of institutional life. Most, if not all, Canadian universities have individualized accommodation programs to which people can apply for individualized services. Yet there is little consideration of how a commitment to the values of equity, accessibility or inclusivity are reflected in the organization of institutional application processes, websites, reading lists and course outlines, library resources, washrooms, classrooms, offices, computer labs, photocopiers and mailboxes, extra-curricular events and all the other arenas for active participation in university life. The solutions proposed in response to the problem of disability in the academy, when it appears, revolve around the use of personal technology to "level the playing field" and "help the individual" maintain the appearance of typical participation in the academy, in effect making disability disappear yet again.

The conversations that produce an official or authoritative sense that someone is a person with a disability happen in particular locations and exert their particular influence. In the academy, the status and identity of each of us as legitimate participants (or not) is constantly being produced through a set of normative demands regarding reading, writing and knowing. While the narrative of accommodation rests upon a conception of disability as outside the boundaries of normal embodiment and knowledge production, many students, faculty and staff struggle with these same demands, albeit in differently positioned ways (Wendell, 1996; Smith & Hutchison, 2004). While producing text is part of the normative orders of education, there are in fact many aspects of university life that make the production of text difficult, for example, workload issues; balancing family, work and school life; computer malfunctioning; economic and time constraints; and access to appropriate support and materials (Acker, 2003; Acker & Armenti, 2004). It is fascinating that Susan's story might well involve all of these uneven distributions of resources, but by becoming a "person with a disability," she is simultaneously produced as *the person with a problem* which then produces other problems, such as computer problems. Today, it is expected that students, faculty, and staff have access to computers as an ordinary technology. Not to have such technology is to be in a troubling situation. Susan does not have such technology. But the trouble belongs only to Susan and not to the situation. In this sense, access and accommodation remain the unique problem of individuals despite the growing number of students, faculty and staff at universities across Canada requiring assistive computer technology.

As we suggested earlier, participation in the academy rests upon a narrow conception of literacy, learning and academic knowledge production. Given the individualized nature of accommodation, different ways of writing, teaching and knowing need not enter the academy; what is needed is that individuals continue to produce texts according to Western writing conventions that deploy a disembodied authoritative voice. The mind–body split, essential to patriarchal and colonialist knowledge regimes, is reactivated by making disability appear as an individual problem known only by the expert. Success in graduate education demands that people fulfill academic obligations in normal time, in normal ways, through normal tasks, accomplished by people who regard all this in a normal fashion: we write, present, publish, teach and do research. All of these activities rely heavily upon our bodies, mythologized as autonomous individuals generating substantial amounts of written text to demonstrate intellectual and participatory competence. In other words, the dominant ways of producing knowledge require for their accomplishment a certain kind of body. Disability can then be read as the scene where, even in the face of feminist gains, anti-racist education and post-colonial studies, the normative order reasserts itself almost without question. Some of the ways we critique these normative demands are limited and constrained. For example, faculty and students alike can question whether the writing demands are too much or too little, but these debates typically occur through an unquestioned assumption of some sort of shared "normal" embodiment that allows writing to take place.[3] The category of disability may sometimes exempt one from normal role responsibilities (Parsons, 1951), but still the normative demands of social and educational environments remain in place.

To learn from disability, however, requires not only that we begin to understand disability as accomplished through articulations and interactions, it also requires that we do something other than reduce impairment to the singular need to seek personalized solutions. Such learning entails acknowledging the embodied relations that we bring to our work in the academy in order to resist the (re)production of disembodied knowledge and oppressive social hierarchies (Ng, 2000). We conclude our chapter now by reflecting upon how the typical concern with *doing something about* disability can and should be denaturalized. To change the meaning and place of disability in the academy, we must theorize how and why disability appears, and appears as a problem.

REFLEXIVE RELATIONS

When disability makes an appearance, a singular type of question often arises: "What, if anything, can be done?" "How much will it cost?" "Who is qualified or worth this expense?" This type of questioning conceals the social practice of making some bodies problems while making the doings and expenses of other bodies seem beyond question. It seems natural that we regard disability as an anomalous rarefied condition found only in a few individuals. So naturalized is this conception that it is difficult to realize that, like everything else that is a human matter, we have already granted our bodies meaning (Butler, 1993: 32). Insofar as daily life insists on employing a conception of disability that is void of the productive practices of culture, non-disability and normal participation are achieved as all the more authoritatively legitimate. It is this process of othering that makes disability void of the necessary relation between self and Other that grounds competency, legitimacy and participation.

A self-reflexive inquiry offers up the possibility of attending to the conversations we have already had such that disability is made meaningful as absence and as an unappreciated one at that. This is not just about making disabled people present and legitimate participants (although this is essential), it is also about turning towards disability as an occasion to reflect upon how we make some forms of absence *absent* from consciousness and to ask how culture, not nature, produces disability as this kind of void.

Disability studies claims that disability is more than a personal problem in need of solutions, such as rehabilitation, technological assistance or accommodative measures. Disability studies starts from the assumption that disability *is* a complex socio-political phenomenon where gender, race and other social differences are reified in unexamined ways. By thinking through bodily differences as part of daily life we can learn about the uneven ground that is the academy and which serves to organize our experiences of disability and knowledge production in general. Uncovering the ways in which disability is always already steeped in practices of social meaning-making can both enhance our understanding of the normative demands of education and lead us to explore transformative possibilities.

Our chapter demonstrates that disability in the academy is a space where the cultural production of social difference is reproduced in ways that often escape critical attention. For this reason, we now return to where we began. Recall the opening quotation from Paulo Freire about the dynamic relation between language and experience. Freire (1983) goes on to suggest that "… we can go further, and say that reading the word is not preceded merely by reading the world, but by a certain form of writing it or rewriting it, that is, of transforming it by means of conscious practical work" (10). The stories we tell ourselves about disability, then, do not only represent what culture has already told us about embodied difference; they are, in fact, evidence that we have already done something with that difference. To suggest that disability finds its expression through the intersections of language, power and embodiment — in those spaces where the material and the imagined meet and also evade one another — is thus to recognize the transformative potential of (re)negotiations grounded in the actualities of our daily lives and scholarly practices. Thinking gender and disability together, we might come to address the many practices that require a mind–body split and masculinized ways of knowing, and thus resist colonial relations to knowledge production that attempt always to tame or to same differences. As feminist anti-racist scholar Chandra Mohanty (2003) argues, to theorize and politicize difference requires that we engage what she calls "pedagogies of dissent" (217), taking seriously the intersubjective relations we bring to both our knowledge-making projects and our classroom and institutional practices, towards the active creation of "oppositional analytic and cultural spaces" (196). On a practical level, we hope that this chapter exemplifies the political necessity of pursing a self-reflexive relation to the conversations that we are all already having with disability. Understanding disability as a conversational achievement that can be traced throughout different social relationships and institutions is productive because it underscores that disability is always a dialogue — a dialogue that precedes any individual expression of disability and one that is carried forward in the writing and reading of this text. It is through this sort of engagement that we might learn to resist the common demand to understand disability only as a problem, and a problem requiring resolution.

Thus, this narrative does not end with the successful acquisition of assistive technology or with the claiming of a new identity; nor does this narrative end with the familiar conclusion that people do respond and adjust in the face of disability and embodied difference. We do not end with these resolutions, even though all such endpoints have been experienced by both of us. The hope of our chapter is, instead, to show that the ways we do end up living with disability are also the beginning places for desiring a self-reflective relation to social and political thought. Through our writing and rewriting of disability, we have sought to demonstrate a commitment to this kind of reflexive resistance that produces a fuller understanding of the social meanings of the contested space of the body in the academy.

NOTES

We thank the editors of this book for their engagement with our chapter and their thoughtful feedback. This work is funded by the SSHRC standard grant "Organizing Disablement: The University and Disability Experience" (#410-2006-2132).

1 According to the Government of Canada, assistive technology refers to "any hardware, software or system that overcomes or reduces the barriers inherent in standard technology" (Government of Canada, 2006).

2 The field of disability studies addresses the socio-political organization of "normal embodiment," for example, Davis (1995); Oliver (1996); Garland-Thomson (1997).

3 For an exception, consider McRuer (2006).

REFERENCES

Acker, S. (2003). The concerns of Canadian woman academics: Will faculty shortages make things better or worse? *McGill Journal of Education, 38*(2), 391–405.

Acker, S., & Armenti, C. (2004). Sleepless in academia. *Gender and Education, 16*(1), 3–24.

Butler, J. (1993). *Bodies that matter: On the discursive limits of "sex."* New York: Routledge.

Davis, L. (1995). *Enforcing normalcy: Disability, deafness and the body.* London: Verso Press.

Erevelles, N. (2000). Educating unruly bodies: Critical pedagogy, disability studies, and the politics of schooling. *Educational Theory, 50*(1), 25–47.

Freire, P. (1983). The importance of the act of reading. *Journal of Education, 165*(1), 5–11.

Garland-Thomson, R. (1997). *Extraordinary bodies: Figuring physical disability in American culture and literature.* New York: Columbia University Press.

Gordon, A. (1997). *Ghostly matters: Haunting and the sociological imagination.* Minneapolis: University of Minnesota Press.

Government of Canada. (2006, November 16). *Accessible procurement toolkit.* Retrieved 2 July 2007 from www.apt.gc.ca/dProdExpandE.asp?Id=260.

King, T. (2003). *The truth about stories: A native narrative.* Toronto: Anansi Press.

Maracle, L. (1990). *Oratory coming to theory.* North Vancouver: Gallerie Publications.

McRuer, R. (2006). *Crip theory: Cultural signs of queerness and disability.* New York: New York University Press.

McRuer, R., & Wilkerson, A. (2003). Desiring disability: Queer theory meets disability studies. *GLQ: A Journal of Lesbian and Gay Studies, 9*(1–2), 1–24.

Michalko, R. (2002). *The difference that disability makes.* Philadelphia: Temple University Press.

Michalko, R., & Titchkosky, T. (2001). Putting disability in its place: It's not a joking matter. In J.C. Wilson & C. Lewiecki-Wilson (Eds.), *Embodied rhetorics: Disability in language and culture* (200–228). Carbondale: Southern Illinois University Press.

Mohanty, C.T. (2003). *Feminism without borders: Decolonizing theory, practicing solidarity.* Durham, NC: Duke University Press.

Ng, R. (2000). Toward an embodied pedagogy: Exploring health and the body through Chinese medicine. In G.S. Dei, B.L. Hall, & D.G. Rosenberg (Eds.), *Indigenous knowledges in global contexts: Multiple readings of our world* (168–183). Toronto: University of Toronto Press.

Oliver, M. (1996). *Understanding disability: From theory to practice.* New York: St. Martin's Press.

Parsons, T. (1951). *The social system.* Glencoe, IL: The Free Press of Glencoe.

Smith, B.G., & Hutchison, B. (2004). *Gendering disability.* New Brunswick, NJ: Rutgers University Press.

Thomas, C. (2006). Disability and gender: Reflections on theory and research. *Scandinavian Journal of Disability Research, 8*(2–3), 175–185.

Titchkosky, T. (2008). To pee or not to pee? Ordinary talk about extraordinary exclusions in a university environment. *Canadian Journal of Sociology, 33*(1), 37–60.

Titchkosky, T. (2007). *Reading and writing disability differently: The textured life of embodiment.* Toronto: University of Toronto Press.

Titchkosky, T. (2005). Clenched subjectivity: Disability, women and medical discourse. *Disability Studies Quarterly, 25*(3). Retrieved 11 March 2008 from www.dsq-sds-archives.org/2005_summer_toc.html.

Titchkosky, T. (2003). *Disability, self and society.* Toronto: University of Toronto Press.

Wendell, S. (1996). *The rejected body: Feminist philosophical reflections on disability.* New York: Routledge.

PART II

NAVIGATING

THE ACADEMY

CHAPTER 4

THE HOT SEAT:

THE BLACK SCHOLAR'S PERCEPTION

OF THE "CHILLY CLIMATE"

Patrice A. White

Canadian campus conflicts revolve around the concept of "chilly climate." The phrase "chilly climate" was coined in 1982 by Americans Bernice Sandler and Roberta Hall to capture the combined effect of a number of practices which ... cumulatively communicate lack of confidence, lack of recognition and devaluation, and which result in women's marginalization.

— Susan Prentice, "The Conceptual Politics of Chilly Climate Controversies"

WHETHER OR NOT A "CHILLY CLIMATE" EXISTS IS A DEBATE THIS CHAPTER does not propose to resolve or make central to its discussion. The fact of the matter is that regardless of the labels they are given, the elements that indicate a "chilly climate" are indiscriminate forms of prejudice. This reality is often lost in the debate, and so too is the notion that female is not a homogeneous label, but rather one that is further deconstructed (and compounded) by race and ethnicity. In fact, "it must be recognized that white/Anglo women have more power and privilege than Hispanas,

Black women, etc." (Lugones & Spelman, 1983, quoted in Jones, 1999: 305). Therefore, women as gender minorities are subject to diverse climates. And while all are potentially troubled by the inequities inherent in their advancement within higher education, skin colour colours similar experiences differently. Within higher education, the rueful discussion of racism ushers in new challenges for the Other, not to mention novel definitions of alienating and isolating acts. That one can be "chilled" by attention that fixates on difference and favours a script of oppression over less controversial intellectual debate is the reality of this post-secondary racialized[1] student.

RACIALIZED

I use the term racialized to capture the socially, politically and economically driven act of identity coercion, as it pertains to the racial segregation that is routinely embedded in the institutions "whose administrative and departmental structures sometimes seem to practice a sort of disciplinary apartheid" (Chavez-Silverman, 2000: 136). That the content of one's interests is often policed and (for the sake of specialization and institutional integrity) hog-tied to one's gender, class, sexuality and race is a reality that is packaged in the term. Certainly, the concept of racialization allows those who are critical enough to enquire the opportunity to understand that the dominant culture has determined that a person of colour's points of reference (and interest) should be her race, followed by the "other hierarchical categories such as gender and class, as is the case in the life experiences of racialized women in particular" (Galabuzi, 2006: 34). It is these standardized barriers to "border crossing" (Chavez-Silverman, 2000: 137) that reminds someone classified in Canadian parlance as "visible/racial minority" that this classification is merely an assignment and reinforcement of her inferiority, and not, as it has been promoted to be, a category "for the purpose of addressing … disadvantage" (Galabuzi, 2006: 31). And so, "racialized" not only exposes how this identity has been negatively coded, but asserts that the status is not "*a* given," but one that has *been* given, or imposed. Therefore, the type of inclusion that is practised in higher education, the sort in which the spotlight binds the Other to a script and performance of oppression and anger, and blinds the spectators to her hybridity and the multiplicity of her interests, also creates a chill.

Higher education's alternative approach of overstudying the Other creates an inverse set of rules, but a similar dilemma. This intense curiosity about the Other not only objectifies her but also mediates a new type of "chilly climate." No doubt, this way of dealing with difference is based on a postmodern teaching methodology designed to open up "discourses so that previously inadmissible questions and unheard voices can have access to it" (Worth, 1993: 61). Nevertheless, when imposed on the Black female student, even if for the sake of fostering an understanding and empathy for her position and stories, the spotlight creates somewhat of a hot seat. This scholarly obligation to be transparent not only runs counter to the culture of privacy and observation that is common to the Black female experience but also violates her (racialized and gendered) body — the canvases and scripts from which she is expected to teach. For Black females, the "chilly climate" of higher education resides in the fact that in order to participate at this level, the Black female scholar must denude her cultural bodies of knowledge. As Bannerji (1991) explains, "this body, along with centuries of 'knowing,' of existential and historical racism, is [her] 'teaching' presence and tool" (6). Even so, such a use of one's body is an uncomfortable and insincere response that betrays a systemic and more insidious type of slavery, one in which study and curiosity (outside of one's racial and gendered identities) is rationed, and the educational harness that keeps one feeding exclusively from the trough of one's oppression is recast as the "Underground Railroad" to racial and gender equality.

CHILLED BY THE SPOTLIGHT

From their first days on campus, women students encounter multiple patterns of gender bias that are liabilities both inside and outside of the classroom. It has been repeatedly documented that women are at a distinct educational disadvantage in the classroom (Chapman, 1989: 287).

Chapman's (1989) overview of the alleged "chilly climate" stimulated my own intimate search for experiences that parallel this claim. Imagine my surprise when the conditions of the "chilly climate" did not immediately trigger flashbacks of subtle acts of oppression. In fact, up until the writing of this chapter, I would have resolutely stated that the institutional efforts and initiatives to address and amend these elements, while not overwhelmingly efficient, have fairly eased my agitation at being silenced and rendered history-less.

The departments in which I have been a graduate student —York University's "Language, Culture and Teaching" and OISE/University of Toronto's "Sociology and Equity Studies in Education" — explicitly frame their mandate of inclusivity and awareness in their department titles. Even so, I am repeatedly stripped naked by the overly earnest efforts to understand the struggle for which I have become a poster child. Whereas the white man and his history have had the luxury of time to be studied, discussed, photographed, filmed and emulated, the well-meaning but somewhat panicked efforts to hastily insert the authenticated voice of the racialized and gendered individual into canons of literature and theory have positioned the Black woman as a specimen rather than a student in the classroom. Having to speak almost exclusively about the Black experience has placed undue pressure on the racialized student who is still becoming acclimatized to the terms of her new acceptance. What's more, being expected (on a moment's notice!) to articulate how dominating discourses have affected our public and private selves is a pressure that racialized scholars must resolve and master at the risk of undoing the ambitious reparations that have occurred within the space of a generation. It is a performance without external props, one that relies on the body for its script, a way of teaching that Bannerji (1991) describes as being both the object and the subject (7). And so, not being able to locate my source of alienation within these elements does not mean that I have developed the "ruthless single mindedness" to which Curthoys (1995) attributes "the success of female researchers" (205). Rather, what it signifies is that I, not unlike Ng (1993),

> … want to draw attention to the interactional dimension of power relations operating as forms of exclusion and marginalization by recognizing that in addition to our structural positions as students, faculty, and staff in the academy, we are at the same time gendered and racialized subjects. (195)

WRITTEN ON THE BODY: PERFORMING BLACKNESS

> Bodies are "maps of power and identity."
> — Donna Haraway, "A Manifesto for Cyborgs"

Bodies cannot be adequately understood as historical, precultural, or natural objects in any simple way; they are not only inscribed,

> marked engraved, by social pressures external to them but are
> the products, the direct effects of the very constitution of nature
> itself.
> — Elizabeth Grosz, *Volatile Bodies*

Interestingly enough, being one of few racialized females in a seminar class has actually garnered me more attention. It has certainly elicited such comments as, "Patrice, you LOOK like you have something to say." Oftentimes, my not verbalizing my feelings has been interpreted as an invitation to politely press me for a response. At first I obliged, apologizing for the fleeting expressions of confusion, anger, surprise and approval that flash across my face and body with some half-baked response. I did it out of a sense of duty to my participation mark and not a mutual desire for "enlightened acceptance of multiplicity" (Jones, 1999: 315); the former might otherwise be compromised by a stubborn silence. In one first-year undergraduate class, this event occurred so frequently that I developed an almost crippling fear of the professor and his class. I actually began leaving between the general lecture and class discussion, fearful that without warning my option to participate would be wrenched out of my control. When the professor called me at home to inquire about my partial absences, I mumbled something about a teaching-related throat illness and began counting down the days to the course's end. In this instant, the chilly climate of being "overexposed" rendered the classroom an intimidating space.

Although I have had my fair share of female professors and lecturers, my never having been taught by more than one racialized faculty (male or female) in almost ten years of full- and part-time studies in Canada's multicultural core (Toronto) is somewhat disconcerting. These absent bodies might be explained by the fact that I rarely gravitate towards the courses with the blatantly ethnic and multicultural titles. On the grounds that they narrowly define and tend to "tropicalize" (Chavez-Silverman, 2000) if not divide the liberal arts student body into distinct camps — the curious and voyeuristic, the guilty and the oppressed — I tend to resist these minority-taught and themed modules. Instead, I prefer to fracture and expose stereotypes by disciplining my body to sit through (and enjoy) Old English studies of Chaucer's collected works rather than an advanced Contemporary Black Authors seminar. Is there self-sacrifice in my decision to meet institutionalized mentors on my own terms and in a desperately indirect fashion? Most definitely! For I hold out hope that one day a Black woman who does not need to publicly work through the intersection of her race and gender before a captive audience of undergraduate and graduate students will lead an enthralling discussion on the "Knight's Tale." I am searching for the role model who does not feel compelled to perform Blackness, the individual who will instead exhibit the breadth of interests that racialized students and teaching faculty pursue outside of their cultural centres.

Higher education, specifically the new rituals of "sharing or talking across difference" (Jones, 1999: 299) in the classrooms of the contemporary university, ignored my desire to revel in the pure and connecting beauty of silence. Jones explains that this practice of making things visible and therefore coherent and accessible is central to the white "cannibal desire to know the Other" (313). It certainly explains why this form of transparency, which is sanctioned by a yearning for progressive pedagogy, sometimes sits uncomfortably with me. What I find most discomfiting about this new pedagogy is that it assumes a cultural knowledge (from the Other) that should be readily articulated. And should she arrive (to academe) ill-equipped, this ambitious curriculum tries to provide her with a script and history of her oppression to which she must adhere. When my autobiographical reading of Rudyard Kipling's *Jungle Book* was met with the suggestion that a colonial reading would have been more appropriate to my own interests — which I had not revealed — I realized that I had somehow flubbed my lines.

This course, taken in the first year of my graduate studies, led us (students) through critical readings of the text and historical contexts of classic children's stories and international fairytales and fables. From *Peter Rabbit* to *Good Night Moon*, we took turns evaluating the stories as both innocent entertainment and potentially subversive tales from a culture mired in racism, sexism, colonialism and capitalism. So, when it came time to choose a student-led seminar topic, I opted to focus on *The Jungle Book* and the autobiographical elements that were woven into the story's characters and plotlines. While the other non-white female student chose to examine and expose the racist elements in *Little Black Sambo*, I decentred the obvious colonialist elements in *The Jungle Book* to offer a less strident but no less equity-conscious critique. While my approach to the text could not sidestep the sexist and racist elements of the narrative, my autobiographical focus might easily have suggested that at least one of two "brown" females had actually veered from the minority-beaten path to choose the road less travelled. We had set out on two separate journeys, facilitated two very different but valid discussions and managed to do both well. Why then did I receive the book *The Struggle: The History of the African National Congress* (Holland, 1989) as a parting gift from the professor? The book disagreed with both my topic and presentation, and so, I was perplexed by the seeming disconnect. It sits unread at the bottom of my bookshelf, a constant reminder that I may have strayed outside the acceptable boundaries of research for a minority female. Doing well in the course did not rescue it from being my least positive and self-affirming experience. You see, this one generous act of gift giving challenged my intellectual self-confidence, reminding me that even within higher education, there are still doors marked "Black Only."

THE HOT SEAT

Though sometimes awkward in its embrace of the oppressed Other, feminist pedagogy, particularly its central act of troubling homogenized and masculine discourses, offers some warmth to the female academic of colour. It is an oddly compelling fire, for it warms the soul of the conscious majority with a sense of justice and "doing good" while "chilling" the benefactors. Finally, it provokes a perplexing mixture of resentment and relief in the victim/ subject of repatriation. As a racialized female, I have been relieved by the effort to understand me, and will often endure — for the sake of knowledge — the curiosity that is made palatable by scholarly pursuits. Still, the effort to understand the neglected Other cannot quite quell the knot of resentment that rises every time the spotlight is shone on my experiences as a Black woman. Invariably, my historical struggle to negotiate a presence and a voice in multiple contexts will define my role in the group, and I am rarely permitted to occupy more than this critical but limiting role. Perhaps I should be happy that I am not subject to the same "questions of ... authenticity" that Susana Chavez-Silverman (2000) endured because "I didn't look oppressed enough for white liberals or black cult nats" (134). Unlike Chavez-Silverman, the colour of my skin does not signal "confusion" (134) about my racial identity, just a perceived disconnect between my non-minority colleagues and me. I am rarely allowed (particularly within my graduate studies) to be a fellow student with the same theoretical quandaries, guilty preference for qualitative research methodologies and predilections for Marxism. I must somehow intersect my beliefs and practice with the identity by which I choose not to be identified, but by which I am forced to identify — Black and under-represented in higher education — in short, the Other. Sometimes the only respite I get from this fixed standpoint is the opportunity to speak from my professional experiences as an "educator," who in seven years of teaching has taught in every division and resisted a dramatic and volatile history of teacher turnovers to become the second-longest serving staff member at my current work site. I relish these moments, even when the topics are mundane. Nevertheless, when conversations in which colleagues' attempts to probe my "true" feelings about being a "Black educator in a diverse classroom" became the after-seminar ritual, I began to understand my participation to be intriguing because my designation is exoticized by my skin colour. It is a reality from which I cannot escape and one that reaffirms my resentment of a culture that wants to understand me on its own terms. Now, that is what kills, no ... chills me.

As an educator, speaking from the "teacher's experience" is not uncommon, particularly in circles where teachers are underrepresented. What I find peculiar, though, is that when there is no short supply of teachers, I am often tagged as the "speaker" for the group. This "hot-seat experience" is recurring, and I am hard pressed to believe that it is because I am an eager or dynamic speaker. I can only surmise that some other factor is demanding repeat performances, a factor that is visible, compelling and even exotic, namely, the colour of my skin and the remoteness/disharmony of my experiences. To be sure, I prefer the ambiguity of positionality, a type of feminist pedagogy that Chavez-Silverman (2000) describes in the tropical classroom to imply "above all, that there is no one text" (145). To me, a Black woman whose "hot-seat" experiences have found me complicit in reproducing tropicalized or hegemonic representations of the Black woman in higher education, the notion of there not being one text is endearing.

CONCLUSION

While Acker (2004) concluded that the work intensification and associated stressors revealed in her research on academics are not necessarily synonymous with chilly climates, my auto-ethnography of the Black female academic's experience suggests a new understanding of the chilly climate, one premised on an intense set of exposures that, by provoking exhaustion, continues to disadvantage the minority female and agent of change.

Within the context of my personal history, "the chilly climate" hides in the shadows of opportunity. Not only does it limit its beneficiaries with expectations that expose and force them to yield control of their bodies, but also denies them access to outside knowledge and of the supposedly progressive rituals of transparency within higher education. This chapter, then, while it recognizes and applauds the equity ambitions inherent in higher education's curricula and practice, also levies a caution that must be heeded. Lest higher education wishes to burn out a generation of racialized and gendered individuals who are now only finding and exercising their voice, unreasonable time frames and expectations of the Other will have to be amended. Indeed, hurried (and harried!) recruitment efforts will not fix years of repression and subjugation. Instead, we — and I include "members of the target groups who are already a part of the campus community" (Valora-Harvey, 1989: 3) — must celebrate and encourage the holistic expressions of the Other. We must also realize that "providing students with role models, preparing minority youth to assume positions of authority, and ... supporting minority-related scholarship" (Valora-Harvey, 1989: 2) can actually limit the scholar's authority to things that pertain only to her gender and culture, which in turn restricts her audience, her power, her flexibility and mobility within higher education. And so, it is not only vital that we increase the transparency of our past but also recognize that how one achieves clarity is controlled by a dominant culture, one that is complicit in maintaining the repression that it is meant to expose.

NOTE

1 Grace-Edward Galabuzi's explanation of the term "racialialized" is here used to describe my understanding of "racialized" as a term that resists and critiques the coded and essentializing category/label, "visible minority." According to Galabuzi (2006), "the term 'racialized groups' is used to describe non-Aboriginal people of colour, also referred to by Statistics Canada and in the *Federal Employment Equity*

Act as visible minorities. Its use here and elsewhere suggests a discomfort with the official use of the term 'visible minority' because it implies a permanence of minority status that is imposed on the population. Racialized denotes that process of imposition, the social construction of the category, and the attendant experience of oppression as opposed to the seemingly neutral use of the terms 'visible minorities' or 'racial minorities,' which have the effect of masking the oppressions" (xvi).

REFERENCES

Acker, S. (2004). Managing in the chilly climate of change: Women academics in leadership positions. In D. Liwiski et al., (Eds.), *Sexism in the academy? 10 years later. Proceedings from CASWE's Tenth Anniversary Institute* (95–102). Winnipeg: University of Manitoba.

Bannerji, H. (1991). Returning the gaze. *Resources for Feminist Research, 20*(3–4), 5–11.

Chapman, S. C. (1989). Helping diverse first year students: Women students. In M. Lee Upcraft & J. N. Gardner (Eds.), *The freshman year experience: Helping students survive and succeed in college* (287–302). San Francisco: Jossey-Bass.

Chavez-Silverman, S. (2000). Tropicalizing the liberal arts college classroom, In S. Gook-Lin Lim & M. Herrera-Sobek (Eds.), *Power, race and gender in academe* (132–153). New York: Modern Language Association.

Curthoys, A. (1995). Taking advantage of disadvantage: Women and research. In A.M. Payne & L. Shoemark (Eds.), *Women, culture and universities — A chilly climate? Proceedings of the National Conference on the Effect of Organisational Culture on Women in Universities* (205–208). Sydney, Australia: University of Technology Sydney.

Galabuzi, G. (2006). *Canada's economic apartheid: The social exclusion of racialized groups in the new century.* Toronto: Canadian Scholars' Press.

Grosz, E.A. (1994). *Volatile bodies: Toward a corporeal feminism.* Bloomington: Indiana University Press.

Haraway, D. (1990). A manifesto for cyborgs. In L. Nicholson (Ed.), Feminism/postmodernism (190–234). New York: Routledge.

Holland, H. (1989) *The struggle: A history of the African National Congress.* New York: George Braziller.

Jones, A. (1999). The limits of cross-cultural dialogue: Pedagogy, desire, and absolution in the classroom. *Educational Theory, 49*(3), 299–316.

Lugones, M., & Spelman, E. (1983). Have we got a theory for you! Feminist theory, cultural imperialism, and the demand for "the woman's voice." *Women's Studies International Forum, 6*(6), 573–581.

Ng, R. (1993). "A woman out of control": Deconstructing sexism and racism in the university. *Canadian Journal of Education, 18*(3), 189–205.

Prentice, S. (2000). The conceptual politics of chilly climate controversies. *Gender and Education, 12*(2), 195–207.

Valora-Harvey, W. (1989). *Affirmative rhetoric, negative action: African-American and Hispanic faculty at predominantly white institutions.* Washington, DC: ERIC Clearinghouse on Higher Education.

Worth, F. (1993). Postmodern pedagogy in the multicultural classroom: For inappropriate teachers and imperfect spectators. *Cultural Critique, 25*, 5–32.

CHAPTER 5

THE INVISIBLE CLOAK:

EXPLORING THE IMPACT OF TRAUMA
ON WOMEN LEARNERS IN HIGHER EDUCATION

Anne Wagner

Trauma is like a big cloak that covers you and that sets you apart and you go through the world under this cloak. So there is that really deep sense sometimes — that I'm not like other people. And other people can go into things with relative ease, but I can't.

— Julia, graduate student

As ISSUES OF DIVERSITY AND EQUITY BECOME MORE FAMILIAR ACROSS Canadian campuses, we increasingly hear about initiatives to remove/reduce barriers for people from traditionally marginalized groups, in order to afford them greater ease of access to sites of higher education. In addition to practical initiatives have come critical scholarly perspectives on the salience of identities grounded in race, class, sexuality, ability and gender (Reay, 1998; Monture-Angus, 2001; Titchkosky, 2003; Acker & Armenti, 2004; Cotterill & Letherby, 2005; Lenskyj, 2005), in which higher education is seen as a contested public sphere and political site for the reproduction of power relations and social inequality. Our knowledge is now sufficiently advanced that we can move beyond simple categorization in terms such as gender and race and begin to explore aspects of those identities that are particularly salient to the experience of higher education. As we know, not all women (or men) are "the same." This chapter is concerned with one group of women students, those who have experienced a particular form of trauma, namely, interpersonal violence — defined here as having experienced either physical or sexual abuse at some point in their lives. This aspect of women's collective reality has not been widely recognized within the context of higher education.

My argument starts from the premise that structural inequality and oppression deeply affect women learners and are embedded in current institutional practices. I see power as manifested through the structures of our educational institutions, the pedagogical practices we engage in and take as "the norm," and the knowledge that is produced both in and out of the classroom. While education is known to instill certain norms and values in students (such as the value of hard work), it plays a more subtle and unrecognized role in reinforcing dominant ideologies and common-sense understandings, some of which can do harm to persons oppressed by other aspects of their lives. How, then, is violence against women understood within the context of academia?

SITUATING THE RESEARCH

Acknowledging that interpersonal violence is a fact of life for many women (Herman, 1992; Brown, 1995), this research was designed to explore how women's experiences of trauma may affect their pursuit of university education. It draws on qualitative interviews with seven diversely situated women students (both graduate and undergraduate) who identify as having experienced violence at some point in their lives.[1] In addition, seven feminist-identified faculty were interviewed, in order to focus more specifically on some of the challenges that experiences of trauma evoke within feminist academic classes. Participants were recruited via posters and electronic postings and were drawn from a variety of social science disciplines. Involving more than one constituency was a strategy to provide a more holistic perspective on how the issue is viewed by differently positioned subjects, what constraints are inherent in the system and how changes might be sought. The faculty perspective also provides a means of identifying structural constraints of which students may not be aware.

Feminist classrooms were of particular interest because of the assumption that such venues may be expected to have the most fully developed analyses of the situation faced by women who have experienced or are experiencing violence. In feminist classes, learners are encouraged to theorize the personal — a situation which can present unique challenges for some students. Such a pedagogical approach does not allow students to remain in the position of passive learners, instead stimulating them to become reflexive about their own positioning in systems of oppression and dominance. This task has not proved to be easy, and theorizing on feminist pedagogy increasingly acknowledges the inevitability of conflict in the classroom.

It is significant that this radical project of feminist pedagogy is situated within a system that has often been described as androcentric, racist and classist (Monture-Angus, 2001; see also Bourdieu, 2001). According to Bourdieu (2001), academia incorporates a masculine order that is naturalized and presented as neutral. Any reality inconsistent with this universalized androcentric vision is denied or rendered invisible through a process of "symbolic domination" (37). Women are expected to adapt to hegemonic practices within the academy that are largely derived from the experiences of white, heterosexual, able-bodied men. This research will use Bourdieu's work as a lens through which to explore the extent to which feminist classes successfully disrupt these oppressive practices, with a particular focus on the perspectives of women who have experienced violence.

STUDENT VOICES

Anne-Louise Brookes (1992) has written compellingly from the perspective of a graduate student about coping with a history of traumatization. One of the most damaging effects she has recalled is the effective silencing that she encountered as a result of the shame and doubt associated with her experiences of violence. As she describes it,

> Relations of power can work to produce the well-kept secret of male violence against women ... And, it is reproduced through schooling practices ... which work only too well to reinforce feelings of fear, inadequacy and contempt — teaching us that it is not nice, not scholarly and certainly not scientific to speak of the personal in an academic context. These social practices work to bifurcate our consciousness, and in so doing, prevent us from actually talking about or knowing the illusions, assumptions and learned values which organize our everyday experiences. These forms work to silence women. (10)

Each of the student participants involved in the research believed that trauma definitely has an impact on a significant proportion of women students. Further, each described her decision to speak about violence as a strategy of resistance, defying cultural dictates to remain silent. Elaine,[2] a mature white student pursuing a liberal arts BA and mother of three, explained that when she was growing up in the 1970s, women who were subject to violence were expected to be ashamed and not speak of it.

> Of course you know you don't question that you deserved it … not that it was right but that it just happens and there's nothing you could do about it. So you're basically given a message that it's just inevitable and that's just kind of your lot in life.

This pervasive sense of guilt and shame was shared by many of the women, who internalized the message that violence was a personal issue which should not be acknowledged within the realm of the public. Reflecting on their experiences in academia, many students felt that these messages were reinforced in mainstream classrooms even today. Such socially sanctioned beliefs, it may be argued, are actively encouraged by a society that does not want to bear witness to such pain and that seeks to erase its complicity by perpetuating systems of oppression and dominance. Horsman (1999) has perceptively noted that a great deal of survivors' energy is directed towards attempting to hide any effects of the abuse, masking their symptoms and diverting energy that otherwise could be used for learning.

Students recounted that by the time they became involved in feminist classes, each had bridled against social dictates and developed a willingness (at some point) to speak of their past within the confines of the feminist class. Hope, a Black undergraduate student and mother of two, remarked, "I'd say I'm pretty vocal now. I'm making up for those six years of living silent." Gilda, a white mature mother of grown children who emigrated from Portugal as a child and is now working towards her BA, attributed her decision to speak out to her current feelings of safety after having left her violent marriage. "I can talk about it now because I'm not in it … I can talk about it because I've been through it." Central to all of the narratives was the contention that each woman was resisting subtle admonishments to remain silent by claiming the space within feminist classrooms to share their experiences.

These decisions were often fraught with difficulties and not without associated costs. Interestingly, undergraduate and graduate students in the study approached the question of disclosure from different perspectives. Those studying at the undergraduate level were much more likely to frame disclosure as an opportunity to share experience, thereby educating others. Amy, a white mature student and mother, espoused a position which was characteristic of many students when she explained that sharing her experiences served as a growth experience for all in the class. In contrast, Erica and Julia, both racially minoritized female graduate students, highlighted some of the dilemmas associated with disclosing their experiences of violence to fellow students. Julia recalled being very open about her experiences as an undergraduate, but later became concerned about the ways in which her revelations were understood by others. Julia's worry was founded on the understanding that many tropes about sexual abuse of racially minoritized women were frequently evoked and, consequently, her past was often understood in very simplistic and superficial ways. In her own words,

> How do I explain the fact that I was treated very badly by my dad and by my uncle ... by Chinese men, within a racist context of other violences being committed by white teachers, by white children. There's just so many complexities. I can't just read my dad or my uncle as just mere "men," the generic male perpetrator. There are lots of things within that as well — about being an immigrant. There's just lots and lots of stuff around it.

Erica concurred with Julia's ideas about the limitations of sharing personal information, further highlighting the personal costs of doing so. Erica also feared that other students read her experiences of violence through her status as a South Asian woman, rather than as a commentary on patriarchy. Erica felt an obligation to the broader South Asian community, as a result of the kind of stereotypical thinking previously described by Julia.

> There is that kind of concern, that if you have been abused, then you have to be careful what you tell people because they may think you cannot be objective. I think I just felt that the classroom wasn't safe and particularly in a white classroom — talking about domestic violence, I hardly ever do that.

Despite the small sample size, which included only one undergraduate student of colour, the distinctions between graduate students and undergraduates seem potentially significant. The graduate students acknowledged the complexity of personal experience and deliberately contested the notion that simply sharing one's history is an adequate tool for learning, especially when experience is reduced to one facet of their identity, which is then interpreted through a dominant (and often misinformed) lens of understanding. Not recognizing the intricacies of women's lives, they countered, obscures structural and systemic inequities, thereby reinforcing current societal hierarchies. Dominant processes of interpretation serve to restrict the agency of these women, accentuating perceived "differences" and construing them as victims of their culture, their level of ability or whatever other social location is being accorded prominence in the formulation (Razack, 1999; Krane, Oxman-Martinez & Ducey, 2000). Potter (1995) suggests that such practices are indicative of an institutional tendency to conceptualize students as disembodied learners, resulting in the decontextualization of their "existential reality" (70). Although women's studies classrooms have realized considerable gains in acknowledging power dynamics and striving to foster inclusiveness, as the experiences of these students attest, further work needs to be done regarding the theorizing and acknowledgement of multiple and intersecting forms of oppression, including experiences of trauma. Otherwise, the result will be continuing "epistemic alienation" (Potter, 1995: 77), where simplistic stereotypes function as yet another system of oppression through which students are forced to manoeuvre.

FACULTY VOICES

Both students and faculty grappled with the tension involved when participating in discussions in which the personal is valued, yet the boundary of how much sharing is appropriate is never clearly evident. As many of the faculty and students acknowledged, it is often difficult to draw such boundaries in the midst of what are often very emotionally laden discussions. Hence, although all agree in principle on the value of the pedagogical practice of sharing the personal, the problems with such an approach are also readily apparent. Teresa, a faculty member who identified as an immigrant to Canada from South America, explained that the issue is even more complicated when we note that the process of discerning social conventions about how much information is socially appropriate to share is grounded in culture and class:

There's an enormous difference of what is private for different people. I come from a culture where nothing is private, where everybody talks about everything. I find that for example in a North American environment, there's an amazing amount of things that are private that I would never think they were. So it's very difficult for people to judge, to have to understand what is private and what is not — what should be said and what should not be said.

Teresa's example illustrates the difficulty faculty face in maintaining boundaries in the classroom for students. In the context of addressing students' histories of violence, faculty must balance the inclusion of personal experience as a valued pedagogical tool with consideration of whether such disclosures are relevant to the point at hand, while linking these reflections to broader theoretical considerations. In order to maintain a balance, faculty often relied on meeting with students outside of class, in order to offer support and referrals, if required, thereby reinforcing what they saw as appropriate boundaries within and around the class. In this way, faculty attempted to validate students' experiences while ensuring that the classroom did not become a space of prolonged personal introspection. For students, such practices are difficult to read, as they might be interpreted as another attempt to silence them.

Faculty struggled with questions of balance. When asked about their perceptions of the unique needs of students who had experienced violence, faculty responses were noteworthy. Although conscious of violence against women as an important social issue, faculty found it challenging to translate this abstract knowledge into examples of concrete practices that inform their pedagogical strategies. Chris, a white faculty member who identified as having an interest in queer activism, was unique in identifying that her own experiences with victimization informed her actions in the classroom:

My own experiences with violence and trauma have definitely informed the kind of topics I bring into the classroom and the choices I'm making in terms of safety for my students and things like that. Recognizing my students have possibly encountered violence also makes me sensitive towards what's going on in their lives and the impact upon education.

It is significant to note that Chris's sensitivity regarding the impact of violence on students was not based on any institutionally supported context. Lorraine, a white faculty member whose teaching experience was primarily grounded in the United Kingdom, concurred that the issue of violence is marginalized in institutional discourse. As many faculty participants noted, institutional support services focus on issues of stress management, skill development and English as an additional language. Tellingly, issues of violence were never acknowledged during the orientations attended by the participants. Perhaps addressing problems of language is less threatening than dealing with something as personal as issues of violence.

Nancy, a white junior faculty member who identified as having a disability, further challenged dominant practices, suggesting that universities often gloss over the differing needs of students, claiming to be equitable by treating everyone in the same way. Although all of the participants acknowledged that staff in academia have been working to support diversely positioned students and gains have been realized, the consensus was that more needs to be done. It was suggested that unless all students perceive that their realities are being recognized, these groups may not feel that they are being accorded a legitimate place within academic structures. Bourdieu (2001) would also frame this situation as reflecting the masculine order of academia, in which certain realities are affirmed at the expense of others, thereby perpetuating "masculine domination" (88).

Faculty were also concerned about how best to respond to student disclosures of violence. The most common practice was to offer a referral, thus connecting the woman to a support while simultaneously maintaining appropriate professorial–student boundaries. Chris was the sole exception, suggesting that working with students to establish immediate safety was within her purview as a professor. Offering an example of a situation in which a student disclosed that her husband had threatened to kill her, Chris explained:

> I also have made a point of knowing what the resources are, so I can say, "Here are resources in the community; here are your rights as a student. Do we need to get your husband banned from campus? Can I take you to the Human Rights Commission so that you … can let them know what's going on and what your rights are. Do you need me to call a police officer on your behalf?" Like, there are all of these things that go on outside of the classroom.

Although acutely aware of maintaining appropriate boundaries once the initial crisis had passed and the woman was connected to longer-term support, Chris clearly felt it imperative to offer practical support beyond the initial provision of a referral. It is possible that her self-identification as a person who experienced violence while a student informed her response.

These differing interpretations of the appropriate role of faculty are noteworthy, since such practices involve not only considerable time commitments but also illustrate the general uncertainty resulting from a lack of clear institutional policy guidelines regarding such sensitive issues. Participants all acknowledged that a disproportionate number of feminist faculty are confronted with these situations, given the nature of their pedagogical commitments and the reality that students approach women faculty more often than men about personal concerns (for example, see Acker & Feuerverger, 1997; Cotterill & Letherby, 2005). It is clear that interpreting one's faculty role too broadly could quickly lead to overwork and burnout. These dynamics are also consistent with Bourdieu's concept of masculine domination evident within the broader institutional context, in which such emotional (and largely female) labour is devalued (Acker & Dillabough, 2007). Faculty did identify tensions between the feminist project undertaken in their individual classrooms and the broader university environs. Despite their efforts to structure their classrooms in ways that affirmed students' diverse identities and experiences, they acknowledged the reality that such practices are not consistently used within the broader university community. Further, institutional realities such as large class sizes also affect the possibility of fully enacting effective feminist pedagogy (Webber, 2006). As a result, feminist faculty are in an untenable situation, forced to function within a system that affords them scant support and often relegates their pedagogical practices to the periphery.

ENVISIONING CHANGE

As institutions increasingly become aware of issues of equity and diversity, this historical juncture offers a unique opportunity to challenge academia not only to acknowledge but also to act on an understanding of the impact that trauma may have on women learners. I recognize that other sources of oppression are equally pressing, and I do not intend to invoke a competing hierarchy of oppressions. As detailed in the feminist literature (for example, see Lorde, 1984; Fellows & Razack, 1998), such tactics have often been used by the privileged to fragment marginalized or oppressed groups, as each struggles to have their reality affirmed. Instead, what is being advocated is a more holistic perspective that acknowledges and values student diversity. Any approach that seeks to conceptualize women's lives must recognize not only experiences of violence but also interlocking sources of oppression.

Many participants proposed the instigation of anti-oppression policies as a strategy to work towards infusing academic practices with an acknowledgement of the diversity among students. While adopting such frameworks is significant, as Ahmed (2007) has painstakingly detailed (see also Martimianakis's chapter in this volume), simply adding equity references to institutional policies is inadequate. Even worse, the development of ostensibly positive initiatives may, in fact, serve to conceal inequities while doing little to challenge the status quo of the institutional culture. Instead of acting as a vehicle for change, dissemination of the policy may become part of the "institutional performance" (Ahmed, 2007: 594), thereby presenting the image that inequity is being addressed without altering the reality.

Accordingly, Helen, a racially minoritized faculty member who identified as having experienced considerable ageism, suggested that policy can only be one component of a larger initiative. In her view, meaningful change would require implementing measures beyond "typical liberal democratic means ... tinkering with the system." Although acknowledging the value of specialized services such as the sexual harassment office, participants noted that such initiatives were underfunded and possibly established as part of the "institutional performance." While not denigrating the work being done by individuals in these departments, some called attention to the value of actually questioning broader institutional and societal practices that continue to place women at greater risk of being the targets of violence.

Interrogating the institutional and societal definitions of violence, according to Kathy, a faculty member who identifies as Aboriginal, would be a useful strategy, challenging us to collectively consider the everyday violence that women endure. For instance, even in the absence of traditionally understood forms of violence, women's position in society may be understood as a source of violence. Offering the example of the impact of inadequate student funding, she explained that students may feel they have no choice but to work in unsafe situations in order to afford their education.

> I had a woman last year who worked at a casino at night and [went] to school during the day, [and did] her placement three days a week … to get herself through school. I admire that determination and that strength but why, you know? Why is it like that?

Kathy clearly questions the accountability of the university and government funding formulas in ensuring that students have equal access to education, irrespective of their class status. Linda, a Jewish lesbian faculty member, identified safety as another significant systemic issue, reflecting on how the physical design of the campus may disadvantage women students. While acknowledging the positive initiatives such as Walk Safe programs,[3] she contended that campuses are "structured around men's reality." As a result, universities present a toxic environment for women, who may feel that they can only access campus resources at certain times of day, thereby limiting their ability to move around freely. Significantly, both of these narratives highlight the necessity of theorizing the need for changes from the perspective of the lived realities of women.

Even when universities focus on women's physical safety through programs like Walk Safe, they continue to ignore other ways in which violence may be intertwined in women's lives, in the process silencing women and contributing to a sense that one's physical, emotional and social safety are being eroded in the university community. Erica, a graduate student, suggested that such negation of women's identities and the concomitant silencing of women's experience do not go unnoticed by women students. Silence about such realities can be seen as a form of symbolic violence perpetrated against women (Bourdieu, 2001).

Thus, conceptualizing change must begin with a consideration of the extent to which education functions to maintain the status quo rather than challenging hegemonic practices and ideologies. This observation introduces an interesting paradox, as institutions of higher education are not only sites of reproduction but also places where ideas about how to challenge these processes can be created and expressed.[4] Drawing upon a fundamental feminist belief that education and curriculum are sites of struggle and teaching and learning are political acts, the goal then becomes to replace accepted ways of thinking with a framework grounded in a vision of social justice. As feminist scholars continue to challenge mainstream/malestream academic practices, acknowledging the diverse lived realities of women students, we may increasingly realize the value of enabling students to develop the "power to perceive critically *the way they exist* in the world" (Friere, 1992: 70, italics in original, quoted in Potter, 1995).

CONCLUSION

In reflecting on the issue of how trauma experienced by women students affects their learning and how violence against women should be understood and combated within universities, it is clear that mere policy changes or liberal reforms will be inadequate. Given the entrenched inequities within the system, introducing meaningful change will require challenging the normative practices that currently force women to remain in a disadvantaged position. Academic practices must be grounded in an understanding that relates women's individual experiences to ongoing conditions of masculine domination (Bourdieu, 2001). By transcending the normative discourse, we are able to shift the focus from the individual characteristics of women and consider the systemic barriers faced by women students.

This chapter is intended to challenge readers to critically consider the significance of experiences of violence and the ways in which these issues are integrally related to broader relations of power and domination both within and beyond academia. Those of us who are educators bear significant responsibility for either supporting or resisting traditional viewpoints of what it means to "do academia," moving beyond an approach that frames violence against women as an individual issue to one that addresses it as a social issue. By not overtly addressing the issue of violence in women's lives or developing effective support strategies, we are impeding women's ability to learn to their full potential, as well as perpetuating a form of symbolic violence by not acknowledging their reality. Teaching a woman-centred curriculum or prioritizing personal experience are not enough without recognizing that women are embodied learners who come to the classroom with a variety of life experiences. As Horsman (1999) has written, by pretending that violence is outside of the realm of most women's experience, we collude in the silencing.

NOTES

1 To reduce women to a sole identity as individuals who have experienced trauma would do further violence to them by categorizing them based on a limited number of social characteristics. This is especially critical in the case of survivors of violence, as once they identify themselves as having been victimized, the victim label often overshadows all other facets of their identity, obscuring their complex social identities. It is not my intention to obscure the fundamental inequalities within which we live by focusing on one area of difference (Bannerji, 1991). Rather, my goal is to acknowledge that an individual's social location with regard to race, class, gender, sexual orientation and disability and their access to power and privilege will necessarily shape their experience of trauma.

2 All the names of participants are pseudonyms to ensure their privacy. The descriptors used are based on the way in which participants chose to self-identify.

3 These programs are available free of charge and offer an escort to students walking on campus after dark.

4 My thanks to Sandra Acker for furthering my thinking on this point.

REFERENCES

Acker, S., & Dillabough, J. (2007). Women "learning to labour" in the "male emporium": Exploring gendered work in teacher education. *Gender and Education, 19*(3), 297–316.

Acker, S., & Armenti, C. (2004). Sleepless in academia. *Gender and Education, 16*(1), 3–24.

Acker, S., & Feuerverger, G. (1997). Enough is never enough: Women's work in academe. In C. Marshall (Ed.), *Feminist critical policy analysis II: A perspective from post-secondary education* (122–140). London: The Falmer Press.

Ahmed, S. (2007). "You end up doing the document rather than doing the doing": Diversity, race equality and the politics of documentation. *Ethnic and Racial Studies, 30*(4), 590–609.

Bannerji, H. (1991). But who speaks for us? Experience and agency in conventional feminist paradigms. In H. Bannerji, L. Carty, K. Delhi, S. Heald, & K. McKenna, *Unsettling relations: The university as a site of feminist struggles* (67–107). Toronto: Women's Press.

Bourdieu, P. (2001). *Masculine domination*. Translated by Richard Nice. Stanford: Stanford University Press.

Brookes, A.-L. (1992). *Feminist pedagogy: An autobiographical approach*. Halifax: Fernwood.

Brown, L.S. (1995). Not outside the range: One feminist perspective on psychic trauma. In C. Caruth (Ed.), *Trauma: Explorations in memory* (100–112). London: Johns Hopkins University Press.

Collins, P.H. (2001). The social construction of Black feminist thought. In K.K. Bhavnani (Ed.), *Feminism and "race"* (184–202). Oxford: Oxford University Press.

Cotterill, P., & Letherby, G. (2005). Women in higher education: Issues and challenges. *Women Studies International Forum, 28*, 109–113.

Fellows, M.-L., & Razack, S. (1998). The race to innocence: Confronting hierarchical relations among women. *The Journal of Gender, Race and Justice, 1*(2), 353–404.

Freire, Paulo. (1992). *Pedagogy of the oppressed.* New York: Continuum.

Herman, J.L. (1992). *Trauma and recovery.* New York: Basic Books.

hooks, b. (1994). *Teaching to transgress.* New York: Routledge.

Horsman, J. (1999). *Too scared to learn: Women, violence and education.* Toronto: McGilligan Books.

Krane, J., Oxman-Martinez, J., & Ducey, K. (2000). Violence against women and ethnoracial minority women: Examining assumptions about ethnicity and "race." *Canadian Ethnic Studies, 32*(3), 1–18.

Lenskyj, H.J. (2005). *A lot to learn: Girls, women and education in the twentieth century.* Toronto: Women's Press.

Lorde, A. (1984). *Sister outsider.* New York: Crossing Press.

Monture-Angus, P. (2001). In the way of peace: Confronting "whiteness" in the university. In R. Luther, E. Whitmore, & B. Moreau (Eds.), *Seen but not heard: Aboriginal women and women of colour in the academy* (29–49). Ottawa: CRIAW.

Potter, N. (1995). The severed head and existential dread: The classroom as epistemic community and student survivors of incest. *Hypatia, 10*(2), 69–92.

Razack, S.H. (1999). *Looking white people in the eye: Gender, race, and culture in courtrooms and classrooms.* Toronto: University of Toronto Press.

Reay, D. (1998). Surviving in dangerous places: Working-class women, women's studies and higher education. *Women's Studies International Forum, 21*(1), 11–19.

Titchkosky, T. (2003). *Disability, self and society.* Toronto: University of Toronto Press.

Webber, M. (2006). Transgressive pedagogies? Exploring the difficult realities of enacting feminist pedagogies in undergraduate classrooms in a Canadian university. *Studies in Higher Education, 31*(4), 453–467.

CHAPTER 6

BRIDGING THE GAP:
I WILL NOT REMAIN
SILENCED

Donna A. Murray

You have to know where you come from to know where you
are going.
— Kim Anderson, *A Recognition of Being*

THIS CHAPTER EXPLORES THE MANY LAYERS I HAVE ENCOUNTERED IN
higher education as a result of becoming aware of my Aboriginal heritage.
First, it reveals the progenitors of my existence based on a Euro-Western
upbringing at the expense of my Native identity. Next, it examines pedagogical issues in higher education, specifically the women's studies classroom, probing the role of both professors and students in making the
space safe or otherwise. Third, it considers power issues and hierarchies
in educational institutions. All of these aspects come together in a discussion of my struggles for identity. The juxtaposition of white versus First
Nations is an ongoing challenge.

EXPLORING THE HIDDEN PAST

I have recently learned that the above quotation by Kim Anderson is a
distinctly Aboriginal way of comprehending how the past, present and
future are inextricably entwined. As an educator, I have always put forth

an analogy, similar in nature, to my students at the beginning of every new class. I was unaware that my hidden "Nativeness" had been surfacing without my knowledge. Sylvia Maracle refers to this manifestation as "blood memory" (Anderson, 2001), the innate ability to carry the memories of one's ancestors. She states that this phenomenon can be physically, emotionally or spiritually driven. Shortly before my return to school to complete an undergraduate degree in my forties, I found out I was of Aboriginal descent. This discovery permanently changed my life and how I viewed the world. As an Aboriginal person, I now fell into the broad category with others in society who were "neither white nor black" (Dyer, 1997). My life had taken on a colour/colourless form, non-white, that began to change my thought processes. How should I refer to my heritage, my identity? Should I call myself an Indian (Status Indian, Bill C-31 Indian), an Indigenous or Aboriginal person, an Irish/English/First Nations (tri-racial) person, or simply a person of mixed race or blood, the latter terms speaking of a more indiscriminate sense of identity? I have never been entrenched in the knowledge of my ancestry, and as a result, I have never fully understood the circumstances that have led to the loss of my "Nativeness" to the world of "whiteness." The implications of discovering that I was "rootless" seemed endless.

In terms of my personal entitlement, I have boldly stated, rightly or wrongly, as a result of the stigma attached to Bill C-31,[1] that I am a member of the Six Nations Tuscarora Nation from the New Credit Reserve that joined the Iroquois Confederacy in 1722 as the sixth tribe member along with five other tribes: the Oneida, Mohawk, Onondaga, Cayuga and the Seneca (Indian and Northern Affairs Canada, 1997). My totem is the turtle.[2] My white Anglo-Saxon appearance, however, affords me the option of adopting or ignoring my Aboriginal heritage, unlike individuals whose Native appearance does not offer them the same opportunity. Bonita Lawrence (2004) refers to the pressure placed upon Aboriginal people in the apartheid situation created by the "colonialist nature of Canadian society, where Native realities are distorted everywhere but in all-Native contexts" (7). Perhaps this is why the maternal side of my family of origin remained what I call "Closeted Indians." I am sure that the options for white individuals offered by the colonized world would have seemed more appealing and less hazardous. I acknowledge that everything we experience influences all that follows, so it is important to validate such an awakening to better understand how the silent pieces of my early life have brought me to where I locate myself within academia.

When I began my research for this narrative, I had not expected it to become so personal, nor had I planned for the possibility of struggling with my identity. There was something enigmatic about this process as I ruminated over past memories. I began to have a better understanding of how dominant patriarchal Euro-Western social forces shaped the experiences of my family's environment, turning it toxic. The subsequent creeping veil of self-imposed silence had cast a long shadow of shame and denial over generations of my ancestors, blanketing and distorting their Indigenous historical gifts of knowledge. As a consequence, I was denied the privilege of knowing about my Indigenous heritage. Both my discovery of an Aboriginal heritage and my Euro-Western cultural experiences have affected how I interpret the socio-cultural aspects of the ivory towers of higher education.

PEDAGOGIES AND SILENCES IN EDUCATION

When I entered university I assumed that one could expect to be treated equally, fairly and respectfully, without prejudice, bigotry and racism. I was wrong. Unfortunately, what I encountered in the classroom was a microcosm of race and gender relations in society with all its complications and paradoxes.

I had high hopes for the women's studies classroom. The intent of women's studies, as I understood it, was to critique and analyze the gender challenges of women's experiences in the androcentric systems of knowledge in higher educational settings. I believe that every woman in a feminist classroom experiences something different, depending on her history, race, age, sexual orientation and economic circumstances. Morra and Smith (1995) state, "… feminism's most basic principle [is that] women are free agents with the capacity to forge their individual destinies" (85). Yet even within feminism, participants have different levels of agency. In some cases, I became more aware that the concerns that pertained to women who were non-white, disabled or otherwise marginalized were not being addressed, even though the class was studying liberal, socialist or radical feminism. These theories are meant to challenge women's oppression in the course of patriarchal domination, including economic oppression, through the analysis of *all* women's experiences.

At the same time, efforts to compensate for prior discrimination and exclusion had the potential to create their own problematic consequences. For example, a particular class discussion centred on the interlocking forms of oppression that women of different races and classes endure in society. The white professor's lecturing style and questions were directed primarily towards the Black women. Knowledge and its presentation, in this instance, were a powerful combination. I could neither comfortably consider myself an Aboriginal student nor a white student. I felt caught between two cultures, which Monture-Angus (1995) believes is the best place to be in terms of "building bridges of understanding" (47), by being able to walk in both directions. At that point, however, I was unable to do so, and I found myself becoming increasingly silent and distrustful. The content and atmosphere of this women's studies classroom did not lend itself to empathy or respect for the experiences of others. I felt more could have been accomplished if the interaction had included all members of the class in the discussion as a tool to bring women of different racial and ethnocultural backgrounds together.

All professors have an opportunity to warm up the chilly climate by making every student's experience more relevant to their needs. Yet, in many cases, the women's studies professors did not humanize the content and structure of their classrooms. I found that their approach did not give the power back to each of the woman's voices, mine included, which subsequently invalidated our experiences. In the process of making people so separate and different, they negated inclusiveness. Trust in the classroom, states Lenskyj (2005), is a shared responsibility among the students and teachers, which allows room for critique to occur. For example, increasing the time that each student is afforded in a classroom can lend itself to building trust. When knowledge and experiences are shared, a comfort with and a sense of connectedness to others deepen.

TENSIONS AMONG STUDENTS

As previously stated, I had expected that the standards in institutions of higher learning would be more inclusive, based on the presence of students of various racial backgrounds. Nevertheless, forms of racism and ageism still operated. As a result of my age and white appearance, some of the younger women students viewed me in ways for which I was not prepared. I had become the Other in the classroom. Acknowledging my

Indigenous heritage was to no avail. I felt I was viewed as part of the first wave of feminism, where white, middle-class feminists were believed to have dismissed, denigrated and denied the experiences of women of different races and classes.

As a consequence, I remained on the outside of many discussions or was vigorously challenged in the classroom about my feminist beliefs. The four characteristics of a chilly climate — "stereotyping, devaluation, exclusion and revictimization" (Wylie, 1995: 1) — were apparent. In hindsight, I believe I was seen as being a proponent of "white solipsism" (Spelman, 1988: 116), a term coined by Adrienne Rich to explain how feminist theory has contributed to imagining, thinking, and speaking as if whiteness described the world. Henry, Tator, Mattis and Rees (1998) state, "anti-racism examines the meaning of [w]hiteness and the power and privilege of [w]hite skin, which is largely invisible to those who possess it" (41). I could not agree more. I suspect that when I was a very young female child, my family was silent about our Aboriginal heritage as a way to protect me from the racism they had experienced.

It had never occurred to me, however, that I would be viewed as a white racist. I was shocked and angered at being perceived as something other than what I imagined myself to be. I had never considered myself to be part of the political movement labelled feminism, nor had I treated the experiences of women of colour, poor women or women with disabilities as being of less importance than my own. Yet, as a result of being challenged, I began to see that I was guilty of white solipsism, for I had not perceived the Other as having Other experiences, different than my own. I had not questioned my social position of privilege, which made me an "oppressor as well as [a] feminist ally" (Maher and Tetreault, 1997: 322).

STRUGGLING FOR AN IDENTITY

As time went on, I began to be aware of two aspects of my identity that negatively impacted my educational experiences: (1) that I was an *Aboriginal* individual in a very Euro-Western educational setting, and (2) that I was *female* in a very patriarchal institution. Moreover, at the time, I was a married, part-time student who had full-time and part-time employment off campus with minimal university life contacts, which in and of itself was an oppressive situation.

Higher education had turned into a double-edged sword. I was struggling both with the dawning understanding of white privilege and the implications of my newfound Native identity. In a study of students in feminist classrooms, Maher and Tetreault (2001) found that "[w]hiteness was assumed to be a normal condition ... not a privileged position within networks of power" (230). When I entered university, my whiteness was invisible to me. I did not equate the race with privilege. I did not recognize that racism was a social construct in which I was embedded. I did not recognize that oppression could be created when gender, class, race, sexuality and ability intertwined. Perhaps it is due to the connected nature of oppressions that I felt my journey was, as Ng (1993) states, "protracted, difficult, uncomfortable, painful and risky" (45) in the classroom, conditions which Ng deems necessary in order to change the status quo.

In university, I discovered that what is classified as being the "norm" tends to depend on who is defining it. In my search for identity, I found, amid the multiple racial backgrounds in the classroom, that a persona was being constructed for me which brought me to a point where I no longer had a sense of who I was. As a result, I kept silent in the classroom and waited for answers as well as a better understanding of the sociological implications of my presence in a women's studies feminist course. Curriculum had become more than an abstract concept. I now understood it as a cultural construct with the power to reproduce cultural and social inequalities. By the end of my undergraduate program, I was more aware of the fact that feminist theory was laden with challenges. As a graduate student, and particularly in my research, I became aware of how important it was to reshape the methods of teaching and practice of feminism in order to lessen the marginalization of women. In the process, the oppressive boundaries that had cocooned me became loosened, as my awareness and knowledge of the lives of other women increased.

At the same time, there surfaced yet another marginalizing obstacle in the classroom, not from other students but from myself — a case of mistaken cultural identity. I had not only just learned that I was an Aboriginal individual but also was learning about the stigma attached to this racial group. A positive self-identity, states Eileen Antone (2000), is "imperative for academic success" (99). I found it challenging to try to assimilate into the Indigenous world. Seemingly caught in the middle, I endeavoured to balance the white world in which I lived with the recently acquired knowledge of the Indigenous world of my ancestors. As such, this ambiguity has undoubtedly created some biases that impacted my identity, my experiences in academia and, quite possibly, my narrative.

HIERARCHICAL POWER STRUCTURES

Denzin and Lincoln (2005) point out that it is important for researchers to identify their ideology and biases because there is no bias-free or value-free design. I accept that my narrative is based on my ideological position and, as such, provides a conceptual framework that is laced with the patriarchal ideology encountered during my upbringing. In an effort to better understand my distrust of the white patriarchal male professors in higher education, I need to acknowledge an experience from the past that involved a white male vice-principal in high school and that was racist in origin. The incident took place at Pauline Johnson High School, named after the famous poetess daughter of the Mohawk Chief of the Six Nations Reserve and an English woman — the irony does not escape me — who grew up belonging to two cultures. The vice-principal berated me in a spiteful, angry voice, and with a look of contempt, for not knowing my true racial origins. I was bewildered and frightened, for I had no idea what he was referring to for he had not actually said that I had Aboriginal ancestry. I did not report this incident to anyone for two reasons: I was anxious that it might escalate and lead to problems for my family, and I did not know my true origin, nor could I ask my parents, which left me powerless in the face of bigotry. However, had he been challenged, he would have undoubtedly, in the words of bell hooks (1988), "denied any culpability" (57).

This snippet of my background actually laid the groundwork for how I came to perceive higher education and the way I came to understand how the system worked. It might be said that my intrinsic Aboriginal characteristics led me to strain against the pedagogical "old ways" of thinking in hegemonic Euro-Western institutions. These old ways have persisted in higher education, as have my views about male academics in positions of power and educational institutions that are invested in maintaining a Euro-Western authoritative voice for themselves. By contrast, the old ways in most Native societies, before white contact, were matrilineal, not patrilineal, and these Indigenous old ways were peaceful and egalitarian. However, according to Weaver (1993), by 1971, patriarchy was so entrenched within Native society that it was seen as a traditional trait, just as patriarchy is deemed to be the norm in Euro-Western culture, including institutions of higher education.

The males in positions of power, whom Lenskyj (2005) labels "gate-keepers — traditionally white, heterosexual men" (150), have controlled the content of the curriculum, the hidden practices and the politics of the university. Acker (2001) likened the "hidden curriculum of the graduate school to an iceberg, with the more overt requirements above the water and the rest submerged" (61). In my experience, I have found the majority of women professors to be consistently open, interested, clear and accommodating to their students, unlike some male professors I have encountered, who would miss scheduled appointments, with no apology or explanation given, or become irritated when enquiries were made about their course content. They made it clear that they did not have the time or inclination to discuss or answer any questions. These are examples of the hidden abuse of power in the academy. Conceivably, more of what the iceberg has been hiding will be readily available as the academic waters heat up, providing equal opportunity for women of every race and class attending university. It is hoped that there will not be as much of a need for a "keen eye or [the] appropriate equipment" (Acker, 2001: 61) to fathom the degree requirements once the current under-representation of women faculty lessens. Yet my experiences at university suggest many challenges remain in fostering the incorporation of non-traditional groups, challenging the pervasiveness of hierarchies and the difficulty of dispelling oppression without creating new forms of it.

BRIDGING THE GAP — CULTURAL (MIS)UNDERSTANDINGS

It is essential to find a way to bridge the chasm that separates one from the Other. It is imperative to develop a more inclusive understanding of all women in academia, and this task begins by challenging those who teach, the way they teach and the language that is used in the classroom. Leclair and Nicholson, with Métis Elder Elize Hartley (2003), referred to a statement of purpose that was created by a circle of Métis women in 1999 that might lead to a better understanding of what constitutes knowledge. In it, they talk about celebrating and reclaiming their cultures, histories and identities. They also want to empower, educate and support Métis women and to "acknowledge the Creator and the wholistic relationship between the Earth and the gifts provided to us" (55).

I would agree there are no easy answers, but I believe their goals would enrich Euro-Western education, were it to include Aboriginal knowledge and practices (see also Baskin's chapter in this collection). This collaboration might initially be feared, for it may be viewed as if night and day are fighting for the same sky when Aboriginal peoples take up the challenge of entitlement. I have viewed and still view the educational arena with skepticism, as it operates in much the same manner as my family of origin. The contradictions and ambiguities that permeated my family also exist within institutions of higher learning. The impact of racism and bigotry on my home life denied me my heritage; in the classroom it rendered me invisible. Unlike the "Closeted Indians," I believe that there are ways to expand the circle of knowledge within the Eurocentric world to include the wisdom of all who wish to tell their stories.

Currently there is a need to find new ways for students and educators to produce curricula and pedagogies that go beyond the predominantly male and white models of the past. The road to change has many obstacles. My journey is but a minuscule example of how racism and bigotry are a plague that needs to be eradicated within institutes of higher learning and society. This "hindsight/post-mortem" of the educational program that I attended provides a cautionary example of the dangers involved and the significance of gender, class, race and age in higher education. I encourage all individuals in institutions of higher learning to face the fear of change, to speak up, to champion inclusivity and to heed Graveline's message: "I will not remain Silenced any more. No More ... Silence to cover Fear. an Old. Deadly. combination" (2004: 149, 158; original punctuation).

NOTES

1 The 1985 *Indian Act* (generally known as Bill C-31) embodied three fundamental principles: "one, that all discrimination be removed from the *Indian Act;* two, that Indian status within the meaning of the Indian Act and band membership rights be restored to persons who had lost them; and three, that Indian bands have the right to control their own membership. The new provisions had a major impact on

entitlement rules and procedures. The most important changes were: women no longer gain or lose entitlement to registration as a result of marriage; the practice of enfranchisement, a process by which Indians could apply to give up status and band membership, is abolished; the marriage of parents is no longer a factor in the entitlement of children; and bands can now choose to control their own membership" (Indian and Northern Affairs Canada, 1991: 21).

2 The totem is a symbol or emblem, usually an animal or plant, of a Nation or family. It is believed to symbolize a mythical ancestor. The turtle "is a very powerful symbol for women. It symbolizes fertility, long life, and perseverance. It is sometimes even considered able to defy death. It is also used as a symbol for the Earth" (North American Indian Tribes of the U.S. and Canada, 2008: 3).

REFERENCES

Acker, S. (2001). The hidden curriculum of dissertation advising. In E. Margolis (Ed.), *The hidden curriculum of higher education* (61–77). New York: Routledge.

Anderson, K. (2001). *Recognition of being: Reconstructing Native womanhood.* Toronto: Sumach Press.

Antone, E.M. (2000). Empowering Aboriginal voice in Aboriginal education. *Canadian Journal of Native Education, 24*(2), 92–101.

Denzin, N.K., & Lincoln, Y. (Eds.). (2005). *The SAGE handbook of qualitative research,* 3rd ed. Thousand Oaks, CA: Sage.

Dyer, R. (1997). *White.* New York: Routledge.

Graveline, F.J. (2004). *Healing wounded hearts.* Halifax: Fernwood.

Henry, F., Tator, C., Mattis, W., & Rees, T. (1998). *The colour of democracy: Racism in Canadian society,* 2nd ed. Scarborough, ON: Nelson.

hooks, b. (1988). *Talking back: Thinking feminist, thinking black.* Toronto: Between the Lines.

Indian and Northern Affairs Canada. (1997). *First Nations in Canada.* Ottawa: Minister of Public Works and Government Services Canada.

Indian and Northern Affairs Canada. (1991). *The Indian Act past and present: A manual on registration and entitlement legislation.* Ottawa: Retrieved 23 January 2008 from www.ainc-inac.gc.ca/qc/csi/intro_e.pdf .

Lawrence, B. (2004). *"Real" Indians and others: Mixed-race urban native people, the Indian Act, and the rebuilding of indigenous nations.* Vancouver: UBC Press.

LeClair, C., & Nicholson, L. with Métis Elder E. Hartley. (2003). From the stories that women tell: The Métis women's circle. In K. Anderson & B. Lawrence (Eds.),

Strong women stories: Native vision and community survival (55–69). Toronto: Sumach Press.

Lenskyj, H. (2005). *A lot to learn: Girls, women and education in the twentieth century.* Toronto: Women's Press.

Maher, F., & Tetreault, M.K.T. (2001). *The feminist classroom: Dynamics of gender, race, and privilege,* 2nd ed. Lanham, MD: Rowan and Littlefield.

Maher, F., & Tetreault, M.K.T. (1997). Learning in the dark: How assumptions of whiteness shape classroom knowledge. *Harvard Educational Review, 67*(2), 321–349.

Monture-Angus, P. (1995) *Thunder in my soul: A Mohawk woman speaks.* Halifax: Fernwood.

Morra, N., & Smith, M.D. (1995). Men in feminism: Reinterpreting masculinity and femininity. In N. Mandell (Ed.), *Feminist issues: race, class, and sexuality* (185–208). Toronto: Prentice Hall.

Ng, R. (1993). Sexism, racism, Canadian nationalism. In H. Bannerji (Ed.), *Returning the gaze: Essays on racism, feminism and politics* (182–196). Toronto: Sister Vision Press.

North American Indian Tribes of the U.S. and Canada. (2008). *Animal Totems.* Retrieved 24 January 2008 from www.aaanativearts.com/animal_totems.htm.

Spelman, E. (1988). *Inessential woman: Problems of exclusion in feminist thought.* Boston: Beacon Press.

Weaver, S. (1993). First Nations women and government policy, 1970–92: Discrimination and conflict. In S. Burt, L. Code, & L. Dorney (Eds.), *Changing patterns: Women in Canada,* 2nd ed. (92–150). Toronto: McClelland and Stewart.

Wylie, A. (1995). The contexts of activism on "climate" issues. In Chilly Collective (Ed.), *Breaking anonymity* (29–60). Waterloo, ON: Wilfrid Laurier University Press.

CHAPTER 7

GENDERED AND QUEER BODIES
IN THE ACADEMY:
PEDAGOGICAL CONSIDERATIONS

Wayne Martino

Once "sex" itself is understood in its normativity, the materiality of the body will not be thinkable apart from the materialization of that regulatory norm. Sex is, thus, not simply what one has, or a static description of what one is: it will be one of the norms by which the "one" becomes viable at all, that which qualifies a body for life within the domain of cultural intelligibility.

— Judith Butler, *Bodies that Matter*

I AM A WHITE, GAY MALE SCHOLAR IN THE ACADEMY WHO ARRIVED IN Canada in 2005 to take up a tenured faculty position in equity and social justice education at the University of Western Ontario. I am conscious of a certain degree of privilege in terms of my gender, social-class status and ethnicity. However, both my Australian accent and my gender nonconformity function in important ways as markers of difference, bodily inscriptions which lead me to be classified or read as both non-Canadian and queer. While feeling free to explain or to talk about my Australianness and to incorporate it into an introductory narrative about myself when I meet my students as an instructor for the first time, I do not feel the same degree of comfort about including narratives about my sexual orientation in the heteronormative space of the classroom. In other words, heteronormativity — that is, the beliefs and punitive social rules that both privilege and compel one to conform to normative heterosexuality, though not always made explicit — has a powerful influence on my pedagogical practices in the academy. I do not attribute this sense of discomfort, pedagogically speaking, to some form of internalized homophobia that I am unable to shrug off. Rather, as I will explain in this chapter, it is more of a concern that my commitment to anti-oppressive education will be framed in essentialized terms and, hence, attributed to the fact that I am merely a gay male with a particular social justice agenda.

At the heart of this polemic is the sense in which my body already speaks over which I appear to have little control or agency. In fact, being able to talk about my Australian accent and my white ethnicity actually enables me to deflect attention away from the potential problematic of my sexuality which appears to function as a lens through which my pedagogical commitment to equity and social justice education is to be understood or framed. There is a notion (and I realize that it is only an illusion) that my being able to draw attention to the fact that I am non-Canadian, my accent being a notable marker of *otherness*, has the potential to deflect attention away from what I perceive to be an all too familiar tendency to frame everything I say through the lens of my sexual minority status. It is this pedagogical significance of the body as a signifier of sexual difference that I want to address in this chapter.

QUEER FEMINIST PERSPECTIVES

In making sense of these embodied experiences, I draw on queer feminist theorists, such as Judith Butler (1993) and Elizabeth Grosz (1995), who write about the body as "a surface of inscription" (Grosz, 1995: 33). I also refer to other literature that deals with the pedagogy of the teacher's body within the academy (Laubscher & Powell, 2003; Cooks & LeBesco, 2006; Ingalls, 2006; Schippert, 2006) to reflect on my own experiences of the gendered body in higher education. In so doing, I hope to draw attention to the norms that govern the surveillance and regulation of the male body and the pedagogical significance of this regulation for me as a male professor who teaches courses about equity and social justice education. It is this focus on the heteronormative framing of the sexed body that is of particular interest to me (see Britzman, 1995; 1998). For example, the privileged status that is accorded to being heterosexual within the academy and the extent to which heterosexuality is institutionalized and functions as a filter for making sense of the social body are central to understanding my own pedagogical experiences in this context. Thus, I raise crucial questions about how teachers' bodies signify (Eastman, 2006). The focus, then, is on trying to make sense of the significance of my own gendered and sexed body as a queer male professor in the academy.

Laubscher and Powell (2003), for example, in reflecting on their own experiences as academics and "multicultural educators," highlight how their own pedagogies are mediated by the ways in which they are *marked* as or in ways they identify themselves as *different* (205). This identification has particular significance regarding the ways in which the queer male body is inscribed and marked as different within the context of a *gendered matrix of relations* that is governed by norms for constituting the male subject according to the dictates of compulsory heterosexuality (Butler, 1993: 7). In other words, the heteronormative requirement to display oneself as appropriately heterosexual is also played out on the site of the gendered male body. At the heart of this compulsion is a "repudiation of the feminine" that has a particular pedagogical significance vis-à-vis the misogynist policing and surveillance of masculinities in male teachers' lives both in schools and in the academy (see Martino, in press, 2008).

THE FEMINIZED MALE BODY

I have written elsewhere about the extent to which the body matters in gay men's lives in relation to how a disavowal of the feminine, which is signified and embodied in the form of the "feminized faggot" or queen, leads to a hierarchical marking of difference amongst gay men (see Martino, 2006). This marking involves a process by which the male body, as a surface of inscription, is invested with a corporeal subjectivity that is constituted in relation to an "outside" that functions as "its own founding repudiation" (Butler, 1993: 3). In other words, to be read as effeminate is to simultaneously constitute the *other* as a basis for determining the domain of cultural intelligibility in terms of what is to count as legitimate masculinity. It is the policing and surveillance of masculinity in these terms that raise important questions about the male body as site for the denigration of the feminine with all of its misogynist associations. This analysis raises crucial questions about the body as a signifier of failed masculinity and, hence, as a surface upon which effeminacy is inscribed according to the regulatory norms governing embodied expressions of idealized hegemonic, heterosexualized masculinity. This perspective is consistent with Grosz's (1995) theorization of the normalization of bodies:

> The body becomes a text, a system of signs to be deciphered, read, and read into. While social law is incarnate, "corporealized," correlatively, bodies are textualized, read by others as expressive of subject's psychic interior. (Grosz, 1995: 34–35)

In this sense, I argue that the male body, as a site for fashioning or performing masculinity, is governed by norms that dictate a psychic investment in embracing an idealized hegemonic masculinity at the basis of which lies the "regulatory apparatus of heterosexuality" (Butler, 1993: 12; see also Connell, 1992; 1995). It is the image of an idealized straight-acting masculinity that is defined against the feminine or effeminate male body that is still central to understanding how some gay men come to regulate or understand their desire for other men. Masculinities thus become eroticized, embodied and objectified for some gay men within the terms set by a heteronormative framework for thinking about sexuality (Martino, 2006). In other words, for some gay men only certain sorts of *straight-acting* bodies — that is, bodies that signify straight as opposed to effeminate or "girlie" masculinity — are desired. Such a framework reinforces rather than subverts gender hierarchies and oppositional categories and helps to explain what Butler (1993) means when she makes reference to "the regulatory apparatus of heterosexuality" (12) in terms of its capacity to determine and limit our thinking about gender and sexuality primarily in binary oppositional terms.

Thus, the spectre of the feminized male body and its disavowed status emerges as significant in terms of understanding "the processes by which the subject is marked, scarred, transformed, and written upon or constructed by the various regimes of institutional, discursive, and non-discursive power as a particular kind of body" (Grosz, 1995: 35). In short, the capacity of the male body to signify effeminacy draws attention to the regulatory norms governing a gendered hierarchical system that produces effects at the level of embodied social and pedagogical relations for both male and female teachers. It is in this sense, as Grosz (1995) argues, that the body speaks:

> Bodies speak without necessarily talking, because they become coded with and as signs. They speak social codes. They become intextuated, narrativized; simultaneously, social codes, laws, and ideals become incarnated. (35)

The potential for the male body to signify effeminacy has implications not only in terms of understanding the regulatory norms and constraints governing the constitution of corporeal subjectivity. In this sense, it is this equation of effeminacy, and thus women, with stigma and lower status that is significant. The processes by which the male body is inscribed and read have a pedagogical significance in terms of their capacity to further illuminate the regulatory force of gender norms that mediate sexual minority male professors' experiences in the academy. Such practices of mediation need to be understood as negotiated within the struggle over *a hierarchy of worth* vis-à-vis the statuses of masculinity that are ascribed, attributed to or projected onto the male body as a pedagogical site within the academy (Laubscher & Powell, 2003: 205).

HOW BODIES MATTER, PEDAGOGICALLY SPEAKING

My own reflections on the pedagogical significance of the body were triggered in response to the Laubscher and Powell (2003) discussion of the signifying practices surrounding their own bodies in relation to teaching multicultural education courses in the higher education context in the United States. Powell writes about her physical difference as a consequence of being born with a genetic condition that resulted in the overgrowth of her hands. Laubscher, "a man of colour from South Africa," writes about the pedagogical significance of his racial identity (see also Mitchell & Rosiek, 2006). Together they highlight how visible markers of difference, as they are signified by their bodies, are immediately identifiable in terms of their gender, the "hue" of their skin and the "shape" of their bodies (209). In fact, they claim other markers of difference, such as religion and sexual orientation, do not have the same signifying potential in terms of being inscribed on the surface of the body, an argument which ignores important considerations surrounding the normative constraints that not only produce but also constrain gendered bodies within highly regulative regimes of compulsory heterosexuality (Butler, 1993). They fail to see how gender non-conformity functions as a means by which to inscribe sexual orientation on the surface of the body. My own reflections at the beginning of this chapter draw attention to the potential of the gender non-conforming body to signify a minority sexual orientation. I draw out further the pedagogical significance of this process in the following section.

What is significant for me about Laubscher and Powell's contribution is that they highlight the extent to which certain markers of bodily difference cannot be erased, ignored or hidden. In fact, they write about their desire to refuse the perpetuation of stigma and objectification that are often ascribed to their visible minority or disabled status. For example, they assert that "under the gaze of a scrutinizing majority," the "accented Black mouth" or the "deformed" hands of the female professor cannot easily escape detection. This assertion raises the sort of philosophical issues identified by Grosz (1995) and noted above about how bodies speak and become coded with signs which set limits to how bodies can be thought into existence. It is in this sense that Laubscher and Powell draw attention to how bodies are textualized and read by others according to reception regimes or ways of thinking that are governed by specific norms for making sense of our bodies.

However, rather than simply subjecting themselves to the normalizing gaze of their students, in which the registration of their bodies is contained, Laubscher and Powell (2003) attach a special pedagogical significance to this corporeal experience of feeling objectified. They explicitly refer to such bodily experiences to create a pedagogical space in their classrooms for interrogating normative constraints around bodies:

> The conversation is not about knowing us. It is rather about what our bodies represent and signify to the questioner, who is trying to clarify or assert schemas within which superficial bodily differences are signs of the "natural" inferiority of their possessors. (214)

Thus, by pointing to the limits of such discursive regimes for marking and coding the body as a signifier, pedagogical spaces can be created for making available alternative readings. Rather than identifying with the projection of *otherness* that is inscribed on their bodies, Laubscher and Powell draw on their experiences of visible bodily differences to create a pedagogical space for interrogating and exceeding the meanings which their students ascribe to such texts: "… the presentation of ourselves and our experiences, as learning texts, open for reading alongside their experiences, facilitates a dialogic transformation into the creation of a new reading, a new joint text as it were" (215).

PEDAGOGICAL CONSIDERATIONS OF BODILY AWARENESS

While Laubscher and Powell deal for the most part with the projection of *otherness* on the basis of physical disability and racial markers of difference, my own experience of bodily difference and its pedagogical significance is directed to a consideration of the effects of the regulatory apparatus of heterosexuality, especially in terms of the normative constraints it has imposed and the anxieties it has incited in me as an educator. It is such an understanding of the embodied semiotics of gender that I want to reflect on here. As Ingalls (2006) highlights, in drawing a connection between her own body size and gendered authority, "the subjectivity of the teacher body" (244) is inextricably tied to the "ever present gaze of students" (245), which results for the instructor in an intensification of bodily self-awareness in the classroom. For me, this self-consciousness produces an intensified bodily awareness of the way in which a regime of heterosexual hegemony constitutes the effeminate male body as a site for projecting the fear and loathing of the "homosexual" subject as the embodied feminine other. In other words, a failure to embody heteronormative or straight-acting masculinity brings with it a certain unease and fear of the surveillance and regulatory gaze of students in terms of their capacity to read my gender non-conformity as a sign of my queer sexual orientation with all the normative constraints that this signification carries. This burden translates into both a pedagogical anxiety and a worry that students will see my support for anti-oppressive education in schools solely as an artifact of my sexual minority status.

While this situation would certainly apply to all visible minority teacher educators and may not necessarily constitute a pedagogical limit, it has forced me to confront what I see as barriers or constraints. These constraints become accentuated in co-teaching situations where I witness straight professors using their personal experiences about life outside the classroom with their partners and children to create comfort and to build warm, personable and positive relationships with their heterosexual students. I have never felt this ease or comfort in these pedagogical contexts, where compulsory heterosexuality is so institutionalized and taken-for-granted, to draw on such personal resources. Perhaps at the heart of such a discomfort is not only a desire to avoid being essentialized as a queer male subject but, more importantly, also the realization of the significance of my embodied masculinity, which is accompanied by a sense of urgency in wanting to deflect or not bring any further attention to the potential of my body as a signifier to incite homophobia and/or intense policing of my masculinity. In other words, it is the capacity of the body to signify effeminacy in the eyes of my students that brings with it an intensified awareness of the significance of embodying what often gets inscribed as a failed masculinity.

GENDER EFFECTS AND THE MATERIALITY OF SEX

This corporeal experience of gender surveillance produces an acute knowledge and awareness of the normative force of power relations operating directly on sexed bodies (Grosz, 1995: 5). Moreover, as Butler (1993) highlights, it draws attention to the extent to which "bodies only appear, only endure, only live within the productive constraints of highly gendered regulatory schemas" (xi). It also foregrounds the significance of the crucial question she poses regarding gender effects and the materiality of sex:

> What are the constraints by which bodies are materialized as "sexed," and how are we to understand the "matter" of sex, and of bodies more generally, as the repeated and violent circumscription of cultural intelligibility? Which bodies come to matter — and why? (xii)

This statement informs directly the concerns I have documented in relation to the regulatory norms that govern the bodily inscription of difference for the gender non-conforming male professor.

In addition, engaging with such queer-feminist theorizing also got me thinking more deeply about the need for conceptual frameworks capable of explaining the bodily significance of different homophobic and misogynist forms of oppression. For example, Grosz (1995) asks provocatively whether "there is such a thing as homophobia and a common oppression for both lesbians and gays":

> Do lesbians experience the same forms of homophobia as gay men? Can we presume that it takes on universal forms? Does the fact that they are women and men (however one chooses to define these terms) alter the forms of homophobia each experiences? (211)

My experiences as a male professor in the academy would tend to support the position that we need more sophisticated analytic frameworks that are capable of explaining both homophobia and misogyny in terms of their specificity and in relation to the experience and inscription of bodily difference. This observation also raises important questions as to whether students' reactions might vary according to their own sexuality, gender or other minority inscriptions. It may well be that my own location at the University of Western Ontario leads me to see students as more homogenous than they are in some other institutions.

CONCLUSION

In this chapter I have offered some reflection on my own embodied experience as a queer male professor in the academy who is also read as non-Canadian. I have drawn on important queer feminist theoretical frameworks and some literature in the field as a basis for addressing the pedagogical significance of inscribing bodily difference and how this inscription relates to questions of sex and gender within the context of "the workings of heterosexual hegemony in the crafting of matters sexual and political" (Butler, 1993: xii). Institutions of higher learning are not immune to the effects of the normative demands of compulsory heterosexuality, particularly in terms of how our experiences as academics are mediated and how we understand ourselves as gendered subjects. I have attempted in this chapter to illuminate the pedagogical significance of bodily difference as a basis for teasing out some of the implications of what it means to teach in the academy, particularly in terms of drawing on one's own personal experiences of *otherness*. As Cooks and LeBesco (2006) argue vis-à-vis "those whose bodies often stand outside the classroom boundaries of normalcy": "The proper teacher embodies all that the culture/society/nation wishes its people to be, and so her body must be scrutinized, her behaviour dissected — held to the dominant standards of (non) conformity" (233).

REFERENCES

Britzman, D. (1998). *Lost subjects, contested objects.* Albany: State University of New York Press.

Britzman, D. (1995). Is there a queer pedagogy? Or stop thinking straight. *Educational Theory, 45*(2), 151–165.

Butler, J. (1993). *Bodies that matter: On the discursive limits of sex.* New York: Routledge.

Connell, R.W. (1995). *Masculinities.* Sydney: Allen and Unwin.

Connell, R.W. (1992). A very straight gay: Masculinity, homosexual experience, and the dynamics of gender. *American Sociological Review, 57,* 735–751.

Cooks, L., & LeBesco, K. (2006). Introduction: The pedagogy of the teacher's body. *The Review of Education, Pedagogy and Cultural Studies, 28*(3), 233–238.

Eastman, N. (2006). Our institutions, our selves: Rethinking classroom performance and signification. *The Review of Education, Pedagogy and Cultural Studies, 28*(3), 297–308.

Grosz, E. (1995). *Space, time and perversion.* Sydney: Allen and Unwin.

Ingalls, R. (2006). Unmasking the brilliant disguise: Smallness, authority and the irony of the teacher's body. *The Review of Education, Pedagogy and Cultural Studies, 28*(3), 239–252.

Laubscher, L., & Powell, S. (2003). Skinning the drum: Teaching about diversity as "other." *Harvard Educational Review, 73*(2), 203–224.

Martino, W. (In press, 2008). The lure of hegemonic masculinity: Investigating the dynamics of gender relations in male elementary school teachers' lives. *International Journal of Qualitative Studies in Education.*

Martino, W. (2006). Straight-acting masculinities: Normalization and gender hierarchies in gay men's lives. In C. Kendall and W. Martino (Eds.), *Gendered outcasts and sexual outlaws: Sexual oppression and gender hierarchies in queer men's lives* (35–60). New York: Haworth.

Mitchell, R., & Rosiek, J. (2006). Professor as embodied racial signifier: A case study of the significance of race on a university classroom. *The Review of Education, Pedagogy and Cultural Studies, 28*(3), 395–409.

Schippert, C. (2006). Critical projection and queer performativity: Self-revelation in teaching/learning otherness. *The Review of Education, Pedagogy and Cultural Studies, 28*(3), 281–295.

PART III

SUPPORTING
THE ENTERPRISE

CHAPTER 8

DISRESPECTIN'
ADMINISTRATIVE STAFF WORK:
CAN WE TALK?

Ann Kristine Pearson

A FELLOW ADMINISTRATIVE STAFF EMPLOYEE ATTENDED A TRAINING
session film some years ago and shared the film's theme with the rest of
us. The main image was of office doors opening, revealing the occupant's
life with its struggles and victories: the professor with elder care issues, the
secretary supporting a disabled child, the cleaner writing letters and send-
ing money to her child whom she hasn't seen in three years, and so on.
The moral: we should all respect and recognize the human being behind
the professional title. We listened with half an ear and smiled acknowledgement of the moral truth with a somewhat wary inner response.[1]

As administrative support staff,[2] we acknowledge an equation in university life: our inner thoughts and the facts of our life challenges are not
perceived to be equal to those academic workers who have more credentials. Our real image as person or professional in the university is fragmen-
tary. Intriguing family histories that we might have, our personal trials
and triumphs, hobbies or talents, all these are merely faint outlines during
a lifetime of work, an accident of an inadvertent half-sentence thrown out
while hurrying to the printer. As Judy Szekeres (2004) points out in her
analysis of how administrative staff are represented in various texts, "in

most cases administrative staff in universities are largely invisible" (387). Similarly, Carole Leathwood (2005), looking closely at women administrators, lecturers and managers as they live their professional lives around gendered, racialized and classed identities, comments that "administrative support staff have received little attention" (391). Professors may know little of the personal lives of other professors, but they generally have a good idea of their research, an indicator of at least one strong life passion. Our image is subsumed into our usages: typists, data enterers, secretaries, liaison officers, business officers and so on.

General support staff have a more detailed image of faculty life. As secretarial support workers, we type faculty manuscripts and our knowledge of faculty research is substantial. We are also more likely to know something of faculty members' personal struggles with their professional lives, since a faculty member in a stressed-out moment will often share her or his angst with us. Unspoken protocol does not usually allow an *equally* reciprocal expression. We are not the star players on this field. Our job is to facilitate and remain in the background. After sixteen years of working in the university, I take it for granted that the wonderfully rich and varied lives of support staff will and do remain hidden behind closed doors.

I would suggest, however, that an even more important aspect of our lives affected by the closed-door image is not the personal: it is the devaluation of our work's worth. Although we do not necessarily expect personal interaction with other university members, the most debilitating part of our experience remains the lack of professional respect. As a member of a large, unionized, predominantly female administrative staff group, I would like to present several scenarios of administrative staff workflow: sketches of the human beings who, though their professionalism is often unrecognized, collaborate with management, instructors, students and each other to make the university function. Though the main image is that of "caring" staff, with implications of traditionalized female qualities such as emotive sensitivity and helpfulness, I would suggest that if we really look at the considerable expertise, knowledge and intelligence involved in support staff work, the image fractures and glints of androgynous transformation emerge. Professional achievement, determination and knowledge are involved in their daily carrying out of their mission: to make it so!

WORKING FOR THE UNIVERSITY

Most administrative job descriptions describe "the ability to multitask," that is, work on several work assignments simultaneously, as a desirable and, indeed, an essential requirement. However, there are still some jobs that involve responsibility in a single type of activity, such as a transcriptionist's job in an academic institution. This involves listening to recorded interviews for research purposes — interviews which are often highly confidential and subject to legal confidentiality protection — and typing them into hard copy. The value placed on multitasking skills often means that single-task jobs and the skills required to do them are less highly regarded. However, when we are working as transcriptionists, we are handling sensitive knowledge as we listen to and absorb several hours of interviews per cassette tape. As transcriptionists, we listen intimately to each word, carefully pushing the pedal to reverse in order to relisten to a badly recorded section so as to capture it accurately. That knowledge is ours, though we may be constrained to be mute about it for reasons of confidentiality. If we type one six-hour cassette per day every work day, we will be typing some 1,320 hours of interviews per year, gaining knowledge of social settings, linguistic minority experiences or whatever social situation is being investigated. We should assume that a transcriptionist's knowledge is actually profound, unless we imagine her as a machine mechanically word processing data without comprehension, but that would be an incorrect supposition, one that portrays (or betrays) the gendered chauvinism underlying it.[3] Not only is the work consistently undervalued, but so is the very consciousness and intelligence of the human being doing the work, whether she is female or male.

A transcriptionist specializes in one particular task. Most university support staff multitask work projects that are ultimately delivered to more than one faculty member, committee or office. The multitasking often involves multiple supervisees. My own job responsibilities offer a good example.[4]

As a departmental student liaison officer working in a department with some 200 graduate students, I work with several committee chairs. These committee chairs will know that I am performing multiple tasks for them, although they will be unaware of many details involved in completing the work. Part of my responsibility is to work as unobtrusively as possible, leaving the chairs free to take care of their own duties. Simultaneously, a busy and continuous dialogue is going on between myself and the Registrar's Office, the Student Services Office, the School of Graduate Studies and sometimes the Dean's Office concerning detailed checkups and urgent problem-solving regarding student registrations, missing grades, admissions status, course scheduling, awards requirements, graduations, oral examinations, institutional events, processing changes, recruitment drives and so on. Staff from all these offices will each have a partial idea of the others' work and be aware that we are all co-dependent on one another. If one person fails at her part of a task, the other one also fails. In a sense, we are each other's real, although publicly unacknowledged, supervisor and we function as a well-oiled machine, accomplishing a great deal of the hidden work involved in maintaining university life. The image is that of a series of coupled oscillators, two objects connected by a spring, the movement of one automatically initiating movement in the other.

If we discover an urgent problem requiring an immediate solution, we will immediately prioritize, drop other work, deliver documentation to various offices, call pertinent administrators, students or organizations for information, plan a strategy for dealing with the situation and then act on it. If we can find a solution without taking up faculty time or attention, we will do so, since it is our duty to shield faculty from unnecessary administrative work.

A liaison officer also works with students. She or he may give at least preliminary degree program counselling, and a faculty member who has met with a student will often send the student back to the liaison officer to check on the viability of a planned academic procedure. Not all faculty members are deeply or equally conversant with university regulations and restrictions. For instance, a faculty advisor, unaware that the student hasn't taken all her required departmental courses, may suggest that a student take a course outside of the department which is relevant to the student's thesis plans. The faculty member's advice makes intellectual sense, but the student may apply to graduate later on and find her graduation blocked. It is then up to the registrar and department liaison officers to try to help the student. Both liaison officers might be receiving agitated emails and telephone calls from the student, especially if the student has a short time limit to prove degree completion. The liaison officers might initiate with faculty a process to document course equivalencies, if there are any. They may even suggest which course is the better equivalency. Failure to achieve a solution within the prescribed time limit will cause the student to graduate one term later than expected with a consequent additional tuition fee of a few thousand dollars. This one example of a small and rather simple task with various tactical manoeuvres *multiplied* by several other interruptive crisis situations is the order of each day. Most staff who interact with students on a daily basis sympathize with a student whose degree is in jeopardy and will try to help them within the confines of university regulations. They also feel a professional obligation to do so.

Now multiply simple scenarios like these — many of them requiring much more extensive knowledge of university regulations and requirements and a stronger perspective on how the regulations intersect with each other — by perhaps five to eight per day year round. Intersperse these rescue events with committee responsibilities that might involve reporting statistics, significant database entering, ghostwriting cases or documents, maintaining sections of a departmental website, communicating with degree and scholarship applicants, calculating grade point averages for scholarship competitions, and so on. Add to this responding to at least thirty-five or more intense emails a day, many of them requiring careful thought to avoid legal repercussions; answering twenty to thirty telephone calls per day; having an open office where twenty-five to forty-five students come in each day for advice for resolving diverse quandaries, some quickly dealt with, many not; and accomplishing many other chores or projects; and you glimpse the complicated responsibility load with which a liaison officer is burdened. Only a convoluted sentence like this one can convey the complexity of the job.

Most support staff hold positions that report to multiple offices and that have the same complex work expectations, many of which include confidentiality issues and liability obligations. For example, staff who word process communications regarding a plagiarism case are legally bound not to disclose this information. Staff in the Registrar's Office are always aware of the legal consequence involved in giving out inaccurate information to a student — if the student is litigiously minded and demands compensation, she or he will be held responsible. If support staff answer queries with curt replies, it is not that they are being inherently rude, as some may suppose; it's that they may have been "burned" by a litigious tangle in the past and are being cautious. An informational error can cost the university several thousand dollars if a student can prove institutional miscommunication. The sense that our every word has legal repercussions is always at the back of our minds. We may answer a query in sophisticated English or not, but the legal consciousness informing either the short or the extensive answer is and must remain firm. There must always be a silent wall behind which we operate in order not to compromise the university. Hence, despite the lack of prestige associated with the position and the invisibility of much of the work, administrative staff are expected to be highly skilled communicators, aware of legal ramifications and able to cope with multiple competing demands in an often chaotic environment.

We interact with and are responsible to multiple sectors within the university, and we may work for several immediate individual supervisors. However, we are not ultimately working for any one person or department. Our ultimate responsibility is to the university, and we have a legal obligation (and liability) to uphold the regulations, confidentiality laws and reputation of the university.

THE GENDERED UNDERWORLD

There is a gendered underworld within the university where harried staff recognize their own professional skills and respect each other's knowledge and expertise. This is a world where we take personal pride in a job well done and know the importance of our work within the organization, a world in which we have knowledge that other constituencies do not have. Before the labour intensification era, our training would have included a demand for the "neat" document — carefully typed out and proofread several times. Work intensification has hurried us all into a "get it done in time some way or other" mode. The new management style derides our worry about this harried work rhythm, with a call for a high turnaround and a quick fix to any errors occurring as a result; we know the mathematical formula attached to correcting errors: one correction equals five times or more the time required to do it right the first time, plus twenty times the number of steps originally required to effect the desired goal. We know that an error does not necessarily speak to our inability or our lower level of intelligence, but rather to badly made managerial decisions to overload us with responsibility. Everyone else just sees the error.

If we in the gendered underworld value our work, why is it that our bosses and supervisors trivialize what we do? Certainly, gender issues play a significant role. As opposed to women faculty who have challenged the formerly male boundaries, support staff have remained in jobs that have been classified as predominantly female, though, ironically, the jobs themselves have evolved significantly. In comparison to faculty and student profiles, the professional persona of administrative staff is practically nil. Our skills are rated as low to general level, requiring little conceptual complexity. We are seen as interchangeable workers, easily replaced by any other trained staff, as opposed to faculty whose research specialization implies a specific discipline or at least interdisciplinary appointment.

We enter the academic world with basic typing, word processing, language and mathematical skills, and are required to have at least a high school or undergraduate degree, depending on the particular job requirements. During the years we spend on the job and through our gendered underworld connections, we acquire and collect data, regulations and laws, general student demographics and management projections for future development. We learn from each other and from our close front-line connection with students. Our fellow colleagues and students' emotional reactions to bureaucracy are our most important instructors. An executive secretary new to the job will often be on the phone to someone in a similar position, asking questions when she first faces tenure review paperwork; a liaison officer will consult registrar staff when confronted with a student's problem which requires a solution involving legal considerations. We also learn by reading university forms and guidelines, calendars, provostial documents as well as regulations that help us determine what certification is required for graduation. We not only develop a large personal network but also a cognitive framework that becomes an internalized map of interrelated organizational regulations, so that we know how they overlap and which ones have priority over others.

As front-line workers relating to students on a daily basis, we also learn from students. When management proposes a fee hike or increased bureaucratic paperwork, we will know how "hot" the student response will be to the proposal based on our daily interactions of dealing with them around the practical issues involved in earning a degree. With these skills and knowledge, we are charged with a duty: to make it so! That is, when university management decides to raise fees, we are the ones who have to "take the heat" and ensure those fees are collected, even if we might personally disagree with it.

Faculty are hired based on their academic competence and original research, not necessarily their administrative skills. It is support staff who keep the less administratively informed ones in line so that the general profile of the department remains professional. Again, this alludes to the invisibility of the work — professional work carried out in the shadows. Hidden but vital tasks that are often undertaken by administrative staff may include tracking faculty members for missing grade submissions, ghostwriting an administrative document requiring legal and organizational structure expertise, shadow editing a badly written document, facilitating the meeting of a PhD candidate with a frequently absent supervisor, spelling out a complicated program to a student, computing international grade point averages and so much more. One employee might enter several thousand data bits into a database under a tight deadline — a task that requires an astute, attentive mind. Yet she won't be credited with this work. If we prepare a complex report, at most, our initials will appear as the typist; or we might be acknowledged for our support in the preparation of a book. In most cases, our presence remains hidden and obscured.

Faculty and student names characterize a university's substantive image. Academic staff are the central players in the university world: their research and theoretical originality functions as the true student recruitment drive; their expertise, their teaching and supervision shape the finished product — graduates. An academic's name might be synonymous with a particular theoretical exploration, whereas the administrative staff's name is linked to a generic job position and refers to a mundane usage: Business Officer, Administrative Assistant, Executive, and so on. Our identity is subsumed into the support we give to strengthen an academic's personality. A card-carrying Conservative secretary can be a good employee in a department whose research bias is Marxist, or vice versa. It doesn't matter. Support staff's professional duty entails neutrality and service. We are not hired to present our own conceptual framework; we are hired to present that of others. It would seem that our work, as opposed to that of the female faculty, has not surged forward into the world of authenticated value. Rather, the support staff role is congruent with that of the old-fashioned housewife: an overshadowed identity that is quietly and inconspicuously supportive.

The administrative job protocol that mutes our public image as professionals is neatly encapsulated by the adjective *support* staff. It implies unobtrusiveness. It follows that we should not bother the academics with the technicalities and complexities involved in our work, and these invisible realities are not acknowledged. However, there are stories, dramas and conceptual explorations in the complications we experience. An employee may receive an assignment one day with the requirement that it be completed the next day. Meanwhile, she or he might discover a glitch in a particular computer program required to complete the job. While notifying the technical support staff, she may also have many other urgent, time-conflicting assignments to finish. When the professor returns for the completed assignment and the employee triumphantly hands over the completed work, she will probably be confronted with a quizzical look, the meaning of which she knows well: "What was so difficult about the task I gave you to do?"

Support staff don't expect faculty to be interested in the details of work technicalities; however, they have long been due some acknowledgement of the intelligence and acumen required to accomplish their work. Administrative staff sometimes resist the undervaluation of their skills by assertive statements directed to faculty members, to their union or their immediate supervisors, but I believe that most often the resistance is visible only to fellow administrative staff. Our internal communication involves complaint sessions, raised eyebrows, groans — hidden language which is often interpreted by the rest of the university body in terms of gender disparagement. For instance, our "complaint sessions" often involve real analysis of the way our work is depreciated and unrecognized, but these sessions, if partially overheard, will most often be labelled as "gossip sessions," a clearly gendered and offensive criticism.

THE CORPORATE UNIVERSITY

The one place where support staff might expect a fair estimation of their skills is the university itself. The university periodically reviews job responsibilities to look for efficiency enhancements. I have experienced two of these formal reviews since my employment began in 1991. Co-workers, management and the technical support staff have been interviewed, so we are aware of the scope of the review. The results of these studies have been labelled "Internal Reports: Confidential." My experience with these job reviews has been fairly positive, though I may have qualms regarding some of their recommendations, particularly the recommendation of enhanced computerization as a method to increase work efficiency in order to deal with the budgetary need to cut staff.

Many recent cost-cutting objectives have been accompanied by an emphasis on making *all* essential university information available on the Internet, which has fostered a general managerial hope that technology upgrades will enable departments to cut support staff positions. Web pages nested upon web pages do contain all the information that an applicant or student might need, and they do complement support staff work. However, many of us have experienced a surprising increase in the volume of student and applicant telephone and email inquiries asking us how to find specific information on these websites since the activation of these technological innovations. Perhaps the electronic method of knowledge-sharing neglects a human biological and pedagogical requirement or perhaps the linearity of pages in a book which you can mark and reread is more compatible with the human mind. Perhaps the human contact which support staff represent is a more effective primary communication tool. Unbeknownst to those in decision-making positions, support staff listen not only to the words of the inquirer but also to their vocal tone and expression, adjusting the answer to the intensity of the questioner and often intuiting the real question that the inquirer is trying to frame. Hence, it is not only our knowledge, but our human awareness and our experience in dealing with many unique situations that make us an essential organizing force in the university. Electronic communication is not necessarily the more advanced methodology when it comes to knowledge transmission — it is limited due to its inability to fully meet the human needs of users.

The increased attention to efficiency and lowering institutional costs is also evident in job reorganization reviews, which are primarily activated by mandated cost-cutting drives.[5] In this highly credentialed environment, support staff know that their positions are the main target for cost-cutting measures. Our tension increases when these reviews are initiated because they place us in a no-woman's land. The invisibility, the confidentiality, the requirement that we work unobtrusively leave us vulnerable. Adding to our tension is the fact that we are in suspension until informed whether or not our job still exists. It would be similar to faculty with tenured positions suddenly being informed that they no longer had tenure and were suspended — until further notice! Often there is a type of bullying that occurs under cost-cutting job reorganization scrutiny: it is one person's word against another's, with no clear-cut guidelines for formulated delineation of work value. Our new job descriptions must state that the tasks involved constitute 100 percent of the workload, no more and no less. The pressure exerted to diminish the time needed for a task is enormous, and if we hope to keep our position at all, we must be able to do more work in less time.

CAN WE TALK?

At the university where I work, many of the predominantly female support staff are roughly the same age as feminist faculty. Many staff members approaching retirement years were involved in the early 1960s feminist movement. At that time, we were all "sisters." Now, we are support staff and "they" are faculty. A division has occurred, driven by either an accidental or volitional separation arising from our personal histories. One group of "sisters" took the career ladder to raise the professional and academic profile of women in society — they followed the "high road" of visible achievement. Long-term administrative staff followed another path, either through personal preference or circumstantial issues. Many of us remember the 1960s dialogue that occurred at that time concerning secretarial work. Cartoons zeroed in on the chauvinistic male boss. With these memories, we have watched what has been a long era of relative neglect in the investigation of support staff work devaluation.

Within our department, staff have, through the years, conducted Internet searches on "secretaries and gender," or "administrative staff and feminist studies," and so on. Perhaps our search words weren't the most appropriate, for we found very little text giving serious consideration to the implications of our work devaluation. In an article analyzing the administrative image in various texts, Szekeres (2004) notes: "It is a telling statistic that, out of all the texts focussed on universities which I have examined, only a small percentage concentrate any serious energy on the life of administrative staff (14 out of over seventy)" (20). From time to time, however, we have found a document pertinent to our situation. Examples include Jane Gaskell's (1987) exploration of the interplay of clerical workers' class and gender positions in the socially constructed de-valuation of their work, and E. Clare Alleyne's (1987) doctoral thesis, which advocates for serious recognition and certification of the student services staff sector, describing them as "competent bureaucrats (and the term here is in no way meant to be pejorative), with important respon-sibilities which form a large part of the foundation on which faculty and students go about building their academic careers" (121).

We have joined the workforce as wage-earners, whether willingly or by necessity, and we are frequently responsible for our own financial sup-port or for income integral to our family's welfare, or even for supporting a family as a sole-support parent. Having bitten off the first part of the feminist agenda, that women should be "out there" as wage earners, we have been left trapped in a humiliating stereotype as lower-class females with no mental acumen. The feminist movement has become irrelevant to our professional needs.

Intellectual honesty demands that the study of the complexity of our work, the knowledge needed to do the work and the knowledge gained by the work itself should involve serious feminist reflection. It is time to make the invisible work that we do visible. The fact is that the work we do has never been simple and the knowledge expectation, both technical and organizational, within our job descriptions has increased consider-ably through the past decade. The mental world of administrative work is uncharted territory. As one of my grandmothers, who had an eighth-grade education and whose own work was as a farmer, saleswoman and mother of seven children, would say, "Folks is folks — there's no call for disrespectin' folks."

NOTES

1 Despite the critical nature of this chapter, I would like to acknowledge the efforts of the department in which I work, the Department of Sociology and Equity Studies in Education, in the face of external pressure, to ensure that our voices and our perceptions count. I especially would like to thank Dr. Sandra Acker, an SESE faculty member, Anne Wagner, a recent PhD graduate, and Kimine Mayuzumi, an SESE PhD candidate, for their unique invitation to share some of my observations on administrative staff work. Finally, I would like to express my deep respect for the work and dedication of administrative staff who work within the University of Toronto.

2 According to the University of Toronto "Facts and Figures 2005," the unionized University of Toronto administrative staff population in September 2004, both full-time and part-time, totalled 3,163 (936 males and 2227 females) (68). Academic staff, not including librarians, totalled 2,982 (1,968 males and 1,014 females) (66).

3 Jane Gaskell (1987) describes the interplay of clerical workers' class and gender positions in the socially constructed devaluation of their work. Though general support staff job descriptions have evolved to include complex duties, conceptual dexterity and technological knowledge, my impression is that the history of devaluation continues in a straight line: these are "women workers'" jobs and therefore preconceived as "easy to do," "requiring very little mental ability."

4 I describe my own job responsibilities in some detail simply because my knowledge of its intricacies is, of course, more complete. There are many other administrative and secretarial jobs that require equal or even more complex multitasking.

5 Allison Dubarry (2007), president of the USW Local 1998 (unionized University of Toronto employees), describes how "over a period of approximately five years during the mid-1990's many administrative and technical staff at U of T directly felt the impact of increased workplace stress as our numbers were cut by approximately 25%." These types of job reorganization reviews are directly focused on cutting positions.

REFERENCES

Alleyne, E.C. (1987). *The preparation and professional development needs of non-academic student services staff in Ontario universities.* Unpublished doctoral dissertation, University of Toronto.

Dubarry, A. (2007). *Overtime.* Frequently Asked Questions (FAQs), United Steelworkers Local 1998. Retrieved 17 June 2007 from www.uswa1998.ca/overtime.htm.

Gaskell, J. (1987). Gender and skill. In D.W. Livingstone (Ed.), *Critical pedagogy and cultural power* (137–153). South Hadley, MA: Bergin and Garvey.

Leathwood, C. (2005). "Treat me as a human being — don't look at me as a woman": Feminist and professional identities in further education. *Gender and Education, 17*(4), 387–409.

Szekeres, J. (2004). The invisible workers. *Journal of Higher Education Policy and Management, 26*(1), 114–125.

University of Toronto. (2007). Facts and figures, 2005. Retrieved 22 October 2007 from www.utoronto.ca/aboutuoft/quickfacts/factsandfigures/factsandfigures2005.htm.

CHAPTER 9

"I'M COCKY THAT WAY ...":

WOMEN'S STUDIES TEACHING ASSISTANTS NEGOTIATING FEMINISM IN THE CONTEMPORARY ACADEMY

Michelle Webber

I'm not like everybody else, I mean, I'm cocky that way ...
— Sybil, teaching assistant

TEACHING ASSISTANTS (TAS) REPRESENT AN OFT-NEGLECTED GROUP OF workers in university life and are the focus of this chapter. In the social sciences and humanities, women comprise the majority of TAs. Teaching assistants are usually hired to support the delivery of undergraduate courses through leading small group tutorial discussions, grading assignments and answering students' questions. The teaching assistants included in this study work in feminist courses (whether housed in women's studies or in other social science departments) with feminist professors. I explore how faculty and TAs communicate with each other regarding pedagogy, outlining the discursive construction of the "good" teaching assistant as one not requiring much effort on a faculty member's part. TAs' understandings of feminist pedagogy and their attempts to alter relations of power and authority with their students are also explored. The last substantive section of the chapter is an account of how TAs incorporate feminist material into their classrooms as well as their experiences of student resistance to such material. I argue that despite their precarious position, TAs are poised to make significant contributions to the legitimacy of feminist knowledges in the academy.

WOMEN, WOMEN'S STUDIES AND THE ACADEMY

Before exploring the TAs' experiences, it is first necessary to provide some context on gender and the professoriate as well as on the position of women's studies in the contemporary academy. Women's presence in the academy has significantly changed over the past few decades. Over time, we have seen a growing representation of women as full-time faculty members (although we still have not reached parity with men). Women's participation as a percentage of all faculty has grown from 12.7 percent in 1973 to 15.2 percent in 1982 (Ornstein, Stewart & Drakich, 1998), to the current proportion of 32.6 percent of all ranks in 2004–2005 (Canadian Association of University Teachers, 2007). While these statistics represent a dramatic improvement, women's participation as faculty remains greater at the lowest ranking levels. Currently, women represent only 18.8 percent of full professors, 34.7 percent of associates, 41.4 percent of assistant professors and 54.8 percent of "other," including lecturers (Canadian Association of University Teachers, 2007).

Sexism and racism are "historically sedimented in the everyday working life and the intellectual practices of universities in North America" (Smith, 1999: 223). Women's studies is meant to represent a space in the academy where students can challenge the regime of rationality that assures the masculine orientation of the academy (Smith, 1992). Women's studies is supposed to provide a space for "social and intellectual transformation" (Braithwaite, Heald, Luhmann & Rosenberg, 2004: 10).

One of the tools for transformation is the use of liberatory pedagogies (or feminist pedagogies). The goal of implementing feminist pedagogies is an important consideration for this essay, as it influences how the faculty members and their TAs interact, as well as how the TAs approach leading their tutorials. Writers on feminist pedagogies tell us that they focus on trying to identify and understand gender relations (with many pedagogues taking an intersectionality approach and linking gender relations with relations of race, sexuality, class and so forth); utilizing people's experiences as important sites of knowledge; recognizing and altering power hierarchies in university classrooms; and engendering social change (hooks, 1988; Briskin, 1994; Morley, 2001).

Despite its promise, "women's studies does not have the status of the mainstream disciplines; the evidence is all around ... the number of faculty ... the reactions of their parents, their peers and faculty members throughout the university" (Heald, 2004: 78). Nonetheless, feminist faculty members carry on with the goal of transformation.

THE PROJECT

Data for this chapter were drawn from a larger study investigating the social organization of feminist teaching (Webber, 2005a). The research site was a primarily undergraduate university located in a medium-sized urban setting in Ontario, Canada. Women's studies courses and courses cross-listed with women's studies have been running in the institution for about twelve years. Cross-listed courses are those courses that are mounted by a department other than women's studies (such as sociology, psychology, economics) but are also listed as available as a women's studies credit. The home department is responsible for the staffing of these cross-listed courses. Interviews were conducted with twenty-two participants (twenty-one women and one man): eight faculty, five teaching assistants and nine students. An in-depth semi-structured approach was used and allowed a dialogue to develop between myself and each participant; interviewees were able to introduce topics and alter the course of our discussion. This qualitative approach to interviewing is widely used by feminist scholars (Reinharz, 1992).

This chapter draws mainly on my interviews with TAs, although faculty material is included where appropriate. I sought to interview all of the current TAs for cross-listed courses in the social sciences. There were only women employed in these positions; hence, the sample is exclusively women. Three of the five TAs (Julia, Arja, Dale) were in their first year in the role, while the other two (Donna, Sybil) had previous experience, with one being quite an experienced TA. Four of the TAs were undergraduate students at the research site (Julia, Donna, Dale and Arja), while the fifth was a graduate student at another Ontario university but was working at the research site (Sybil). I also interviewed the faculty members who were currently teaching cross-listed courses in social sciences, all of whom were women. Faculty members were drawn from across the ranks: one stipend instructor (Sue Ann), two lecturers on contractually limited term appointments (Tina, Bettina), one assistant professor on a contractually limited term appointment (Jordan), two tenured associate professors (Ilana, Rosemary) and two tenured full professors (Cara, Paula). All of the TAs and faculty members were white women. One limited term faculty member identified as Jewish. One TA and one faculty member identified as lesbian and one TA identified as bisexual.

BACKGROUND – USE OF TEACHING ASSISTANTS

It is important to understand how TAs are used at this university. TAs are drawn from several groups: undergraduate and graduate students as well as past graduates and graduates from other universities. Although most literature on TAs assumes they are graduate students at their university (Calkins & Kelley, 2005; Jensen et al., 2005; Punyanunt-Carter & Wagner, 2005), this is not the case at the research site. TAs are typically found in undergraduate classes with enrolments greater than twenty students. They lead one-hour weekly tutorials, which supplement two-hour weekly faculty lectures. TAs are usually contractually required to fulfill a range of duties, including attending lectures, leading tutorial discussions, proctoring exams, collating grades, answering student queries and grading student papers, examinations and tutorial participation.

TAs at the research site are governed by a collective agreement outlining maximum hours of work, processes of seniority in hiring (and preference for students currently enrolled at the university) and other relevant aspects of the organization of their work. With this union contract come particular dilemmas for feminist faculty. It is already a challenge to institute a more flexible pedagogy consistent with feminist pedagogical ideals in large undergraduate settings. Now consider adding an extra layer of managing TAs to this already difficult, though not impossible, task. Further, most of the faculty members interviewed work with undergraduate students as TAs for their undergraduate courses. Few faculty members are fortunate enough to hire the much-coveted graduate students for their courses as there are just not enough of them available to cover all of the tutorials. Consequently, in large introductory courses, one faculty member can find herself managing up to fifteen different TAs who are often themselves undergraduate students.

TAs are used widely in undergraduate classes (both at the research site and in other universities), yet they are not typically discussed in the feminist pedagogy literature (see Lathrop & Connolly, 2000, for an exception). In the next sections I report on the various aspects of TA work that surfaced in the interviews.

AUTONOMY VERSUS DIRECTION

TAs were asked to recall directions given to them by their supervising faculty members regarding expectations of pedagogy. The TAs also responded to questions about how they saw themselves as "instructors" in their tutorials and the kinds of relationships that they tried to cultivate with their students. My presumption was that because feminist pedagogical literature highlights the importance of process in pedagogy, feminist faculty members would be keen to provide direction to their TAs, especially those in their first year of such work. However, many faculty members, especially "junior" faculty, do not have the "time, experience or incentive to work with their TAs beyond a simple supervisory role" (Calkins & Kelley, 2005: 262). The reality of the contemporary organization of academic life is that many academics shift their time to research over teaching (Taylor, 2001) and in teaching they shift to content over process (Crabtree & Sapp, 2003). The historical male norms of independence and autonomy prevail over ideals such as mentoring novice TAs. Common to all of the interviews with the TAs was the claim that their supervising professors provided little direction about appropriate tutorial content or the pedagogy. For example,

> She kind of left us on our own, which I kind of liked, and if I had any questions or anything I would go to her and talk to her about it. (Julia)

> Actually, I've been surprised working as a tutorial leader, how little … direction you're given and I've found that to be the same when I've worked as a marker, for example. (Dale)

> I could do whatever I wanted. (Arja)

As Grant (1997) argues, there is an image of a "good" student operating discursively in the academy — one who is competitive, independent, rational and so forth. An analogous argument can be made about TAs. There is a discursive construction of what it is to be a "good" TA, including characteristics such as being competent, able to work on one's own and not undermining the faculty member's work in the course. This normative construction is known by both TAs and faculty.

Grant (1997) describes the personal qualities of the "good" student as including a "fierce kind of individuality in which the strong survive and the weak fall by the wayside" (102). The same construction seems to be at work for the TAs. TAs are not given much institutional support in the form of training or other resources. The novice TA is given a class list, a room assignment and a course outline and is left basically to sink or swim, or as Calkins and Kelley (2005: 266) put it, she is given a "trial by fire." Cazden (1988) refers to this scenario as performance before competence. The act of being a teaching assistant serves as the means to competency (Grossman, Smagorinsky & Valencia, 1999).

While it seems that faculty members should be concerned about the lack of attention given to teaching assistants (although faculty did not express concern), the teaching assistants themselves generally appreciated the autonomy granted them by their course supervisors. For example, Julia stated, "It was nice because it gave me the confidence to know that she trusts me with her classes and that's very important for me in the classroom, to know that I, hopefully, ... have her approval."

Duffelmeyer (2003), in the context of classroom composition, argues that learning as you go can actually be a useful process, so teaching assistants would develop confidence precisely because they are not following rigid guidelines. Along the same lines, Dale indicated that if she hears nothing from her faculty supervisor, she assumes everything must be fine with the way she is running her tutorials. "For me, I don't mind [autonomy] because if I'm given a job I just go ahead and do it, and then if someone feels that something's not working out okay, then I just assume that they'll come and we'll talk about it." It is possible that other disciplines have different norms for faculty directives with TAs; but I cannot tell whether this is the case.

NEGOTIATIONS WITH THE PROFESSOR

What happens, though, when the teaching style of the professor clashes with the teaching preference of the TA? Is there potential for a disjuncture between the feminism of the professor and the feminism of the hired teaching assistant? The issue of difference in style/approach arose in several of the interviews. Most of the faculty commented on how nice it was when they had the opportunity to work with the same TA more than once, especially if it were someone who seemed to share their feminist pedagogical and theoretical outlooks. On the other hand, most faculty did not get this opportunity, partly as a consequence of the union contract governing the hiring of TAs (and many TAs only work for one year as MA students or in their last year of undergraduate studies).

At my research site, TAs are unionized, as they are at other universities, and tensions can emerge as unionization changes the character of relations between TAs and their supervisory faculty members (Park, 2004). Unions, however, have brought positive elements for TAs, as they now enjoy health benefits, employment security through seniority and participation in collective bargaining processes (Park, 2004). The union contract privileges the university's own full-time students (graduate and senior undergraduates) with students typically beginning to TA in their final year of undergraduate studies. From the faculty side, this practice typically means that they are continually dealing with assistants who have no prior teaching experience. One faculty member who stated clearly that she was pro-union also pointed out that the process for hiring is so complex that there is not much flexibility for faculty to choose their preferred candidates. Consequently, the candidate hired might not approach the course content from the same theoretical or political stance as the professor. For example, Cara said, "She could be a non-feminist, anti-feminist, I mean, you know that's possible." For these cross-listed courses, staffing decisions are made by the home department mounting the course, and prospective TAs make their applications directly to these departments.

Due to such bureaucratic processes, being able to hire a candidate who is the "best fit" for a course or a professor is an issue that is not easily resolved. In some instances, faculty spoke of having to work in situations where their TAs and themselves did not see eye to eye. Effective supervisory relationships are typically based on successful interpersonal relationships between faculty supervisors and their TAs (Park, 2004), and when this does not happen, tensions arise. Cara, a full professor, encountered a situation where two of her TAs accused her of not being feminist enough in her teaching and even approached the director of women's studies in an attempt to have her removed from the course. In this instance, the TAs were both graduate students and were quite experienced. Their challenge to Cara's authority is an interesting example of how TAs are able to exercise power, despite being in a subordinate position.

Cara described the situation as being uncomfortable and unpleasant, and explained that the textbook she was using for the class had "feminist" in the title and that she was one of the book's co-authors. She described her approach to feminist teaching as carefully introducing her students to feminism and not using her authority to enforce a feminist point of view:

> I'm acutely aware that I do have power in the classroom ... I don't see that I'm going to coerce them into adopting any particular point of view. I see them being exposed to things and making up their own minds.

Cara had made it explicit to her students that she would not evaluate them in terms of their agreement with her or with the textbook. However, the TAs wanted Cara to be more assertive with her students about feminism, echoing hooks's (1988) pedagogy of confrontation:

> They definitely wanted me to be much more [assertive]. They said, "We want you to talk about feminist perspectives," so I did. I went to the class the very next day and talked about the different feminist perspectives, including postmodernism and all of which was in the textbook, and I don't like to lecture from the textbook ... But they definitely had this image that it should be much more political ... I feel I know how to teach an intro class. I've done it a lot and I have particular goals in mind here. So the gist of what I got is that it wasn't [challenging] enough [or] in your face [enough], and so forth and so on.

This scenario speaks to how power operates. Taking a relational view of power, we can understand how Cara as a professor could still be subject to the teaching assistants' power to resist Cara's assumption of power. For Foucault (1980), where there is power there is also the possibility of resistance. Further, this experience highlights women's position as contestable authority figures in the academy. It is unlikely that TAs (both men and women) would be as willing to critique a male professor's pedagogical approach.

Other faculty members also spoke about working with teaching assistants who did not match their pedagogical approaches, although none had a story as dramatic as Cara's. Bettina talked about one TA who was much more aggressive with the students than she likes to be. Bettina believes it is not a professor's place to alienate her/his students. In this situation, the TA had little patience for students who did not share her perspective. I happened to interview this same TA (Sybil); she spoke in her interview about considering a professor's teaching style as part of her decision of whether or not to apply as a TA for that course. Sybil also considers the status of a professor (whether tenured or not, limited term, etc.) when making her decision. She describes herself as "cocky" and often tries to do her "own thing" in tutorials. She sees sessional instructors as being "more bendable" than tenured faculty members. Her use of the descriptor "cocky" highlights her gender transgression of being an assertive woman, understanding the academic hierarchy and being willing to use such knowledge in a way that improves her own working situation. This level of confidence and knowledge was not common across the TAs.

TAs negotiate between the pedagogical approach and theoretical positions of the professors they are working for and their own desired teaching styles and theoretical orientations. The above examples illustrate that, despite being institutionally located in assistant positions, TAs are able to use power/resistance in beneficial ways. Additionally, because feminist teaching is sometimes considered less authoritarian than traditional modes of teaching and is compounded by women's secondary position within the academy, women and especially feminist faculty may be challenged by TAs (and students) in ways that men are not.

FAMILIARITY WITH FEMINIST PEDAGOGY

Through the course of the interviews, it became obvious that the teaching assistants at this university are not offered much training (formal or informal) with respect to "teaching" in general, let alone "feminist teaching." This lack of training for teaching assistants is a well-documented pattern in the literature (Duffelmeyer, 2003; Park, 2004; Jensen et al., 2005; Oberlander & Barnett, 2005). When asked about their understanding and familiarity with feminist pedagogical principles, three of the five TAs admitted that they were not well versed in feminist pedagogy.

Oh, I've heard that term, but why don't I know it? I should know it, but I don't. No, I'm going to say no. (Julia)

I'm going to say off the top of my head, no. (Donna)

I don't know. I'm not sure I can answer that. (Sybil)

Another TA, Dale, read up on feminist pedagogy on her own initiative. Arja was the sole TA in the study who was majoring in women's studies, and was, therefore, the only one familiar with feminist pedagogy.

Her knowledge of feminist pedagogy, though, was a result of her own schooling rather than a result of any institutional training or instruction from her supervisory faculty member. For Arja and Dale, the vision of what feminist pedagogy is closely mirrors academic literature on feminist pedagogy (Shrewsbury, 1998; Morley, 2001), including the positioning of feminist teaching as less authoritarian than traditional models of teaching. Dale and Arja both spoke about recognizing and acknowledging that there is a person behind the student, a person who has competing demands on his/her time. For example, Arja said,

> If a student came up to me and said, "I'm a mom, my kid was sick ... can I have an extra day?" on the day the paper's due [that's one thing and I'm not sure I'd cut her slack], but [if] it's due next week and life has happened, I think I would, especially with women's roles like that, cut [her] some slack, that sort of thing.

One of Dale's concerns was the importance of respecting the diversity of her students. She wants her students to engage with course materials that introduce world views different than their own, but to do so in a careful and considerate way, akin to Shrewsbury's (1998: 168) desire for a "mutual exploration of diverse experiences." Dale explained:

> I want to be able to get through to people and be able to expand their minds, and expand their way of looking at life and get them dialoguing, but in that process, always, always preserve their dignity and treat them as valuable.

Dale's objective of getting her students to critically engage with course material is one of the main tenets of feminist pedagogy (Manicom, 1992; Briskin, 1994).

PRACTISING POWER

As demonstrated earlier, TAs are enmeshed in webs of power with their supervising faculty members. These power dynamics extend to the TAs' relationships with their students. Even though the TAs interviewed want to fulfill the feminist mandate of the courses they teach, there is a tricky line for them to negotiate. This negotiation of authority is especially salient for the undergraduate TAs. Using undergraduate TAs creates a situation of peers teaching peers. Students generally judge undergraduate TAs as lacking the "maturity and sophistication needed to make and support subjective judgments about their peers' assignments. From their peers' point of view, they lack credibility" (Rieber, 2004: 177).

The TAs incorporate various strategies to attempt to alter the power relations in the tutorials. Sometimes they are successful, sometimes they are not. Arja, an undergraduate student herself, is one TA who makes little to no attempt to change power relations in her tutorials. She enjoys the "power" that comes with her position. As she says, "Whoever sits at the front and opens their mouth, [that's when] others stop talking." Arja wants to have respect from her students for the position that she occupies. She attempts to treat her students as responsible adults, but finds this difficult when they are "being whiny and irresponsible. I have a hard time," she says, "being kind of polite."

Someone like Dale takes quite a different perspective. She acknowledged that power comes with her position, but she does not enjoy that power. In keeping with Briskin's (1994) account of power and feminist pedagogy, she described herself as trying to "give it away." She thinks that it is important "that other people feel empowered, feel like they have a say." She understands that because of her position as a teaching assistant, she must assign grades: "That's the system, but I'm not a person that expects them to jump through hoops for me." Dale tells her students that she hopes they are in class to learn something and that they want to be there as opposed to her forcing their presence by dangling grades over their heads: "Holding some sort of power over them, like if you do this for me, you'll get 0.5 [marks] but if you do this you'll get 0.75 [marks], because that's a false relationship." Her strategy during tutorials has been to talk as little as possible: "I'm the one who has to facilitate and keep things on topic and on course and so forth, but it's amazing, you give people the opportunity to do the [talking] and off they go." Yet Dale's perspective of "giving away power" masks important power dynamics at play in her tutorials. She seems to think of power as a zero-sum game — one either has power or one does not have power — rather than thinking of power as relational and always operating.

The TAs' middle-ground attempts at altering power dynamics is best illustrated by Donna's approach. Donna was aware of the difficulty of balancing her position as one institutionally infused with power with her attempts to cultivate some power among the students. She reflected that there is "a delicate balance that you want to walk between, control and authority and giving your students some autonomy and power." She has tried to make sure that all her students experience some degree of autonomy and power in the running of the tutorials.

NAVIGATING FEMINIST CONTENT AND RESISTANCE TO FEMINISM

Feminist knowledges are often disavowed in the academy (Webber, 2005b). This disavowal has consequences for how TAs then navigate feminist course content in their tutorial discussions. One strategy that teaching assistants have used in their classes is to not explicitly label feminist material as such. Donna talked about introducing feminist content without identifying it by name:

> There are really negative stereotypes and negative reactions to feminism, so if you sort of go out and hang out this sign saying "feminist, this is feminist content" you immediately lose the students, or not all of them, but a fairly large portion ... just saying feminist will shut them down, they stop listening and you lose credibility if you sort of push blatant feminist content at them.

It may seem surprising to learn that students in a women's studies course are not expecting a feminist course. However, the courses under exploration in this chapter are cross-listed courses, and the students overwhelmingly register for them under the home departments' labels. Many students are unaware that the courses are cross-listed (despite being labelled as such in the undergraduate calendar) with women's studies, and are, hence, feminist courses. According to recent research, female TAs already have a "credibility" issue, which demonstrates that students evaluate female TAs as being less effective than male TAs (Punyanunt-Carter & Wagner, 2005). I asked Donna to expand on her notion of losing credibility:

> What you get is the "Oh, that's just a feminist ranting again." And that's where you lose the credibility because it gets turned into this, as if it's some sort of annoying as opposed to a valid point that has something important to say, or bring to the discussion. It's just an easy way of shutting somebody down and in that sense I think that you lose credibility, you lose the ability to dialogue.

Other TAs supported Donna's recollection of students responding to feminist material by dismissing it as a feminist rant. Arja talked about seeing students roll their eyes or just keeping their heads down to avoid eye contact. Dale has graded exams on which comments were made on the answer sheet about feminists.

I even had some of my exams where they were asked to discuss welfare reforms from a conservative, centrist and ... liberal feminist perspective and you know, a lot of them were going, "Oh well, the conservatives, they have it right, we need to get all of these people off of welfare," and I can think of two actual exams where people wrote, basically verbatim, you know, "Oh, the feminists ... they're just blame, blame, blame, blame."

Sybil, the TA who described herself as being "cocky" and being very upfront about feminism in her tutorials, has routinely had students say that the tutorial is "male bashing." TAs' responses to such resistance vary: Arja's prior teaching experience has helped her navigate such resistance, and Dale has found that her age works to her advantage. Dale has also used humour to diffuse situations: "In the same way that they throw these comments out as joking, I throw it back as joking too ... Because to challenge it seriously is to act like it's something worth challenging seriously, and I don't think it is."

When students do not see feminism as an academic discipline, they are able to regard discussions of gender issues as non-intellectual or non-academic enterprises (Bauer, 1990). Dale mirrors Donna's sentiments and approach. She too has not explicitly named the course material as feminist. Students have participated in her class discussions more actively when "feminism" was not made explicit in the readings or in Dale's statements. As argued elsewhere (Webber, 2005b), this bowing to conservative students' interests can actually serve to reproduce the sentiment that feminist perspectives are not valid forms of knowledge.

Anderson and Williams (2001) argue that in order to claim an identity it has to be declared valid by others. While they are writing about identity, their argument can be applied to many students' visions of feminism. Some students are turned off when feminism is mentioned because of the current culture of dismissing feminist ideas (Letherby & Shiels, 2001). Alternatively, the students might be afraid of saying something "wrong." Like most of the faculty members I interviewed, Dale's goal as a TA was not necessarily "convert" her students to the "feminist side" but to get them to "engage in the conversation" and to perhaps think differently about the world around them than they had before taking the cross-listed course. While both men and women students "resisted" feminist content, the TAs recalled that the resistance came mainly from their young, white male students. Sybil recalled one of her male students stating, "I'm ready to get trashed today," as he walked into the classroom.

While student resistance can make spaces uncomfortable for teaching assistants and other students, it is important to understand that resistance can be theorized as productive (Foucault, 1980). Some even argue that resistance is necessary (Bauer, 1990; Titus, 2000). Resistance indicates that students are thinking about the material and that it is indeed challenging their taken-for-granted assumptions of the world.

However productive it might be, TAs need know how to navigate such student resistance. As the "front line" to students, TAs often have the opportunity to challenge the marginalization of women's studies and feminist knowledges in the academy and to encourage students to see what both women's studies and feminism have to offer.

CONCLUSION

Teaching assistants occupy a difficult position in the academy. They are teachers in a middle space between faculty supervisors and their students. They are seen as doing important work in universities (they basically fulfill the exact same duties as faculty members themselves — see Oberlander & Barnett, 2005), yet our institutions do not seem to care enough about the quality of teaching in classrooms and infrequently require any training for a TA position. Teaching assistants are just expected to "deliver the goods." Nonetheless, TAs come into contact with the majority of undergraduate students in universities and therefore play a crucial role in academic settings. In terms of feminist spaces, TAs also play a pivotal role in the acknowledgement of feminist knowledges as legitimate forms of knowledge. Faculty members need to actively support the work of teaching assistants by being clear about our feminist pedagogical principles and engaging teaching assistants in appreciating feminist approaches to knowledge production.

REFERENCES

Anderson, P., & Williams, J. (Eds.). (2001). *Identity and difference in higher education: "Outsiders within."* Aldershot, UK: Ashgate.

Bauer, D. (1990). The other "f" word: The feminist in the classroom. *College English, 52*, 385–396.

Braithwaite, A., Heald, S., Luhmann, S., & Rosenberg, S. (2004). "Passing on" women's studies. In A. Braithwaite, S. Heald, S. Luhmann, & S. Rosenberg (Eds.), *Troubling women's studies: Pasts, presents and possibilities* (9–41). Toronto: Sumach Press.

Briskin, L. (1994). Feminist pedagogy: Teaching and learning liberation. In L. Erwin & D. MacLennan (Eds.), *Sociology of education in Canada: Critical perspectives on theory, research and practice* (443–470). Toronto: Copp Clark Longman.

Calkins, S., & Kelley, M. (2005). Mentoring and the faculty–TA relationship: Faculty perceptions and practices. *Mentoring and Tutoring, 13*(2), 259–280.

Canadian Association of University Teachers. (2007). *CAUT almanac of post-secondary education in Canada.* Toronto: CAUT.

Cazden, C. (1988). *Classroom discourse: The language of teaching and learning.* Portsmouth, UK: Heinemann.

Crabtree, R., & Sapp, D. (2003). Theoretical, political and pedagogical challenges in the feminist classroom. *College Teaching, 51*(4), 131–140.

Duffelmeyer, B. (2003). Learning to learn: New TA preparation in computer pedagogy. *Computers and Composition, 20*, 295–311.

Foucault, M. (1980). *Power/knowledge.* New York: Pantheon Books.

Grant, B. (1997). Disciplining students: The construction of student subjectivities. *British Journal of Sociology of Education, 18*(1), 101–114.

Grossman, P., Smagorinsky, P., & Valencia, S. (1999). *Appropriating conceptual and pedagogical tools for teaching English: A conceptual framework for studying professional development.* Albany: State University of New York Press.

Heald, Susan. (2004). "Just my opinion?" Women's studies, autobiography and the university. In A. Braithwaite, S. Heald, S. Luhmann, & S. Rosenberg, *Troubling women's studies: Pasts, presents and possibilities* (45–90). Toronto: Sumach Press.

hooks, b. (1988). *Talking back: Thinking feminist, thinking black.* Toronto: Between the Lines.

Jensen, M., Farrand, K., Redman, L., Varcoe, T., & Coleman, L. (2005, July/August). Helping graduate teaching assistants lead discussions with undergraduate students. *Journal of College Science Teaching,* 20–24.

Lathrop, A., & Connolly, M. (2000). Feminist theory and collaborative learning in seminar contexts. *The International Journal for Academic Development, 5*(1), 61–67.

Letherby, G, & Shiels, J. (2001). "Isn't he good, but can we take her seriously?" Gendered expectations in higiher education. In P. Anderson & J. Williams (Eds.), *Identity and differences in higher education: "Outsiders within"* (121–132). Aldershot, UK: Ashgate.

Manicom, A. (1992). Feminist pedagogy: Transformations, standpoints and politics. *Canadian Journal of Education, 17*(3), 365–389.

Morley, L. (2001). Mass higher education: Feminist pedagogy in the learning society. In P. Anderson & J. Williams (Eds.), *Identity and difference in higher education: "Outsiders within"* (28–37). Aldershot, UK: Ashgate.

Oberlander, S., & Barnett, J. (2005). Multiple relationships between graduate assistants and students: Ethical and practical considerations. *Ethics and Behavior, 15*(1), 49–63.

Ontario Confederation of University Faculty Associations. (2006). Brief to the Standing Committee of Finance and Economic Affairs. Retrieved 16 November 2007 from www.ocufa.on.ca/briefs/brieeffeb2006.pdf.

Ornstein, M., Stewart, P., & Drakich, J. (1998). The status of women faculty in Canadian universities. *Education Quarterly Review, 5*(2), 9–29.

Park, C. (2004). The graduate teaching assistant (GTA): Lessons from North American experience. *Teaching in Higher Education, 9*(3), 349–361.

Punyanunt-Carter, N., & Wagner, T. (2005). Communication-based emotional support differences between professors and teaching assistants. *Education, 125*(4), 569–574.

Reinharz, S. (1992). *Feminist methods in social research.* New York: Oxford University Press.

Rieber, L. (2004, January/February). Using professional teaching assistants to support large group business communication classes. *Journal of Education for Business,* 176–178.

Shrewsbury, C. (1998). What is feminist pedagogy? In M. Rogers (Ed.), *Contemporary feminist theory* (167–171). Boston: McGraw-Hill.

Smith, D. (1999). *Writing the social: Critique, theory and investigations.* Toronto: University of Toronto Press.

Smith, D. (1992). Whistling women: Reflections on rage and rationality. In W. Carroll, L. Christiansen-Ruffman, R. Currie, & D. Harrison (Eds.), *Fragile truths: Twenty-five years of sociology and anthropology in Canada* (207–226). Ottawa: Carleton University Press.

Taylor, J. (2001). The impact of performance indicators on the work of university academics: Evidence from Australian universities. *Higher Education Quarterly,* 55(1), 42–61.

Titus, J. (2000). Engaging student resistance to feminism: "How is this stuff going to make us better teachers?" *Gender and Education, 12,* 21–37.

Webber, M. (2005a). *Claiming feminist space in the university: The social organization of feminist teaching.* Unpublished doctoral dissertation, University of Toronto.

Webber, M. (2005b). "Don't be so feminist": Exploring student resistance to feminist approaches in a Canadian university. *Women's Studies International Forum, 28,* 181–194.

CHAPTER 10

"A PRETTY INCREDIBLE STRUCTURAL INJUSTICE":

CONTINGENT FACULTY IN CANADIAN UNIVERSITY NURSING

Linda Muzzin & Jacqueline Limoges

USING A FEMINIST METHODOLOGY, VARIOUS TEAMS WORKING WITH Linda Muzzin explored the largely "invisible" (Church, 1999) or "hidden" (Rajogopal, 2002) academic lives and power relations experienced by non-tenured faculty. This analysis is based on the careers and experiences of forty nursing faculty in a national Canadian study of 160 contingent faculty and academic administrators across various professional fields.[1] Included were four nursing deans or directors, three full-time tenured or tenure-stream and thirty-three sessional, part-time or permanent non-tenured faculty. One man participated. Though we searched for nursing educators of colour, all but three participants were white, even in Aboriginal nursing programs. One of the three was no longer at the university, with the others considering leaving.

The comment in quotation marks in the title was made by a faculty member in nursing who was problematizing the sectors of the academy that operate disproportionately with faculty who are variously called permanent non-tenured, contractual, sessional, adjunct, clinical or casual.

Contingent teaching has long been a permanent arrangement in law, nursing and dentistry where practising lawyers, dentists and nurses introduce students to the practice of their professions through part-time teaching in the upper years of study. In mainstream social sciences and humanities, which do not require preparation for professional practice, sessional teaching is also pursued by a few graduate students and new doctoral graduates intending to apply for tenure-stream faculty positions. According to Rajogopal (2002) and our more recent observations in specific fields, there is also growth of contingent faculty in areas of the retrenchment of the 1990s. These areas include nursing, the humanities and social sciences. In these fields, higher education restructuring in the 1990s was acute, and our evidence suggests that contingent pools of faculty swelled during that period and have remained.

As outlined elsewhere (Muzzin, 2008), in these fields, a teaching/administrative stream of full-time non-tenured faculty has been growing in the traditional academy, and adding scores of part-time and casual faculty makes it possible for the schools to deliver their curricula. As U.S. data clearly show, this teaching stream is disproportionately feminized (National Education Association, 2001). A Canadian survey (Smallman, 2001) similarly shows a feminization of the "other" category of faculty. In Smallman's table 3, the category "other" includes all faculty not listed as tenure-track full, associate or assistant professor and thus is comparable to the group in our study.

In this chapter, when we critique the use of particular discourses, such as the reference to non-tenure stream faculty as "other," these words are placed in double quotation marks to denote our problematization of the expression. This is important in critical feminist research, since we are not assuming neutrality — indeed, we believe with Haraway (1996) that there *is* no neutral position.

Nursing faculty in the non-tenured professoriate perform a variety of tasks from paid full-time administration and teaching to unpaid intermittent supervision of students in clinical placements on a casual basis. While there is some merit in separating the full-timers from the casual workers in this group when looking at specific working conditions and equity considerations, this will not be done here, since most incumbents and administrators agreed that the situation of contingents represented "a pretty incredible structural injustice," whether the faculty were full-time or not. Also, as has been explained elsewhere, "part-time" is a misnomer, in that these faculty largely work full-time or beyond — only the salary is part-time (Rajogopal, 2002; Muzzin, 2008).

Using our critical feminist approach, we call into question the conditions under which these faculty work. We begin by describing the historical conditions that have led to their oppression and link the oppression of contingent faculty in nursing education to the move to the university in Canada, with its research emphasis. We conclude by speculating about the future as nursing struggles for its professional status; as collaborative programs with colleges work to upgrade the basic nursing credential to a baccalaureate; and as programs gear up to meet the contemporary shortage of nurses.

BACKGROUND

In a historical collection on the professoriate in Canada, Bruneau (2006) emphasizes that there is very little scholarship on a central aspect — the lives of university faculty and their identities and contributions. He calls for detailed studies of faculty lives so that we can get some sense of the central impact that they have as professors or even what it is *like* to be a professor in a university. Such studies are necessary, he argues, since the North American higher education literature tends to focus rather bloodlessly and mechanistically on admissions, hiring and other institutional processes rather than on those who people the institutions and their experiences.

Another problem with the higher education literature is that it does not tend to relate the academic profession to professions or work in general, so that we have to search elsewhere for some insight into how things work politically, economically and culturally in the academy. The Canadian sociological literature on professions is somewhat more progressive, with numerous gendered studies on individual professions, including dentistry (Adams, 2000); clergy (Mellow, 2006); engineering (Ranson, 2005); law (Backhouse, 1991); nursing (McPherson, 1996; Rankin & Campbell, 2006); medical laboratory technology (Grant, 2005); midwifery (Nestel, 2004); pharmacy (Muzzin, Brown & Hornosty, 1993; Muzzin, Sinnott & Lai, 1999); social work (de Montigny, 1995); and teacher education (Acker & Armenti, 2004; Acker & Dillabough, 2007). These monographs provide useful insights into the exigencies of the power relations oppressing nursing, the hierarchies in dentistry/hygiene and medicine/pharmacy, and the effects of 1990s restructuring on feminized professions such as nursing and medical laboratory technology.[2]

As in other professions and occupations (Reskin & Roos, 1990), one of the significant changes in academia in Canada over the past thirty years has been large-scale entry of women as students and professors, and the literature has begun to reveal how the academy works from the perspective of women. A start has been made with research on women faculty in particular fields, which provides revealing glimpses of what it is like to be minoritized or treated as a second-class citizen (for example, Ainley, 1990; Hannah, Paul & Vethamany-Globus, 2002). These studies also touch on other dimensions of discrimination experienced by faculty related to ethnoracial, sexual or disability identification (for example, Bensimon, 1997; Margolis & Romero, 1998; Monture-Angus, 2001; Michalko, 2003). Being a non-tenured faculty member is itself a form of minoritization, a point often identified in the stories that faculty tell.

The numbers are useful in showing just how minoritized women are in the Canadian professoriate: a "pyramid" handed out at the 2007 meetings of the Congress of the Humanities and Social Sciences shows that women now constitute almost 60 percent of undergraduates and over 45 percent of PhD students, but only 18.8 percent of full professors and 13 percent of presidents (See Ollivier et al., 2006, for a discussion about the listserve where these results and discussion have been posted). Unfortunately, Statistics Canada does not collect information on tenure versus non-tenure stream numbers, but senior professors and administrators who were interviewed in this study insisted that the numbers of contingent faculty have grown and reliance on them has persisted (see below). But as Bruneau (2006) argues, numbers alone do not reveal how things really work. In our study of women (and men) professors, we focused on the lives and experiences of professors with the intention of explaining how things work, using equity as our starting point.

A BRIEF HISTORY OF ACADEMIC NURSING IN CANADA

It is beyond the scope of this chapter to do a full review of the history of academic nursing in Canada, but a few brief comments can serve to place into a historical context the contemporary situation in which contingent faculty in nursing find themselves. For about 100 years in Canada, nursing education took place "on the job" in hospitals. For the first few decades from the establishment of these hospital schools in the late 1800s, student nurses provided "free labour" in the "schools," where they were placed in order to be trained for nursing (McPherson, 1996). But as feminist scholars have amply documented (for example, Coburn, 1974), instruction was at a minimum and the "students" were largely under the control of physicians rather than nursing teachers (McPherson, 1996).

The fact that the vast majority of nurses have been trained in colleges or hospitals rather than universities for much of the past century in Canada is in contrast with other professions such as dentistry, medicine, law and even pharmacy, all of which until recently have been male-dominated. Thus professional education is clearly gendered, with mid-century mainstream sociologists reinforcing this discrimination by insisting that female-dominated occupations such as nursing were only "semi"-professions (Etzioni, 1969). The nursing literature itself is replete with debates about whether nursing is "really" a profession (Limoges, 2007). Much has changed, though arguably, in the contemporary scene, with the continuing support of the state, biomedicine and physicians continue to dominate the health sector, complicated by the economic events of the 1990s (Limoges, 2007).

In our visits to twelve of thirty-eight Canadian university schools of nursing (which took place prior to full initiation of many of the collaborative college-university programs now under way), administrators and other senior faculty reported that during the 1990s and beyond, they had experienced very severe cutbacks. Beginning in the early 1990s in Alberta, followed by Ontario, these cuts were catastrophic for nursing in hospitals and in higher education. At least one school had been in repeated danger of closing and administrators calculated that up to 80 percent of the curriculum there was taught by non-tenured faculty. Thus, the traditional reliance on the health sector for clinical instructors was strained, since both were short of funds. In the words of one administrator:

> Our clinical faculty [are] part-time ... salaried and they are part of the hospital ... We've been getting [them almost for] free, but because of the crunch in the hospitals with budgetary cuts and the shortage of nurses ... [we'll have to start paying them what they are worth] ... I think that the non-tenured faculty will likely be a category that we will end up with. I'm not sure if we'll ever be able to get rid of it.

It is thus difficult not to see contemporary nursing education in Canada as a continuation of its oppressive past. Not so long ago, nurses staffed entire hospitals for "free" to obtain an "education." And, like other working women, they experienced low pay, since they were considered to just be doing what women did for "free" in the home. Armstrong and colleagues (1993) have documented that union activity of nurses has resulted in net gains in salary and job security for some nurses over the past decades, despite the cuts. However, the move to a profession with a baccalaureate as the standard entry to practice in Canada has had some unintended consequences. This upgrading of nursing credentials can be seen as a coming of age on the part of nursing vis-à-vis the other health professions, where the baccalaureate has been standard for many decades (Limoges, 2007). Unfortunately, the move to credential nurses and their educators, who now routinely require master's degrees and beyond, also followed cutbacks both in the profession and in nursing itself. That is, when restructuring hit the health care system in the 1990s, nurses turned to colleges and universities for part-time work, thus providing the proverbial (largely female) "reserve army of labour," ripe for exploiting. Our interviews took place long after these events began occurring, but they are still being played out, as comments made to us by both faculty and administrators make clear.

THE RESEARCH-INTENSIVE UNIVERSITY AND CONTINGENT STAFFING

Although there are hundreds of colleges and private postsecondary institutions in Canada, there are only about seventy-five universities (Jones, 1997). The system is currently in transformation, with each institution negotiating a bewildering array of inter-institutional diplomas and degrees. This complexity can immediately be glimpsed through visits to post- secondary websites. In contrast to teaching-intensive community colleges and private institutions (the latter still in the minority in Canada), universities tend to be research intensive.[3] As explained elsewhere (Muzzin, 2005), this situation puts cost-intensive academic professions, which must produce practising health professionals, and nursing specifically, at a severe disadvantage.

First, central university administrators look askance at expensive teaching programs, which they tend not to see as cost effective. Dentistry might run a university clinic to recover some of the costs of educating dentists, but this is not an option for nursing. As one dean put it,

> Our clinical costs money ... We're a thorn in [the university administration's] side from that perspective ... [In addition,] the collaborative program [with local colleges] is costing every university money. It's a money loser.

Second, in the case of professions outside of medicine, research funding is a challenge to obtain. Part of the issue is that medicine is well established in research and has disproportionate control of the funding system (evident in the struggle that changed the former federal Medical Research Council to the Canadian Institutes for Health Research). But part of the problem, relevant in the case of nursing, is that credentials are important in obtaining the funding that is the lifeblood of research universities, and nursing is new on the scene.

What effect has this situation had on academic nursing overall? Although traditionally, faculty in the male-dominated professions have been valued for their practical experience in a profession, and have thus routinely only been required to have a master's degree, there is now pressure towards a doctorate and research training for the tenure stream. Nursing, by throwing its lot in with the university, has been required to fall in line by also requiring these credentials for academic positions (Greenslade, 2003). Thus, in university nursing faculties, incumbents in the tenure stream, which is necessarily very small, tend to have doctorates or be in the process of obtaining them, while contingent faculty are required to obtain master's degrees.

As the numbers cited above show, the situation for women seeking graduate credentials is improving, and most contingent faculty in our study either had master's degrees or were in the process of obtaining them. But this achievement is still a challenge, and out of reach of most nurses: sessional faculty in our study pointed out that they could ill afford to return to school for another degree or multiple degrees, which involve both the cost of education and the forgone income in what may be the only, or the crucial, family income in a restructured economy. One contingent instructor in a nursing school observed that "during the time that I was a lecturer, it was made clear to me that a master's degree wasn't good enough to compete for a tenure-track position." Another remarked:

> I hadn't finished the MN at that point in time when I asked first and didn't have a BN. *(LM: So they wouldn't hire you as a sessional?)* So they

wouldn't hire me as a sessional ... People who didn't have master's degrees who were teaching at the School of Nursing were told, "Get your master's degree or you're out."

One of the nursing directors pointed out that she generally had no trouble strictly enforcing that contingent faculty have this credential, though she was forced to "lower the standard" for the introductory years of the program because of a shortage of faculty: "I made one instructor go back to do her MN before hiring her. An MEd is not acceptable ... although I allow them to teach in the first three years."

Another admitted that obtaining multiple credentials would be difficult for most nurses, and that she tried to provide support for these efforts. But overall, she did not see contingent workers as more oppressed than the full-time faculty. In her words, "You need [the tenure stream] to do the research and to keep the reputation of the school up, so they're in a tight bind too." By this she did not mean that part-timers were complainers, nor that the two groups were in opposition to each other. But she was subtly dismissing the idea that the non-tenured group were disadvantaged relative to the tenure-stream group, since she thought that getting tenure was a very difficult hurdle.

JOB (IN)SECURITY AS A PERMANENT FEATURE
OF UNIVERSITY NURSING SCHOOLS

Once they have obtained or are obtaining the required credentials, what are the experiences of contingent faculty in nursing? One immediately obvious problem, glimpsed right at our first meetings with them, was their poor working conditions. For example, one pointed out:

> We have a sessional office, but there's ... seven or eight [faculty in there] ... It's pretty cramped this year, actually, because there seems to be more sessional instructors than there used to be ... We have one phone for the office ... and the computer doesn't work very well ... [and] it's tricky to take vacation because we're paid from September when we start till the end of April.

Descriptions such as these were common across all the fields that we studied, where many contingent workers did not have privacy to meet with students, telephones, travel money to remote campuses, professional development funds or time to attend conferences, or even offices or desks to put down a few items while teaching. Hiring faculty who are excluded

from benefits because they work less than the minimum required to receive them was often seen by the faculty as a purposeful strategy on the
part of university administrators to save money, as was cramming faculty
together in a single office. As a nursing contingent faculty member remarked: "[We have] no privacy at all [with shared offices. We are hired]
to avoid paying benefits ... with no mentors or support." Indeed, in the
larger study, university restrictions on the numbers of courses that could
be taught by individual part-time instructors were reported within and
across universities in particular regions of Canada, ostensibly for the purpose of circumventing the payment of benefits and the acquiring of status
that accrues to those with permanent status in the academy. In nursing,
this might be framed as the need for "flexibility" that goes along with the
restructured academy under globalization.

A movement to unionize contingent faculty was under way during the
time when our interviews were conducted, but union representatives were
frustrated by the fact that because of their atypically high hours of work,
nursing sessionals could not be covered under a blanket policy proposed
for other sessionals at the university. That is, unlike other sessionals, such
as those in sociology who teach students in large classes, sessional clinical
nursing faculty were required to travel to several hospitals where small
numbers of student nurses were placed for individual supervision. This
made their workload much higher than other sessionals at the university.
As one participant put this, "If there are benefits from [being in a union],
the majority of them don't apply to us."

An administrator admitted that the position of contingent faculty in
nursing is fraught with insecurity: "I would have to say that sessionals do
not get sick [and] if they do, their income doesn't continue [and so] they
may as well have been fired." In fact, extreme insecurity, including not
having a contract well into the teaching of a course, or no contract at all,
was sometimes reported by contingent faculty. Alternatively, they were
treated as "just-in-time" faculty who might have to take on a course the
weekend before it was to be taught. As one remarked: "We never know
when we're going to get rehired ... [We are] hired on the basis of numbers
of students ... [and work] under major stress."

Depending upon the risks they wished to take, the extreme insecurity
made a few contingent faculty wary of demanding any consideration from
administrators or even expressing an alternative view. As well, they might

be apologetic about not having very much information, as an outsider, about how their school ran. Contingent faculty often chose to be interviewed away from the campus since they expressed fear of repercussions if it were found they had been interviewed. Overall, in the national study, academic freedom, or the freedom to teach according to one's expertise, even if the material is controversial, was found to be largely non-existent for contingent faculty — a problematic situation in a country like Canada (Muzzin, 2006). In nursing, those contingent faculty planning to go on to the doctorate and apply for the very rare tenure-stream positions tended to complain about not having a voice, but not in the traditional sense of academic freedom. Rather, they were concerned about the practical problem of not knowing what they were going to be asked to teach "from one year to the next." One full-time non-tenured faculty member working on her PhD explained:

> At times we're very frustrated because of the fact that we seldom have a voice in how courses are planned. We aren't responsible for the majority of the training or for the course outlines ... I think those of us who are sessional and who want full-time work have found it frustrating ... It's ... just the feeling that ... there's no permanence to it ... I think part of the frustration relates to people who teach the same course that I do who make a lot more money than I do ... I'm certainly hoping that once I get through [my graduate program] ... things will change. I think that I ... am part of the team, it's just that I feel at times that they can easily get rid of me [when they don't] need as many sessionals.

Although the experiences of contingent faculty are presented as part of a critique here, it is worth emphasizing that in most interviews with nursing contingent faculty, they were not bitter about a lack of academic freedom, insecurity or working conditions. That is, even when they stated that they were working an extra eight hours a week over the twenty-two they might be paid for, this was not expressed as a demand or a complaint. They explained that they just hired babysitters, worked after their children went to sleep and generally found a way to put in the extra time that was needed for the job. Their altruism is reminiscent of professionals in other feminized fields (Acker & Feuerverger, 1996; Broadbent & Laughlin, 1997). Contingent workers in nursing tended to feel confused and saddened by the fact that they were treated with so little respect. Like other contingent faculty in other fields that were researched, the nursing contingent faculty insisted that they were unanimously nurtured by their teaching experiences while at the same time tortured by how little value they seemed to represent to the institution despite their numbers. As one suggested,

I feel like I have so much knowledge to share with the students and I love doing it. I *love* to see the lights come on ... I would like clinical instructors to be respected for what it is they do ... Nurses have no power and autonomy ... I would say the majority of the undergraduate program is being taught by [sessionals].

Another mused:

There are ... faculty here who appreciate what we do and respect our opinions and there are other faculty who really consider us just an addendum if we end up teaching part of the course that they're teaching.

But most recognized that the problem was not so much disrespect from their nursing colleagues as from the university as a whole. One observed:

Most of our money is not ... baseline funding university money. It's like we're a temporary kind of strategy that they hope they'll eventually not need, and so they're not willing to make a long-term commitment to us ... There's never been an interest in the Faculty of Nursing [here] in looking after its own ... We're in debt ... We have a fair number of sessionals and they come and go ... I doubt they get any more than $4,000 max to teach a course.

In some cases, the disrespect might even find its way to the level of the student:

Some of the students will actually open the door and walk in. You know, they'd never do that to a professor ... [Citing a list of benefits that accrue to tenure-stream but not contingent faculty,] I would have to say all those things tell you that you're maybe not quite as valuable as a professor would be.

The participant who gave us the title for this chapter made the same point, but included nursing administrators as part of the problem:

On some levels I think they have a lot of respect for what we do. On another level I don't think they've worked hard enough to try to rectify what I think is a pretty incredible structural injustice. They seem content to let business go on as usual.

In her school, the nursing administrators refused to participate in the project, and we suspect that they were well aware of the discontent being expressed by their contingent faculty. At the same time, we were hard pressed to find nursing administrators who considered governing a large group of contingent workers as "business as usual." One insisted that some improvements came about when "faculty lecturers on contract" were allowed to "stay indefinitely," where previous regulations had required that they either join the tenure stream or leave after a few years. Another nursing administrator, frustrated by the situation, complained that she was in an untenable situation with respect to running a nursing school with this many insecure and part-time faculty. In her words:

> [Sessionals] are invited [to faculty meetings] but don't come … They have no vote … but we welcome their input … Preceptors are not even paid … though sessionals have a subcommittee in the union … I've gone $17,000 over budget to pay them … We were on the verge of canceling one of our clinicals, starting next week, because we couldn't find the teachers … [There are] over 50 percent sessionals at this school … Our numbers were down and we couldn't hire them … So they went out and took other jobs … Nursing lost out in university restructuring because they were not strong in research.

Contingent faculty were not routinely invited to faculty meetings across the twelve campuses we visited. Where they were excluded, at least a few felt that this indicated that they were "not as much a part of the university" as the full-time faculty. In the comment above, the administrator does not seem to have an awareness that part-time faculty may be cobbling together several jobs with no benefits, such that they may wish to attend meetings but not be able to do so. In no case did we encounter the idea of remunerating faculty for attendance at meetings. In some departments and schools, administrators were recognizing the difficulties of administering a "transient" workforce and were handing out one or two permanent positions or one- to three-year contracts to the "teaching stream." However, as we have emphasized here, this does not solve the "incredible structural injustice" for the other contingent faculty.

CONCLUSIONS

When we began the interviews for this study in 1999, there was still an expectation that the large-scale hiring of contingent faculty on Canadian campuses would be a temporary blip. But as we did our concluding interviews in 2003, we realized that the large-scale use of contingent faculty had become a permanent feature of feminized parts of the university campus, perhaps nowhere as much as in nursing. We have argued here that the structural inequity described by contingent faculty in nursing is a continuation of the gendered history of nursing education, which held nurses back from the professional status that male-dominated programs claimed as the basis for professional education. Now, as nursing struggles for its professional status at the university, it must conform to the expectations for all faculty there. As we have mentioned, upgrading the basic nursing credential to a baccalaureate may be seen from a feminist perspective as nursing's coming of age. It may indeed contribute to easing the shortage of nurses that we are currently experiencing. But this happens at a cost to the largely invisible contingent faculty who participate in the professional project, reproducing once again a gendered past. The contingent faculty are doubly marginalized, first, by being nursing educators at universities and second, by being altruistic and self-sacrificing contingent faculty within nursing.

NOTES

1 Law, optometry, dentistry and pharmacy, as well as nursing. SSHRC funding for this project allowed multiple site visits from 1999 to 2003. Sociology and anthropology were added to the list for comparison. The cognate fields differ from the professional fields, which allowed a wider perspective on issues facing contingent faculty; for example, consciousness of equity issues was low in the health-based academic professions (Muzzin, 2008).

2 This literature, as well as the feminist critique of science (for example, Hubbard, 1995; Haraway, 1996; Harding, 1998), influenced the choice of fields in this research: academic health (science-based) professions with various levels of feminization were chosen, and cognate social sciences were added to explore differences across the science-social science divide. Nursing is an interesting hybrid because while it is a health-based academic profession, more social science can be found in its curriculum than in the other health professions. It is also the most feminized of the fields studied in the project.

3 Overall, academic professions are more likely to be found at research-intensive than at teaching-intensive universities. In addition, practical nursing (or what used to be called nursing assistant programs) is still taught at community colleges alongside collaborative university-college nursing programs.

REFERENCES

Acker, S., & Dillabough, J.-A. (2007). Women "learning to labour" in the "male emporium": Exploring gendered work in teacher education. *Gender and Education,* *19*(3), 297–316.

Acker, S., & Armenti, C. (2004). Sleepless in academia. *Gender and Education, 16*(1), 3–24.

Acker, S., & Feuerverger, G. (1996). Doing good and feeling bad: The work of women university teachers. *Cambridge Journal of Education, 26*(3), 401–422.

Adams, T.L. (2000). *A dentist and a gentleman: Gender and the rise of dentistry in Ontario.* Toronto: University of Toronto Press.

Ainley, M. (1990). *Despite the odds: Essays on Canadian women and science.* Montreal: Vehicle Press.

Armstrong, P., Choinière, J., & Day, E. (1993). *Vital signs: Nursing in transition.* Toronto: Garamond Press.

Backhouse, C. (1991). *Petticoats and prejudice: Women and law in nineteenth century Canada.* Toronto: Women's Press.

Bensimon, E. (1997). Lesbian existence and the challenge to normative constructions of the academy. In C. Marshall (Ed.), *Feminist critical policy analysis: A perspective from post-secondary education* (141–156). London: Falmer Press.

Broadbent, J., & Laughlin, R. (1997). "Accounting logic" and controlling professionals. In J. Broadbent (Ed.), *The end of the professions? The restructuring of professional work* (34–49). New York: Routledge.

Bruneau, B. (2006). Quiet flow the dons: Towards an international history of the professoriate. In P. Stortz & L. Panayotidis (Eds.), *Historical identities: The professoriate in Canada* (31–62). Toronto: University of Toronto Press.

Church, J. (1999). Laboring in the dream factory, part 2. *Qualitative Studies in Education, 12*(3), 251–262.

Coburn, J. (1974). I see and am silent: A short history of nursing in Ontario. In J. Acton, P. Goldsmith & B. Shepard (Eds.), *Women at work: Ontario 1850–1930* (127–163). Toronto: Canadian Women's Educational Press.

de Montigny, G. (1995). *Social working: An ethnography of front-line practice.* Toronto: University of Toronto Press.

Etzioni, A. (1969). *The semi-professions and their organization: Teachers, nurses, and social workers.* New York: Free Press.

Grant, M. (2005). Professional ideology and educational practice: Learning to be a health professional. In P. Tripp & L. Muzzin (Eds.), *Teaching as activism: Equity meets environmentalism* (80–94). Montreal: McGill-Queen's University Press.

Greenslade, M.V. (2003). *Faculty practice as scholarship in university schools of nursing.* Unpublished doctoral dissertation, University of Toronto.

Hannah, E., Paul, L., & Vethamany-Globus, S. (2002). *Women in the Canadian academic tundra.* Montreal: McGill-Queen's University Press.

Haraway, D. (1996). Situated knowledges: The science question in feminism and the privilege of partial perspective. In M. Keller & H. Longino (Eds.), *Feminism and science* (249–263). Oxford: Oxford University Press.

Harding, S. (1998). *Is science multicultural? Postcolonialism, feminism and epistemologies.* Bloomington: Indiana University Press.

Hubbard, R. (1995). *Profitable promises: Essays on women, science and health.* Monroe, MN: Common Courage Press.

Jones, G.A. (Ed.) (1997). *Higher education in Canada: Different systems, different perspectives.* New York: Garland.

Limoges, J. (2007). *The hospital work experiences of new nurses: Power relations and resistance within the professional project of caring.* Unpublished doctoral dissertation, Ontario Institute for Studies in Education, University of Toronto.

Margolis, E., & Romero, M. (1998). The department is very male, very white, very old, and very conservative: The functioning of the hidden curriculum in graduate sociology departments. *Harvard Educational Review, 68*(1), 1–32.

McPherson, K. (1996). *Bedside matters: The transformation of Canadian nursing, 1900–1990.* Toronto: Oxford University Press.

Mellow, M. (2006). *Defining work: Gender, professional work, and the case of rural clergy.* Montreal: McGill-Queen's University Press.

Michalko, R. (2003). I've got a blind prof: The place of blindness in the academy. In D. Freedman & M. Holmes (Eds.), *The teacher's body*, 69–81. Albany: State University of New York Press.

Monture-Angus, P. (2001). In the way of peace: Confronting "whiteness" in the university. In R. Luther, E. Whitmore, & B. Moreau (Eds.), *Seen but not heard: Aboriginal women and women of colour in the academy* (29–49). Ottawa: CRIAW.

Muzzin, L. (2008). How fares equity in an era of academic capitalism? The role of contingent faculty. In D. Fisher & A. Chan (Eds.), *The exchange university* (105–124). Vancouver: UBC Press.

Muzzin, L. (2006, June). The significance of contingent faculty in the academic freedom equation. Paper presented at the Annual Meeting of the Society for the Study of Social Problems, Montreal, Quebec.

Muzzin, L. (2005). The brave new world of professional education. In P. Tripp & L. Muzzin (Eds.), *Teaching as activism: Equity meets environmentalism* (152–169). Montreal: McGill-Queen's University Press.

Muzzin, L., Brown, G., & Hornosty, R. (1993). Professional ideology in Canadian pharmacy. *Health and Canadian Society, 1*(2), 319–345.

Muzzin, L., Sinnott, P., & Lai, C. (1999). Pawns between patriarchies: Women in Canadian pharmacy. In E. Smyth, S. Acker, P. Bourne, & A. Prentice (Eds.), *Challenging professions: Historical and contemporary perspectives on women's professional work* (296–314). Toronto: University of Toronto Press.

National Education Association, Higher Education Research Center. (2001). *Part-time faculty: National education association updates.* Retrieved 30 April 2006 from www.org/he/heupdate/vol7no4pdf.

Nestel, S. (2004). The boundaries of professional belonging: How race has shaped the re-emergence of midwifery in Ontario. In I.L. Bourgeault, C. Benoit, & R. Davis-Floyd (Eds.), *Reconceiving midwifery* (287–305). Montreal: McGill-Queen's University Press.

Ollivier, M., Robbins, W., Beauregard, D., Brayton, J., & Sauve, G. (2006). Feminist activists on-line: A study of the PAR-L Research Network. *The Canadian Review of Sociology and Anthropology, 43*(4), 445–463.

Rajogopal, I. (2002). *Hidden academics: Contract faculty in Canadian universities.* Toronto: University of Toronto Press.

Rankin, J., & Campbell, M. (2006). *Managing to nurse: Inside Canada's health care reform.* Toronto: University of Toronto Press.

Ranson, G. (2005). Gender among the "guys": Reflection on work, family life and retention of women in engineering. In L. Biggs & P. Downe (Eds.), *Gendered intersections: An introduction to women's and gender studies* (222–226). Halifax: Fernwood.

Reskin, B., & Roos, P. (1990). *Job queues, gender queues: Explaining women's inroads into male occupations.* Philadelphia: Temple University Press.

Smallman, V. (2001). Closing the equity gap: A portrait of Canada's university teachers, 1996–2001. *CAUT Education Review, 6*(2), 1–5.

CHAPTER 11

GENDER AND THE CHAIR

Sandra Acker

CHASE (2005) DESCRIBES NARRATIVE AS "RETROSPECTIVE MEANING-making ... a way of understanding one's own and others' actions, of organizing events and objects into a meaningful whole, and of connecting and seeing the consequences of actions and events over time" (656). My narrative of the three years I spent in the role of department chair in a Canadian university focuses on the gendered aspects of being an academic administrator. As data for this chapter, I have a few written documents (memos, notes, annual "activity reports"), three audiotapes of lengthy semi-structured interviews — and my memory. The interviews were conducted with me by Johanna Wyn in 1999 and 2001, and by Mary Fuller in 2002. (Quotations in this essay are taken from these interviews.)

My account is no doubt influenced by my position as a white, middle-aged Jewish woman who grew up in the United States. It is shaped by years of reading feminist literature as well as my own research on gender, careers and workplace cultures of teachers, academics, administrators and students (S. Acker, 1994, 1999, 2005). I draw on a large literature on gendered cultures in organizations (Martin & Collinson, 2002) — indeed, as Joan Acker notes, workplaces suffused with race and class relationships too (J. Acker, 2006) — and on the difficulties of holding contradictory subject positions of "woman" and "manager" (Hughes, 2004). Related lines of work that have influenced my thinking are the idea that the self is a dramatization or presentation (Goffman, 1959) and that one's emotions are controlled and manipulated in the process (Hochschild, 1979). Particularly compelling for me is Virginia Olesen's (1992) concern with embodied experience and the transformation of self that occurs after a crisis such as an earthquake or an illness. Olesen's terms, "vulnerable self" and "biography of vulnerability," are powerful ones and, I argue, applicable in other situations such as the ones I am about to describe. My narrative has aspects of performance, emotional management and gender-stereotypical ways of working, and more than a hint of a vulnerable self.

EXPERIENCES OF CHAIRING

I became chair of the Department of Sociology and Equity Studies in Education at the Ontario Institute for Studies in Education of the University of Toronto, in July 1999, at age fifty-four, after having been an academic for thirty years, including two in the U.S., nineteen in Britain and nine in Canada.

The early months presented plenty of challenges: trying to locate a colleague who had stopped working and could not be found; responding to student grade appeals; writing a departmental report for a university-wide strategic exercise. The most bewildering part of that first summer was that I did not know where to locate relevant policies or even whom to ask. I found myself newly disturbed by the appearance of the department and the lack of amenities. Thinking new carpet might raise morale, I did a "carpet survey" of offices in the department, happily using my newly acquired pass key. The very worst ones were replaced, as they could be argued to be a safety issue, but most remained untouched, a financial issue. Another early memory was going around the department and taking down two-year-old notices, adding tape or pins so posters would be more firmly fixed, trying to improve the generally chaotic and drab look of the place. I had seen the same behaviour from the head teacher in my research primary school (S. Acker, 1999). It is as if the department/school is your *house* (you being the *housewife*) and you *must tidy it* or *what will people think?*

My husband died unexpectedly on 30 November 1999, five months after I had begun chairing. My compassionate leave consisted mostly of Christmas vacation and I returned for the start of the new term in January, shaky but convinced I had to be there, as there was a teaching assistant strike and a search was on for a new faculty member. In losing my husband, I also lost my emotional and domestic support system. At a mundane level, I had to spend more time cooking, cleaning, shopping and sorting out finances. Ten months later, my daughter left home to do a master's degree in another province. So in the middle of the new world of being a chair, I was also living alone for the first time in my life.

Three years earlier, a merger between the Ontario Institute for Studies in Education (OISE) and the University of Toronto's Faculty of Education (FEUT) produced OISE/UT, a multi-purpose faculty of education with five departments. (The title has since reverted to OISE.) A major challenge of chairing was keeping my department independent and viable. Because of its relatively small size, and the merger fever gripping the place, there was continuous pressure on my department to amalgamate with another one. I also seemed to be losing faculty members. A few retired and one died; one took up a 50 percent directorship elsewhere in the university; two others transferred to other OISE/UT departments. I had colleagues on sick leave, maternity leave, long-term disability leave, study leave, compassionate leave and unpaid leave of absence. Consequently, I frequently found myself negotiating with the dean trying to get full-time or contract or stipend teaching positions.

I was lucky to find a hitherto undiscovered surplus of money in the department and I spent what I could of it before the balance was clawed back by OISE/UT. That aspect of chairing made me happy: "I loved that part of being chair, I loved spending money — it was like going shopping" (2002 interview). I added:

> I started doing things like providing refreshments at meetings, to oil the wheels, although people rapidly began taking it for granted and complain that there needed to be coffee, decaf coffee, tea, decaf tea and more chocolate chips! I think they were on the whole pleased … I put a lot of emphasis on food.

By the time I finished my term, I had developed new skills and knowledge, gaining increased confidence in my ability to solve problems and make decisions. Faculty, staff and students in my department were becoming increasingly diverse in terms of race/ethnicity and gender, making us a leader in the university in this regard. The student computer room had been upgraded and we had an agreement in place for a corridor of classrooms to be converted into offices. We had hired some new colleagues. I had, I thought, created a better balance between areas of specialization in the department and changed some counterproductive internal policies. I had systematized some of our procedures. I had mentored junior faculty. I introduced a course on Jewish issues, an area hitherto neglected in our equity-focused curriculum. I did many small things to help individual faculty members get something they wanted or needed. One of my biggest accomplishments was what *didn't* happen: the department did not get merged or closed.

Yet, on reflection, I am not at all sure that the tremendous amount of energy and emotion that I poured into trying to succeed at being a chair was matched by commensurate accomplishments. The work itself was incessant, a phenomenon known as "intensification," an aspect of the globalized university way of doing things that is shaping contemporary academic administration. There are expressions of distress in the October 2001 interview, conducted a little over two years into my three-year term, such as "my own role as a chair has been an incredibly difficult experience, and I'm still trying to figure that out; why has it been so hard?" I worried that I was "mired in this everyday web of responsibilities and problems and people … heavily involved in individual people's issues and problems." I was surprised at the high degree of conflict, which could concern any combination of faculty, staff and students, and to realize that people relied on the chair (however untrained in this regard) to sort out minor or major disputes.

On the few occasions where some collegial anger or distrust was directed at me, I was highly distressed. One critical incident was a day-long faculty meeting in the spring of my second year as chair. A group of colleagues brought up a contentious item without notice to me and near the end of the meeting. At the time, I felt that they had intentionally bypassed the normal procedures and that their strategy indicated a lack of trust in my good intentions towards them. I was forced to think on my feet and defend a university policy that they were proposing to reject. I did not understand why they did not consult me first, as my view of my chair-self was one of someone who would strive to understand and, if possible, put into effect the wishes of others. By the end of the meeting, I was in tears.

Most situations were not this tense. But relationships with colleagues were different than in the pre-chair days. Much of what one learns and frets about as chair cannot be shared with others in the department because of confidentiality concerns. The chair's ability to be "friends" with colleagues declines, as friendships are based in part on sharing without holding back so much, and a new reference group of other administrators emerges.

BEING A CHAIR/WOMAN

As relative newcomers to academe, women scholars have already overcome many barriers and are frequently pioneers in their field. It is likely that many, like me, have a heightened sensitivity to performance and achievement and the way others see them. In this section, I focus more explicitly on those aspects of chairing with a gendered inflection.

A concern with appearance — my own and the department's — was evident in the interviews. In the October 1999 interview, I tell Johanna about the orientation for new administrators I had just attended, saying:

> The people that are, you know, in the very high up positions, I'll never feel like I'm one of them … [The women] must spend most of their income on these suits and it's not only the suits. They have the high heels and the scarves and the earrings, and it's just, you know, something I couldn't aspire to if I wanted to.

My solution: "I can still wear pants/trousers and a blouse but I'll have a blazer with it."

That interview was early in my tenure as chair and I expressed a somewhat facetious wish to be taken in hand and told what to wear and where to shop. I continued:

> Well, I coloured my hair. I mean, that's part of it. It's now back to the colour it was once upon a time. It's not grey anymore. That's part of the strategy but at another level, you know, I'm enjoying that too. I'm enjoying looking younger and being the centre of attention. I like the public side of this job, sort of making a little speech to the new students and things, being the public face of the department. It's a bit like when I used to play the piano. It's the performing side that I do like.

Another gender-related area is "being emotional" and the difficulty in regulating emotional display. In the 2001 interview when discussing the incident of conflict I alluded to briefly above, I described myself as feeling angry, betrayed and ashamed that I had reached the point of tears. This was a case of "emotion work" — controlling one's own feelings and the public expression of them — that had not succeeded (see also Hochschild, 1979). I felt that I had violated Rule Number One of the code for (women) managers. In the words of Sachs and Blackmore's (1998) title, "you never show you can't cope."

Negotiating with the (male) dean also had gendered dimensions. I was the first woman chair in the merged institution, although the former OISE had several. The way in which OISE/UT was constructed meant that chairs often had to have the dean's approval for things they needed to do. I think it came more easily to me than to my male colleagues to ask for help. When I could not directly access the dean, I relied on his assistant. I became aware that this dean, as well as other senior managers, was surrounded by female assistants who shouldered much of the administrative and relational work in the university. As Kristine Pearson comments in this volume, administrative staff are schooled to keep quiet, yet to multitask to solve a myriad of problems on a daily basis: they are like the housekeepers for the faculty.

Stepping across Bloor Street to the main University of Toronto campus showed me that life outside OISE/UT was gendered too. At the time, in 1999, women made up a little over a fifth of academic directors, chairs and associate deans at the university (University of Toronto, 2007: 19). By 2006, greater gender balance was more apparent in the three groups of managers for which statistics are presented: directors, chairs and associate deans (29 percent), principals and deans (44.4 percent) and the top management group of president, provost, vice-presidents and vice-provosts (50 percent) (University of Toronto, 2007: 18); the overall figure was 32.3 percent. Visible minorities made up 8 percent of academic leaders.[1]

Another aspect of gendered work is evident in the familial metaphors I used in the interviews, for example in 2001:

> I look upwards and there's the father, the dean, who I desperately need things from — merit, resources, a dependency relation. If he praises me, I'm so excited. Then there's all of the "children" in the department who are treating me like a parent figure, they want something from me, they sometimes hang on my words as if I'm full of wisdom.

In the words of an academic administrator in one of my research projects, was I "mother to the faculty"? As mother, I could be the target of resentment as well as devotion. I put a lot of emphasis on interpersonal relations, being concerned about colleagues, helping and caring for others. This approach could be problematic. In my bleaker moments, I saw myself as constantly giving and the faculty, with notable exceptions, as constantly taking. There are structural reasons for differences in perception, as I noted in the 2002 interview:

> There is a kind of built-in clash between an administrative way of operating and an academic one and I've understood it over time ... Because there are limits on what can be done, people have to make choices about where to put their energies ... It would seem counterproductive, if not totally irrational, to say "I won't put in a grant proposal this year, I'll take on the chairing of the admissions committee," but on the other hand, the department can't run unless some people actually say that. So you're right in the middle of a paradox, all of the time.

There is no easy way for colleagues to distinguish between a routine act (say, signing a form) and an exceptional one (arguing with the dean, with supporting evidence, that someone's salary is too low and getting it adjusted). Moreover, each person sees his/her own situation but not the totality of the work being done. The same analysis can be extended to administrative staff and students.

Mary Fuller, who conducted the 2002 interview, commented:

> You have talked about many acts of kindness and hard work on behalf of people that they probably don't know about, and that's your way of working. It leaves you vulnerable to people not knowing what you've done ... it's a management style ... you're talking about behind the scenes mentoring and facilitating.

If leadership activities at this middle-management level are perceived as a variant of mother's (selfless) work, it is not then surprising if the effort is not recognized or reciprocated (Fletcher, 2004). My reliance on "acts of kindness and hard work on behalf of people" not only sounds a lot like feminist leadership theories (Madden, 2005) but also bears a more than accidental resemblance to the relational work that feminist organizational theorists such as Eveline (2004) and Fletcher (1999) have described as "getting disappeared" within the organization (i.e., not credited, not recognized) despite that work's contribution to the well-being of the organization.

Moving into a year's sabbatical after completion of chairing was more than welcome. As the sabbatical proceeded, I travelled and wrote and felt much more relaxed, although as the new academic year approached, I became nervous about returning to my department, as if it were the scene of a crime. To my surprise, colleagues greeted me in a friendly manner in September, as if the three years of chairing had been a dream. I was one of them again.

CONCLUSION

The emotional quality of academic managing has been greatly underestimated. Women in prominent positions, more so than most men, put their bodies "on the line" to be judged. How do they look, how are they dressed, how do they handle conflict, how do they manage authority, how do they cover up their feelings?[2] Can any disability or personal crisis be kept under wraps (Kolodny, 1998)? Fletcher (2004) comments that "the body in which we do something influences how it will be perceived" (654), while Bannerji (1991) describes her experience as a South Asian woman talking about race relations in a Canadian university lecture theatre as a "body in a space." For academic managers who are not from the mainstream white male cohort, vulnerability is prominent as there is no obvious recipe, no way to know how to do something for which there are few models and precedents. It is like improvising a part in a play where others have a script. At the same time, it can be very stimulating to be at the centre of things and challenged by the adrenalin rush that comes with drama and crisis.

Any such experience takes place in a set of contexts. There is, for example, a *global context* that has created major changes in recent years in the ways universities operate (Morley, 2004; Blackmore & Sachs, 2007). While I knew that intensified workloads, cutbacks, mergers, corporate thinking and accountability processes all had roots in bigger social forces, I nevertheless could not avoid being preoccupied with "the everyday." In the 2001 interview, I comment that "the local is so overwhelming when you're in it, you tend to think that it's the dean who's doing this to you … or it's a consequence of what's happened to certain people in the department, or whatever. It's really hard to see it as this wider phenomenon."

The *institutional context* certainly made the work more difficult. Heading OISE/UT's smallest department in an era of merger frenzy and continual cuts in resources created an aspect of vulnerability that shadowed my authority. Worries about resources, space, departmental traditions, office appearances and so forth were very specific to the times I was in. In many university departments, a new head drawn from the ranks would already have had insider knowledge of the wider university that I lacked. I was chair before the university instituted a regular program of workshops for academic administrators and before policies and procedures were easily accessible on a website.

Finally, there is a *personal context.* I have emphasized gender in this narrative but other identities will also have impinged. I cannot know what I would have made of administration had I been from a different cultural group. Reading Roger Simon's chapter, "Face to Face with Alterity" (1995), where he is concerned with "teaching as a Jew" (94) and "the difference that difference makes" (92) for pedagogy, I wonder if I had been "managing as a Jew" and what that might mean. As Simon reminds us, many Jews have learned to keep their identity muted; on the whole, that was my usual way of being. When the issue arose while I was chair, it tended to be uncomfortable (questions around anti-Semitism; white privilege or marginality for Jewish students; Israeli–Palestinian relations) and often unresolved.

My bereavement also shaped my experience as chair. In the instance mentioned above where I dissolved into forbidden tears, I was also experiencing what is called a "grief attack," in this case triggered by something in the immediate situation but extended by a wave of distress. The vulnerable self, we can see, is shaped by events and interpretations, but it is also shaped by the context of institutional (and wider social) frameworks as well as the whole set of personal life events that are often excluded from academic accounts.

My narrative suggests points of tension that should be eased if we want our institutions to be run by those traditionally outside the corridors of power. Currently, the emotionally intense feelings and vulnerabilities that new academic administrators may face remain a taboo subject, rarely featured in any leadership development efforts, perhaps because it is of most concern to those who come from the margins to the centre.

NOTES

1 Figures for gender and visible minority status are given separately; other groups have very small representations — persons with disabilities, 1.1 percent; sexual minorities, 3.4 percent; Aboriginal people, 0 percent (University of Toronto, 2007: 18).

2 As I write, the media coverage of Hillary Clinton's campaign to be the Democratic candidate for U.S. President provides a perfect illustration of this point.

REFERENCES

Acker, J. (2006). Inequality regimes: Gender, class, and race in organizations. *Gender and Society, 20*(4), 441–464.

Acker, S. (2005). Gender, leadership and change in faculties of education in three countries. In C. Reynolds & J. Collard (Eds.), *Leadership, gender and culture* (103–117). Maidenhead: Open University Press.

Acker, S. (1999). *The realities of teachers' work: Never a dull moment.* London: Cassell/ Continuum Press.

Acker, S. (1994). *Gendered education.* Buckingham: Open University Press.

Bannerji, H. (1991). Re: turning the gaze. *Resources for Feminist Research, 20*(3/4), 5–11.

Blackmore, J., & Sachs, J. (2007). *Performing and reforming leaders: Gender, educational restructuring, and organizational change.* Albany: State University of New York Press.

Chase, S. (2005). Narrative inquiry: Multiple lenses, approaches, voices. In N. Denzin & Y. Lincoln (Eds.), *The SAGE handbook of qualitative research,* 3rd ed. (651–680). Thousand Oaks, CA: Sage.

Eveline, J. (2004). *Ivory basement leadership.* Crawley: University of Western Australia Press.

Fletcher, J. (2004). The paradox of postheroic leadership: An essay on gender, power, and transformational change. *The Leadership Quarterly, 15,* 647–661.

Fletcher, J. (1999). *Disappearing acts: Gender, power, and relational practice at work.* Cambridge, MA: MIT Press.

Goffman, E. (1959). *The presentation of self in everyday life.* Garden City, NJ: Doubleday.

Hochschild A.R. (1979) Emotion work, feeling rules, and social structure. *American Journal of Sociology, 85,* 551–575.

Hughes, C. (2004). Class and other identifications in managerial careers: The case of the lemon dress. *Gender, Work and Organization, 11*(5), 526–543.

Kolodny, A. (1998). *Failing the future: A dean looks at higher education in the twenty-first century.* Durham, NC: Duke University Press.

Madden, M. (2005). 2004 Division 35 presidential address: Gender and leadership in higher education. *Psychology of Women Quarterly, 29*, 3–14.

Martin, P.Y., & Collinson, D. (2002). "Over the pond and across the water": Developing the field of "gendered organizations." *Gender, Work and Organization, 9*(3), 244–265.

Morley, L. (2004). *Theorising quality in higher education.* London: Institute of Education, University of London.

Olesen, V. (1992). Extraordinary events and mundane ailments: The contextual dialectics of the embodied self. In C. Ellis & M. Flaherty (Eds.), *Investigating subjectivity: Research on lived experience* (205–220). Newbury Park, CA: Sage.

Sachs, J., & Blackmore, J. (1998). You never show you can't cope: Women in school leadership roles managing their emotions. *Gender and Education, 10*(3), 265–279.

Simon, R. (1995). Face to face with alterity: Postmodern Jewish identity and the eros of pedagogy. In J. Gallop (Ed.), *Pedagogy: The question of impersonation* (90–105). Bloomington: Indiana University Press.

University of Toronto. (2007). *Employment equity report, October 1, 2005 — September 30, 2006.* Retrieved 2 May 2007 from www.hrandequity.utoronto.ca/Assets/reports/ee/2006?method=1.

PART IV

FINDING
SOURCES OF
STRENGTH

CHAPTER 12

THE SACRED AND RESISTANCE WITHIN THE "PRISON": THE NARRATIVES OF RACIALLY MINORITIZED WOMEN FACULTY

Kimine Mayuzumi & Riyad A. Shahjahan

The university, that place is prison ... So how do you feel when you're in prison? I worked in a ... women's prison, I know how [the women] feel in prison. But we share a lot in common ... You know, the surveillance, very similar dynamics ... But I refuse to have [the academy] destroy my spirit ... They can take everything away from me physically, if they want to. But they can't touch my spirit, 'cause I won't let them. I'm going to keep taking care of my spirit.

— Resilient Woman

THESE POIGNANT WORDS WERE SHARED BY A SELF-IDENTIFIED, spiritually minded and racially minoritized female faculty member while reflecting on her experiences in the academy. Resilient Woman,[1] an Aboriginal scholar in the field of human services, is emphasizing the necessity of spirituality in her academic life. She is part of a group of racially minoritized women faculty[2] who represent only 3.4 percent of full time and only 10.3 percent of all faculty positions in Canadian universities

(Samuel & Wane, 2005; Canadian Federation for the Humanities and Social Sciences, 2006). Her struggles within the academy are echoed by many scholars who describe the chilly climate faced by racially minoritized women faculty in the North American academy. Like Resilient Woman, other racially minoritized women faculty experience barriers that decrease their visibility, voice and power in the academy (Turner, 2003), as they encounter sexism, racism and classism (Ng, 1993; Luther, Whitmore & Moreau, 2003). This chilly climate has not changed significantly over the past few decades (Samuel & Wane, 2005; Spafford et al., 2006).

While most of the literature focuses on analyzing and describing the chilly climate that racially minoritized women faculty experience, less attention has been paid to understanding how racially minoritized women faculty cope with and/or resist this climate. Samuel and Wane (2005) argue:

> As women of color in the academe aim to carve out critical spaces for themselves, important questions arise … What does it mean for women of color to inhabit institutional space of a predominantly White Canadian university? … What strategies do they employ to challenge a Eurocentric curriculum, endure resistance, mainstream students, tolerate unfair evaluations, and suffer lack of administrative support? (77)

In this chapter, we explore an area — spirituality — that has often been ignored in the literature. While acknowledging the gendered and racialized nature of experiences of racially minoritized women faculty, we wish to extend the discussion by centring our analysis on the sacred aspects of their academic life and highlighting their agency. Specifically, we ask: How does a group of spiritually minded racially minoritized women faculty use their spirituality to resist and survive within the chilly climate of the academy?

This chapter is drawn from a broader study (Shahjahan, 2007) based on interviews and document analysis with fifteen self-identified spiritually minded activist[3] scholars (ten women and five men) in Canada, which took place between February and September in 2005. Participants were racially minoritized university faculty members who self-identified with the following criteria: (1) they see themselves as spiritual beings; (2) they teach about and/or do research on gender, class, race, sexuality, disability or anti-colonialism issues; (3) they believe that spirituality informs their social justice work; (4) they do not consider their spirituality as dogmatic or evangelical; and (5) they are conscious of integrating spirituality into their academic activities. The narratives of six female spiritually minded activist scholars[4] are presented in this chapter. These narratives will provide a critical perspective regarding the challenges and possibilities of spirituality in the academic lives of racially minoritized women faculty in the Canadian academy.

Spirituality, in this chapter, refers to a way of being in the world where an individual is connected to one's cultural knowledge and other beings (which includes one's community, transcendental beings, other parts of creation) and which allows one to move from inward to outward action. Furthermore, spirituality can be conceptualized as difficult — not an easy journey (Shahjahan, 2007). The word "Sacred" refers to those interconnected metaphysical spaces and forces within materialist-social realities that cannot be captured by the empirical and rational eye. We capitalize "Sacred" to be consistent with the terminology used by Alexander (2005).

First we will outline our epistemological framework. We will then present the participants' narratives and our analysis of how spirituality was essential to the survival and healing strategies of these scholars. Finally, we will conclude with a discussion of the implications of the study.

CENTRING SACRED SUBJECTIVITY — EPISTEMOLOGICAL FRAMEWORK

We centre the concept of "Sacred subjectivity" in our epistemology, mainly drawing on Alexander's (2005) work on transnational feminism in order to understand and interpret the experiences and narratives of our participants. Alexander asserts that subjectivity is not only composed of social relations but also of the Sacred, which is embodied in human beings' lived experiences. In more detail, she indicates five interrelated elements in the concept of Sacred subjectivity:

> The idea that Sacred energies intervene in the daily lives of human beings; they surround, protect, push, strengthen, and bring a sense of purpose so that the individual is attuned to the Soul's purpose; they are present both everywhere in the Wind, and at specific moments, as in dreams; they mediate a process of interdependence, of mutual beingness, in which one becomes oneself in the process of becoming one with the Sacred; and they manifest their sacredness in nature as well as their relationship with human beings, both of which take shape in a process of mutual embodiment. (301)

Drawing on the above quotation, we also consider the Sacred as a key to looking at lives, experiences and knowledges of the participants in our study.

With the Sacred at the centre of the analysis, secularism that denies or undervalues the Sacred becomes an ideology to be contested. The recent work of a number of feminist scholars questions secularized constructions of womanhood based on liberal, individualized and materialist concepts of "modernity." For instance, Alexander (2005) criticizes feminists who have resolutely seen the "self" as secular. Instead, she argues that "a transnational feminism needs these pedagogies of Sacred ... because it remains the case that the majority of the people in the world — that is, the majority of women in the world — cannot make sense of themselves without it" (15).

Such scholars argue that secular theories have been dominant in feminism and have excluded spiritual ways of knowing and finding agency in women's lives. In attempting to develop "spiritualized feminism," Fernandes (2003) emphasizes that existing theories of power tend to focus only on the material realm and "the possibilities of spiritual power are usually missing in both modern and postmodern views" (17). African-American women scholars Dillard, Abdur-Rashid and Tyson (2000) point out that, while spirituality may be optional for many in the secular academic context, for minoritized women like themselves "whose cultural norms dictate the centrality of spirituality" in their lives, it is a necessity to deal with multiple oppressions and it cannot simply be ignored, as it "has been and continues to be ... our path to self-liberation and self-discovery" (449).

It is important to keep in mind that this concept of Sacred subjectivity is not only grounded in the individual level but also produces social effects. Fernandes (2003) calls this idea "spiritual responsibility," which "unlike conservative discourses of 'personal responsibility,' confronts the fundamental linkages between self-examination, self-transformation and individual ethical action on the one hand, and the transformation of larger structures of oppression on the other hand" (16). Thus, while this concept of Sacred subjectivity recognizes the existing feminist arguments on oppression as relevant, it also deepens these concepts by highlighting the ideas that *the personal is not only political but also spiritual*, and moreover, *the spiritual is also political* (Alexander, 2005). Hence, we will also look at each individual's narratives as part of a collective struggle. What compels us to write this chapter? As Collins (2000) states, "Knowledge without wisdom is adequate for the powerful, but wisdom is essential to the survival of the subordinate" (208). For those of us who are racially minoritized, the academy needs to be contested through the production of knowledge about the chilly climate, but we also need *wisdom* from those who are within it in order to nurture our spirits of survival and resistance. This chapter is a means of documenting some of that wisdom. To this end, in the narrative section, we will share three themes that emerged from our analysis: (1) resistance from students; (2) the secular chilly climate of the academy; and (3) moving beyond academic capitalism.

THE NARRATIVES OF RACIALLY MINORITIZED WOMEN FACULTY

Resistance from Students

Spirituality was integral for the participants in the study in coping with the student resistance against them as teachers (see also Njoki Wane's chapter in this volume). Student resistance to minority faculty is one of the systemic issues grounded in the social construction of minority female bodies by sexism and racism (Bannerji, 1991; Ng, 1993). In this section, we describe how participants in our study used their spirituality to deal with resistance from their students.

In the study, an Asian woman faculty member in social work named Hoi recounted how she experienced student harassment in the classroom due to her gender and race: "As an Asian woman who looks young, the power in the classroom plays out in different ways." She shared a story about experiencing resistance from twelve white students she was teaching. As a new faculty member, she lacked experience with the grading scheme and, as a result, some misunderstandings around marks arose. A group of white students complained to her director about her marking scheme, while her students of colour had no problems once they understood why she marked a certain way. She stated, "The director told me at the time they were saying horrible, terrible things about me."

Hoi echoes the struggles that other Asian women faculty experience around racism, sexism and ageism (Arisaka, 2000; Li & Beckett, 2006). While Hoi was aware that she was being harassed because of her race, gender and age, she tried to heal from the situation. Her spiritual epistemology allowed her to see things larger than herself. She said, "Well yes, definitely there [are] all these racial politics going on … [But] I also [reflected saying,] 'Now [there] was also a structural piece that I brought in. I don't see these people only as themselves. They are in the larger structure as well.'" However, she needed a further healing journey as the pain from this incident still continued. On the same day of the incident, she was walking a route where she encountered boulders. This encounter was significant in her healing journey:

> I went over and I touched one of the [boulders] … it was a magical moment … [I told myself,] "Wow! These things have been around for millions of years! What you are going through right now is very tiny."… So then again, I [saw] something larger. And everything suddenly [was] put into perspective … "Don't worry, it's okay."… I [didn't] get myself caught in … hating my students. Because I [saw] something larger than that. And … I also [got] to a place where it [was] something larger [that held] me.

Through her encounter with the boulders, Hoi learned to reframe the situation around the incident by drawing on a spiritual world view during the slow process of walking. Hoi's acknowledgement of her mutual beingness with the boulders reminded her of a sense of purpose embedded in the Sacred. It allowed her to surrender. Hoi argues that when you are only involved in worldly matters and you are not "spiritually grounded," you don't see the emancipation that allows you to release something you are trying to hold onto, such as anger, and you are able to move onto the next step. As Hoi remarked:

> When you are in [that emotional state], it's big. It consumes you. But when you see the [situation], larger than you are, you come back to that centre and then you are like, "Oh, okay. Hold on."… You don't get consumed. You begin to know what is the most appropriate thing to do right now and right here.

What Hoi had was the agency to choose to see the larger dynamic through her Sacred subjectivity. The Sacred energies intervened in her life to strengthen her, to bring meaning, and helped her refrain from "hating" her students. Hoi's assessment of the situation indicates that things are temporary, static and therefore not significant enough to consume her. It seems that being spiritually grounded and looking at the whole picture rather than sticking to fragments of emotions and incidents has become her strategy to heal, rather than just to put aside a difficult situation.

Resilient Woman, introduced earlier, points out that spirituality is essential not only for getting through the barriers and systemic discriminations that are already there but also for *preventing* them from emerging. In this sense, her spirituality is not for *emergency and crisis*, but is embedded in her everyday life. She described an incident that occurred in her class on the same day that she forgot to do her prayers before she came to the university.

> I didn't take the time to pray [before class]. I didn't take the time to protect myself spiritually … because there are very evil spirit forces that work in this place. So I have to use my protection medicine. Well, that particular day, I didn't do that. And I paid big time.

Resilient Woman, who taught from an anti-colonial perspective, constantly faced resistance from students who did not accept her authority and the curriculum she taught. That particular day, she came across a number of students who challenged her authority, to which she responded, out of fatigue from a family crisis, by making an inappropriate comment. The students mobilized and reported to the professional degree co-ordinator. Resilient Woman admits that she made an inappropriate comment in class and immediately apologized in class. After that incident, she had to face repeated backlash from students and colleagues. She emphasizes that her spirituality has allowed her to survive in the climate of "evil spirits":

> [Spirituality is] an armour, it's an armour of righteousness. It's an armour of love. It's an armour of truth. It's an armour of integrity. If I don't wear that armour, then I become exactly what they say I am. I become angry. I become difficult. I become bitter. I become hostile. I become like a raving lunatic. "See, is she ever," you know.

Being a racially minoritized woman and being challenged by her students could have disturbed her authority and self-esteem as a faculty member in the classroom (Hoodfar, 1992; Ng, 1993). Furthermore, Resilient Woman could have internalized the oppression posed by the students and the androcentric, Eurocentric institutional structures that subjugate her. It might have even affected her teaching practice as well, by making her "bitter" towards the students. However, her spirituality helped her stay resilient and move beyond internalizing oppression and feeling hostile. She argues that if one becomes consumed by fighting the androcentric colonial system and gets physically ill as a result, as she has seen with a feminist colleague, then it doesn't help equity projects in the long run. "I'm not going to get ill for them. How is that going to help Native people? How is that going to help the healing of the earth?" In short, spirituality provides Resilient Woman a daily form of protection, a source of strength and a sense of calling which is attuned with her political mission to "help Native people."

Both women faculty members navigate the chilly climate not by suppressing their emotions but by transforming them through their Sacred subjectivity. Working from a "spiritually centred paradigm," they do not "foreground power issues" embedded in structural relations of the ruling in the academy, but instead choose "balance and harmony" as "their analytic lenses of choice" (Dillard, Abdur-Rashid & Tyson, 2000: 451). Restoring balance and harmony within themselves enables them to resist being consumed by such oppressive situations.

Secular Chilly Climate of the Academy

The participants in this study mentioned another dimension of their identity, beyond their race, gender and class, that they found difficult to bring into the academy — their spiritual identity. Here we call this barrier the "secular chilly climate."

Addon, a Black Christian faculty member in education, commented that through several encounters with colleagues, she came to understand that her spiritual faith was not appreciated in the academy. Addon shared the story of an incident that happened in the staff room, where "somebody was talking about … religion and one of the professors commented, 'Well, people really don't believe that stuff now, do they?'" Addon referred to the academic dominant culture where "… anyone who believed in anything spiritual was … seen as … uncritical or brainwashed and non-academic." Since Addon's spirituality is essential in her daily life, she feels fragmented in such an environment. From Addon's observation, it is almost taboo to talk about spirituality on a personal level in the academy because someone's spirituality is considered to be too private, too subjective and therefore "non-academic."

Some of the participants pointed out that there was a certain kind of stigma associated with faith-based spiritualities in the academy. Khadija, a South Asian Muslim scholar, believes that there is a growing "negative essentialism" around faith-based spirituality in the academy. She saw evidence of people taking "the more extreme orientations of [a] faith" and essentializing it "when it's a minority view." She saw this kind of negative essentialism making it harder for someone like herself to express her spirituality. Addon believes that negative essentialism is applied particularly to Christianity. She pointed out, "I can't talk about the fact that [my spirituality] is Christ-centred. So sometimes it ends up getting masked under other names and labels." Addon further argues that coming from a Christ-centred perspective, she is automatically suspected of being someone who is evangelical and ready to convert everyone into Christians. She emphasizes that her faith is quite different from white Christianity, as hers is rooted in a community of African Canadians. Black Christianity was developed as a resistance to how white Christianity was practised.

Our participants have also experienced gendered stereotyping when expressing their spiritual identities through their attire. Khadija and Ayesha, both Muslim, expressed how wearing a hijab generates gendered Islamophobic labels and stereotypes such as "conservative," "traditional or extremist" and "oppressed." In this regard, Zine (2006) argues that Muslim women must navigate through multiple ideas about veiling not only because of religious but also social, cultural, racialized and gendered meanings attached to it. Khadija said:

> So they [people] assume that you have to be a certain kind of Muslim to wear hijab. You must represent certain dominant norms and views about Islam. And that became also burdensome because that wasn't who I was. I wasn't supporting the dominant ... patriarchal, kind of, narratives that were very common in our community and in fact began challenging those ... The fact that you're no longer in control of the meanings that get attached to your body.

In this case, even bringing a spiritual symbol to the academy is not easy, and the reactions can be quite harsh. However, as a spiritual political project, Khadija sometimes tries to disrupt the stereotypes by wearing a hijab in an academic setting. She added:

> There are times where saying what you do wearing hijab ... actually I think empowers what I say sometimes. And I like that, ... because they don't expect it coming from you ...for example, when I'm on different panels and things, the particular view I'll bring they won't expect from the stereotypical Muslim woman. So I'm shattering stereotypes and that's kind of fun to do. I like doing that.

In such an environment, Khadija seeks to renegotiate her own spiritual identity from within rather than be consumed by labels placed on her by others.

Creating one's own spiritual space in the secular chilly climate seems to be an uneasy act that requires a concerted effort. For example, Ayesha keeps spiritual symbols in her office to remind herself of the Divine. She puts prayers on various spots such as the wall, the door, and her computer. Similarly, Hoi explained that she has a bell sound ring every hour in her office computer as a reminder that she needs to stop and breathe. The act of stopping and consciously breathing reminds Hoi "to [come] back to our true home, [which] ... is our breath and breath is where life [began]." This system helps Hoi see things larger than herself, and it is part of her spiritual practice in the academy. Resilient Woman preserves her spiritual self through prayers and smudging. These practices attest to the degree to which little reminders of the sacred are needed in these scholars' work environment in order to nurture their spirit within it.

Despite the secular chilly climate of the academy, these participants are trying to assert and reclaim their spiritual identities as a means of sustaining their spirits. Addon emphasizes that for her to heal, she needs a space to proclaim how spirituality has shaped her life and subjectivity. She cannot be defeated even within the secular, androcentric chilly climate, but can sustain herself spiritually. In her words, "The more it [spirituality] seemed to get pushed to the back it was really the thing that sustained me." Lotus, an Asian faculty member in the health sciences, also talks about how significant her spirituality is in her academic life when she encounters struggles, or what she calls "suffering." She said, "My spirituality made me very strong. And whatever happened, I'm very optimistic, and I accept failure very readily and I accept all kinds of experiences readily and I wasn't defeated [but felt] strong, competent each time [suffering occurred]." It seems that Lotus's spirituality provided her with what Asante (2003) calls a "victorious consciousness" (65), a hopeful point of view.

For these women faculty, spirituality is a source of power that helps them survive, nurture themselves and thrive in the material world; it is at the centre of their subjectivities. The spiritual identity of scholars has not only been ignored in the academy but has also been marginalized and sometimes undervalued by the community. The fact that it still stays strong in the scholars' spirits and is a key to their healing on a daily basis attests to its centrality in their lives.

Moving beyond Academic Capitalism

For at least the past decade, forms and responsibilities of academic institutions have been affected by the global phenomenon of capitalism and commodification of knowledge (Slaughter & Leslie, 1997; Mohanty, 2003). The academy is becoming more profit oriented, and therefore demands that faculty in teaching and research meet corporate and utilitarian needs (Turk, 2000). Within such an environment, it is becoming difficult for equity-seeking scholars to conduct social justice projects in their teaching, research and service (Nast & Pulido, 2000; Hornesty, 2004). While the wind blows strong against them, there are scholars who try to push into the wind even harder by pursuing their commitment to something beyond the material world (Dillard, Abdur-Rashid & Tyson, 2000).

Some participants, grounded in a spiritual self, have resisted the forces of academic capitalism imposed on them. They have done this by working on research projects that pose risks to their professional status. As spirituality is a subjugated form of knowledge in the colonial androcentric academy, obtaining funding has been a major challenge to pursuing spirituality aligned projects (see Shahjahan, 2005). Here we share the case of Lotus, an Asian female scholar in the health sciences, to illustrate our point. Lotus argued that within the health professions, "it's very hard to get funding [for spiritually minded research, which] ... is very important in a research university." In her words,

> People, especially from science, couldn't understand [my research proposal] ... [People consider] spirituality [as a] soft science and they don't like [it] ... So no matter how [well] you write ... your proposal, ... people just have a different opinion ... Some people just don't think [spirituality is a topic that is] rigorous enough to talk about.

Lotus's experiences illustrate Greenwood and Levin's (2000) argument that research proposals that are not framed in the dominant paradigm — that is, positivist science — "will not receive funding" and that "the peer review system mainly guarantees that research will be kept fully under the control of the elite (and older) members of the academic professions" (88–89). Furthermore, Lotus's experience also reflects the dominant "Eurocentric masculinist knowledge-validation process" which, as Collins (1996) points out, uses positivism as an epistemological standard to negate alternative knowledge systems (225).

Lotus felt that her own challenges and risks in resisting these trends, as an immigrant Asian woman who was an untenured assistant professor, were far greater than those of a white Canadian-born faculty member. She added, "[White Canadian-born faculty] have ... better language skills ... and they are Canadian. They know the Canadian [context] very well." Lotus's quotation highlights that how one communicates English is "one of the socially constructed determinants of who is [a] 'Canadian' and who is [an] 'immigrant'" (Mayuzumi, 2005: 6). Lotus expressed the language struggle, shared by other immigrant women faculty in Canada, for whom English acted as a hurdle in their academic careers. She also emphasized that, because she is an untenured faculty member, she does not have the privilege of a secure position that allows her to pursue her research interests in spirituality. While Lotus problematizes the gendered, racialized and linguistic systemic barriers to engaging her research interests, she still sees her scholarly work as an integral part of a larger spiritual mission that is not governed by the institutional criteria of tenure and professorship. In her own words:

> I have a mission. I [have] not come here because I have to get tenure ... the professorship or whatever. I know a lot of people ... [are] interested in spirituality but they have to compromise [for] academic success ... But I think life is joy and each period of my time I have different plans, although the plan is not necessarily [what] I ... plan. I mean I have to surrender to God's will ... So, my vision for this time is [to] promote spirituality in academia ... We are going to publish [on spirituality] and discuss all kinds of methods that we can [use to] research spirituality.

Lotus's struggle as a non-tenured faculty member resonated with other scholars, such as Resilient Woman and Addon, who recounted how doing work from a spiritual paradigm is a risky endeavour for junior women faculty. Spiritual ways of being helped these faculty resist the pressures to conform. Lotus, for instance, is transgressing being complicit with regimes of power and truth in the academy through her spirituality derived from Asian wisdom traditions. As she argues, all these forms of competition and pressures are really "emptiness." Her vision allows her not to "react to that" but to continue to "do what is important." Her spiritual world view allows her to construct a Sacred subjectivity that assists her in transgressing these seductive forces.

Thus, our participants find the strength to problematize the dominant academic culture and knowledge production as well as see spiritual visions guiding their presence and their work in the academy. In summary, Sacred energies are interceding in the daily academic lives of the participants to "push, strengthen and bring a sense of purpose" which is consistent with their "Soul's purpose" (Alexander, 2005: 301).

CONCLUSION

In this chapter we demonstrated how spirituality provides spiritually minded racially minoritized women faculty with an alternative world view to reframe oppressive situations and avoid spirit injury. It also helps them to prevent and understand the negative energies engulfing the academy, providing them with the will to assert their own spiritual identities in various ways, even as their spiritual identity becomes a site of interrogation, racism, sexism and negative essentialisms. Spirituality is central to a different understanding of academic life, away from the pressures of tenure and promotion, so that one can sustain oneself to carry out spiritually aligned equity projects in academia.

It is important to highlight how considering a Sacred subjectivity is critical for understanding the agencies and resistances of the faculty in this study. Ignoring Sacred subjectivity would ignore the spiritual amputation that these women go through, as well as the daily resistances they pose to the chilly climate that is crushing them. One may also argue that these women's resistances contribute to social change. These women are disrupting the status quo; it is not easy, but they have found means to transgress through their philosophy of possibilities. Resistance needs to be conceptualized at the micro-level, not just as an organized collective action (Lattas, 1993). These micro-forms of spiritual resistance need to be acknowledged from the perspective that all these small acts of resistance contribute to the collective transformative change of the dominant social order. In short, for these spiritually minded racially minoritized women faculty, the personal is not only political, but the spiritual is also a political part of their academic life.

NOTES

1 The names of participants in this study are identified through the use of pseudonyms to protect their privacy and anonymity.

2 We use the phrase "racially minoritized women faculty" to refer to both women of colour and Aboriginal women faculty.

3 The term "activist" refers to the fact that they were actively involved inside and/or outside the academy in advocacy for equitable policy initiatives and/or validating subjugated knowledges and experiences.

4 From this point onwards, we use the phrase "participants" to refer to these six spiritually minded female faculty members.

REFERENCES

Alexander, M.J. (2005). *Pedagogies of crossing: Meditations on feminism, sexual politics, memory and the sacred.* Durham, NC: Duke University Press.

Arisaka, Y. (2000). Asian women: Invisibility, locations, and claims to philosophy. In N. Zack (Ed.), *Women of color and philosophy: A critical reader* (219–223). New York: Blackwell.

Asante, M.K. (2003). *Afrocentricity: The theory of social change.* Chicago: African American Images.

Bannerji, H. (1991). Re: turning the gaze. *Resources for Feminist Research, 20*(3/4), 5–11.

Canadian Federation for the Humanities and Social Sciences. (2006). Feminist & equity audits 2006: Selected indicators for Canadian universities. Retrieved 28 May 2006 from www.fedcan.ca/english/pdf/issues/FEAAuditpostcardEng.pdf.

Collins, P.H. (2000). *Black feminist thought: Knowledge, consciousness, and the politics of empowerment,* 2nd ed. New York: Routledge.

Collins, P.H. (1996). The social construction of black feminist thought. In A. Garry & M. Pearsall (Eds.), *Women, knowledge, and reality: Explorations in feminist philosophy,* 2nd ed. (222–248). New York: Routledge.

Dillard, C., Abdur-Rashid, D., & Tyson, C. (2000). My soul is a witness: Affirming pedagogies of the spirit. *International Journal of Qualitative Studies in Education, 13*(5), 447–462.

Fernandes, L. (2003). *Transforming feminist practice: Non-violence, social justice and the possibilities of a spiritualized feminism.* San Francisco: Aunt Lute Books.

Greenwood, D.J., & Levin, M. (2000). Reconstructing the relationships between universities and society through action research. In N.K. Denzin & Y.S. Lincoln (Eds.), *Handbook of qualitative research*, 2nd ed. (85–106). Thousand Oaks, CA: Sage.

Hoodfar, H. (1992). Feminist anthropology and critical pedagogy: The anthropology of classrooms' excluded voices. *Canadian Journal of Education, 17*(3), 303–321.

Hornesty, J. (2004). Corporate challenges to academic freedom and gender equity. In M. Reimer (Ed.), *Inside corporate U: Women in the academy speak out* (43–66). Toronto: Sumach Press.

Lattas, A. (1993). Essentialism, memory and resistance: Aboriginality and the politics of authenticity. *Oceania, 63*, 240–267.

Li, G., & Beckett, G.H. (Eds.). (2006). *"Strangers" of the academy: Asian women scholars in higher education.* Sterling, VA: Stylus.

Luther, R., Whitmore, E., & Moreau, B. (Eds.). (2003). *Seen but not heard: Aboriginal women and women of colour in the academy.* Ottawa: CRIAW.

Mayuzumi, K. (2005). Breaking the silence: Immigrant women faculty, Canadian academy, and the nation-state. Paper presented at the Annual Meeting of the American Educational Research Association (AERA), Montreal, Quebec.

Mohanty, C.T. (2003). *Feminism without borders: Decolonizing theory, practicing solidarity.* Durham, NC: Duke University Press.

Nast, H.J., & Pulido, L. (2000). Resisting corporate multiculturalism: Mapping faculty initiatives and institutional-student harassment in the classroom. *Professional Geographer, 52*(4), 722–737.

Ng, R. (1993). "A woman out of control": Deconstructing sexism and racism in the university. *Canadian Journal of Education, 18*(3), 189–205.

Samuel, E., & Wane, N. (2005). "Unsettling relations": Racism and sexism experienced by faculty of color in a predominantly White Canadian university. *The Journal of Negro Education, 74*(1), 76–87.

Shahjahan, R.A. (2007). *The every day as sacred: Trailing back by the spiritual proof fence in the academy.* Unpublished doctoral dissertation, University of Toronto.

Shahjahan, R.A. (2005). Spirituality in the academy: Reclaiming from the margins and evoking a transformative way of knowing the world. *International Journal of Qualitative Studies in Education, 18*(6), 685–711.

Slaughter, S., & Leslie, L. (1997). *Academic capitalism.* Baltimore: Johns Hopkins University Press.

Spafford, M., Nygaard, V., Gregor, F., & Boyd, M. (2006). "Navigating the different spaces": Experiences of inclusion and isolation among racially minoritized faculty in Canada. *Canadian Journal of Higher Education, 36*(1), 1–27.

Turk, J. (Ed.). (2000). *The corporate campus: Commercialization and the dangers to Canada's colleges and universities.* Toronto: Lorimer.

Turner, C.S. (2003). Incorporation and marginalization in the academy: From border toward center for faculty of color? *Journal of Black Studies, 34*(1), 112–125.

Zine, J. (2006). Unveiled sentiments: Gendered Islamophobia and experiences of veiling among Muslim girls in a Canadian Islamic school. *Equity and Excellence in Education, 39,* 239–252.

CHAPTER 13

CONTESTED SITE, CONTESTED TOPIC:

TEACHING ANTI-RACIST STUDIES IN A TEACHER EDUCATION PROGRAM

Njoki N. Wane

THIS CHAPTER EXAMINES THE DYNAMICS INVOLVED IN TEACHING ABOUT diversity and social justice in a teacher education program. I draw from my own experience as a visible minority female professor in a program where the majority of students and faculty are of European descent. I provide an analysis of my teaching experience and examine the various forms of resistance that I have encountered, describing my mechanisms of coping and ways of healing the spirit's injuries that I have experienced in this position teaching controversial and contentious topics.

It is not usually necessary to be a trained teacher in order to teach at the university level. However, I was fortunate enough to undergo five years of teacher training, including four years in a Bachelor of Education program, specializing in business studies and management, and one year in an intensive business education teaching diploma course. In addition, my graduate education is extremely diverse, and as a result I am a jack of all trades in terms of what I can teach. It was because of this background that I did not hesitate to agree to teach both in a graduate and teacher education program and in particular to teach general courses in teacher education. I knew I could use my training to develop a syllabus that would engage students with the material, which addressed issues of justice that were significant to our schools.

My commitment in teaching and writing is to an anti-colonial theoretical framework that recognizes intersecting forms of inequality and questions the role of power in the perpetuation of racism, criticizing racialized inequalities and white supremacy (Walcott, 1994). Gender is a key form of inequality, and gender and race must be considered together. Yet we must not oversimplify. Black women in Canada are a varied group of people from diverse backgrounds, cultures and situations. According to the Canadian Health Network (2007), an estimated 54 percent of Black women in Canada are immigrants who mostly come from African and Caribbean countries, as well as Bermuda. Like other minority groups in this country, the situation of Black women in the Canadian landscape continues to be mediated by characteristics such as race, class, gender, religion, age, sexuality and ability, among other aspects of difference.

This argument is taken up by Mohanty (1995), who states that racialized women are usually situated on the bottom rank of each society, whether they live in North America or in other parts of the world. Bannerji (2000) points out that "diversity is not equal to multiplied sameness" (41). In other words, while gender specificity is necessary in any analysis of a situation, it should not be oversimplified. As a result, it is important for me to situate this chapter in a framework that recognizes race, gender, colonial history and anti-colonial thought. Both gender and race are very central, as both are physical attributes which become identifiers that people may apply to describe a woman of African ancestry teaching a homogeneous student population. I cannot escape from my reality as an African female, born and raised in a neo-colonial state — Kenya — where the aftermath of colonial history lingers to the present day; my presence is visibly identifiable.

DIVERSITY AND TEACHER EDUCATION

Given the background and commitments described above, I believe that teacher education programs need to address issues of educational equality, equity and social justice. I use the phrase "contested site, contested topic" to indicate the difficulties of pursuing such reform. Acknowledging the complexity of such teaching, how might we introduce diversity and equity discussions without injuring the spirit of the parties involved?

I write this chapter with the awareness that educational arenas are important sites for understanding how diversity works. I also write knowing that there has been unprecedented internationalization within communities, especially urban areas. It is therefore not unusual to have an encounter with cultural difference in one's daily interactions. As Carson and Johnson (2000) have written, the increased diversity in society is bound to have profound effects on how we educate teachers. It is also common knowledge that preparing teachers for culturally diverse classrooms raises many difficult questions for teacher education, which has traditionally prepared educators to teach from what they call a "curriculum of sameness" (76). According to Carson and Johnson (2000), "The curriculum of teacher education has been traditionally structured around an array of commonalities of normal child development, learning theories, provincially mandated programs of studies, instructional planning procedures, and the identification and measurement of expected outcomes" (76).

Given this reality, what can we say about diversity in the preparation of teachers? As someone who is very conscious of diversity in our communities and who has consistently encountered resistance to nonmainstream approaches on the part of some students, I find this question integrally important. I also find it essential to reflect on the various forms of resistance that I see enacted in the classroom. I will return to the issue of resistance in a later section of the chapter.

SPIRITUALITY AS ANTI-COLONIAL FRAMEWORK

In confronting the concepts and conditions of colonialism and neo-colonialism, I wish to move beyond overworked metaphors of integration, acculturation, multiculturalism or the Canadian mosaic. While thinking through this chapter and the anti-colonial framework, I knew that I could not write about the present without making reference to the past. Within the African world view, there is the notion of Sankofa philosophy, which stresses the need for people to look back at their history in order to make sense of their current situation. I could have easily looked at writings on colonization, colonial education and neo-colonial education that can be found when we enter those terms into a search engine. However, for this chapter, I decided to use reflective anti-colonial spiritual knowledge. For me, spirituality is essential as a method of survival, and it provides sustenance for my psychological well-being. When I light a candle, either at the beginning of a class discussion or at home after a hard day's work, it is my way of putting my fragmented self together, of coping with stress. The silent moments provide a space for me to step out of the rat race to which so many of us have become accustomed.

Whether coming from eastern, western, northern or southern parts of the world, colonial and neo-colonial practices disturb and disorient most of us in one way or another. What is emerging, however, are voices, desires and bodies of knowledge that reveal a sense of culture as well as a politics of history and identity that can no longer be disregarded. These voices and politics demand that we engage in dialogue to try and come up with some understanding of how we are all implicated in this process of suppressing truths and how we can stop the circle of oppression, marginalization and spirit murder. Given the technological advancement of the modern day, which means that the world enters our living rooms and offices, we can no longer ignore the violence, famine, poverty and genocide taking place in different parts of the world.

In my own experience, spirituality guides my quest for greater meaning in life. It enables me to search for answers to conflicting messages that may come from new knowledge being created on a day-to-day basis. Spirituality is also significant to my professional practice, as it provides me with the healing necessary to adapt coping strategies wholeheartedly.

It is important to remember that spirituality cannot be taught, since it is a biologically built-in constituent of what it is to be human. Watson (2003) argues that spirituality at its best fosters growth and helps the individual to search for meaning in his/her life. This may be understood as a process of struggle and self-recovery, and a path to follow in order to become whole and liberated. In other words, spirituality lies at the heart of being human. When I make reference to spirituality, I "do not mean the creed-based formulations of any faith traditions" (Wane & Neegan, 2007: 29). I am making reference to the ancient and abiding quest for connectedness with our own souls, with one another, with the worlds of nature and with the mystery of being alive (Palmer, 2000).

Spirituality is not only a refuge for me. I also see it as a means of engaging my students. When I began teaching in the program concerned, I decided to explore issues of diversity and how colonialism has been used as a tool to divide and conquer the minds and souls of people. Further, I intended to analyze how these divisions have been normalized. As only a select group of students would be exposed to my teaching, I was conscious of the need to make it memorable, in order to increase the likelihood that the students would incorporate these principles of diversity and equity into their own teaching practices. Consequently, I decided to place a discussion of spirituality within an anti-colonial framework. I used spirituality because I wanted to engage my students holistically. In the next section I give an example of how I have attempted to accomplish this objective.

TEACHING ACROSS BORDERS

For a number of years I taught students in the business department of a Kenyan university who were from different ethnic backgrounds, religions and geographical regions. Teaching in a Kenyan university was quite different from teaching in a Canadian one. I was quite successful in my few years of teaching in Kenya, where I used passion to evoke the everyday realities of students and to challenge the biases of class, gender, ethnicity, religion and disability (there was very little mention of race). When I started teaching in Canada, I thought I would use the same techniques that I had successfully employed while teaching in Kenya.

However, I began to realize that not all students were comfortable with my approach. In other works (Wane, 2002a, 2002b, 2002c), I have talked about rituals of border-crossing as an approach that may be applied to a situation that is controversial or tense. I visualize this approach as having three circles, which do not intersect. The students occupy the circle on one side, and I, as teacher, stand in my own circle on the other. The students and I look at the middle circle, which in the initial stages is empty. In order for a meaningful dialogue to take place, participants in the two outer circles must be willing to step into the middle one. For the purpose of explaining the ritual of border-crossing when dealing with sensitive issues in a classroom, I offer the following example, which took place in a Canadian university.

It was a Wednesday morning, 8:30 a.m., and it was our third class. The first two meetings had dealt with generalities of teacher education in Canada, colonialism and the notion of absences. Our topic on this particular morning was entitled "We Are all Implicated: The Discourse of Equity and Diversity in our Schools and Society." On this particular day, I read a passage from Satish Kumar's book *You Are Therefore I Am* for reflection. The passage I read was about a mango seed and how, when it was fully grown, it would provide shade, food, fuel and a home for birds, insects, worms and people. My intention in selecting this passage was to try and draw parallels between nurturing of students' minds and caring for a mango tree. The mango seed is planted, and if watered properly, it grows into a flourishing tree. The same is true with children — if they are nurtured and exposed to different ways of knowing, they grow up to nurture the minds of those who cross their path regardless of ethnicity, gender and so on. If, however, this nurturing does not occur, they grow up thinking only about their world and never step out of their box. Students, too, need to begin with the self and to blossom into full-fledged teachers. I reflect on my own self, and how, as an individual, my actions have huge implications for student teachers' lives.

Some of the students could identify with the analogy of a mango tree, while others resisted it and wanted to distance themselves. After about thirty to forty-five minutes of an open-ended discussion where I watched to see who was stepping into and staying within the mutuality circle, I ended the dialogue, taking up my position as a facilitator, coach and guide.

RESISTANCE

Students are often uncomfortable with my conscious decision to adopt the role of a facilitator, learner and navigator, instead of the expert that the education system prepares us to be. Some of the comments that I have encountered over the years include:

- Why do we have to talk about diversity? We get along fairly well with everyone.

- Is there any need to talk about race and racism, sexual orientation or even disability when most of us do not experience them?

- Why do you have to bring issues that are not relevant to our teaching?

How can I answer these questions? Many times, I feel like I am climbing a very steep mountain and every time I take one step higher, I slide back two or three. A discussion on diversity is always heated unless issues of race and sexuality and, more recently, religion are left out. These conversations are necessary if we want to be sincere in our scholarship. When we fail to provide space for such discussions, we participate knowingly or unknowingly in silencing others, participating in spirit injury and maintaining the status quo.

As I ended the discussion described above, I had a thousand and one questions racing through my brain. Why the resistance? Was it related to my being African and female? Did some students see authority as typically embodied in white male figures? What is this new world, the world that I find myself part of, going to be like in the next hundred years? As I engage in this reflective exercise, I am forced to think of my birth place, where I came from and what I am bringing to my new home. Why do we, as individuals, deny the injustices in the world? Why is it that most cannot see the absence of voices or the scarcity of information about people of non-European descent in our own schools? Why is there so much resistance? Who bears the burden of these forms of resistance?

As I reflect on this last question, I wonder if I am taking this response too personally. Further, to my great surprise and dismay, when I shared my experiences and frustrations with some of my colleagues, their comments were not very encouraging. Common responses included "maybe you are being too sensitive," or suggestions that perhaps the students were simply overworked and overtired, rather than expressing resistance to my teaching approach.

Yet every year that I teach in the pre-service program, I witness various forms of resistance to discussing diversity issues. Even if I discount these negative attitudes, my body and spirit cannot ignore them. The impact is mostly invisible. What follows is an example of my own reflections as I ponder my interactions with students and while I prepare for various rituals to restore my spiritual and intellectual balance.

THOUGHTS ON BIAS

Why are there so many negative perceptions about others in the world and, in particular, in my classrooms? Canada has a reputation as an egalitarian and compassionate country, committed to ensuring that its citizens receive an education that is truly reflective of the principles of equality and social justice. In that context, it is puzzling that students in a pre-service classroom find it so difficult to have an open and frank discussion about how equity and diversity issues affect all of us in our daily lives. How can I engage in dialogue with resistant students without injuring my spirit? Is there a better way to approach the students, keeping in mind that they may simply be resisting what is unfamiliar to them?

I have travelled extensively in Africa, Europe and Central Asia, and have read widely about the various ancient civilizations of the world. I have read most of the sacred texts that many religions follow and have come to conclude that we, as occupants of this planet, strive for peace, and that we are very spiritual people. I know whoever reads this may ask, "What is she talking about?" My answer to this would be to ask the reader to sit still and see the world as you would like it to be. Then ask yourself, why is it not the way you have imagined it? Why the chaos? The answer lies in our own midst. The answer is within you. However, we are too scared to reach into the deep self because, many times when we do, we are confronted with a great deal of resistance. Many of us are burned out by the struggle against resistance. When one is talking about the same issues all the time, one simply gets tired.

As a result, I have to constantly remind myself that I cannot succumb to the stress of the modern world. I have to ensure that I survive the turmoil. Many times I ask myself, why can we not see beauty in diversity? I am not the first, nor will I be the last, to ask these questions. What would be the best way to sustain my interest and commitment in this work that is so important? How can I ensure that I give 100 percent of myself in teaching — because teaching for me is not a career, but a calling? I consider it a calling because no matter how much I resisted becoming a teacher, I found myself drawn to the profession. Teaching is my destiny, and I teach because I love it. I want the students who pass through my class to have a meaningful dialogue with themselves. I want each one to reflect on how they can engage in transformative work as educators, facilitators and coaches for tomorrow's citizenry.

CONCLUSION

No amount of training would have prepared me adequately for the challenges I faced in a pre-service class. During my first encounter with students, I realized that in all my graduate education both in Kenya and in North America, I was never given the tools I needed to teach issues of diversity. Initially, I could not make sense of why the students resisted my approach to teaching when the course mandate ensured issues of diversity were central. My naive assumption was that we would begin from a shared basis of understanding, and therefore much of the content would simply reinforce what they already knew.

I now realize that students' resistance may be partially grounded in discomfort with unfamiliar patterns of thought. Further, I am fully conscious that such learning is more psychologically and emotionally demanding than traditional mainstream approaches. As a teacher, as I have described, I personally experience an emotional, psychological and physical drain trying to teach this subject. Yet it is essential to find a way to create a dialogue that will broaden student understanding of stereotyping, perceptions, biases and misunderstanding, to make them aware of some of the political, social, economic and emotional antecedents of racism, as well as the sources and impact of gender and other forms of bias. If the debate is conducted appropriately, it will make the students aware of the dangers of indifference, intolerance and historical amnesia. However, if the issues are not taken up in a sensitive way, discussions can actually traumatize students and cause further damage to their psyches.

As a professor, I need to understand the sources of resistance. It is important to remind myself that students may have biased sources of information, including stereotypical, homogenized understandings of racial and cultural groups. That is, students' knowledge of equity and diversity may be derived from media or everyday unsubstantiated comments from colleagues, friends, acquaintances or even strangers. For instance, the criminalization of Black males through the media, or the subservient roles that Asian women occupy in movies, normalizes our stereotypical way of thinking in terms of these two groups of people. These images provide a partial story, and rarely are students challenged to contextualize or historicize the circumstances under which these images are produced and packaged for consumption. Relying on stereotypes fails to acknowledge that society does not provide equal opportunities for all its members. In addition, there is the absence of voice from the marginalized segments of our society. Teacher candidates need to be exposed to theories that take them beyond their starting points and challenged to incorporate the implications of interlocking sources of oppression into their developing practice. For me as a professor, this requires affirming students' experiences, acknowledging their individual pain and /or oppression and supporting their efforts to deal with that pain.

I have also described something of my own pain and the spiritually based means I have used to respond to it. I have learned from my students that a lot of work needs to be done within the school system, as students should be exposed to issues of diversity from elementary school onwards. It is unfortunate that so much of the curriculum is taught from a Eurocentric perspective. What is important is that we acknowledge the challenge and then find ways of teaching that are not confrontational or counterproductive and that reduce rather than increase resistance. Despite the difficulties, I have learned much from my students and colleagues about how to approach issues of diversity. There are also many pleasures contained in the teaching journey, especially when students grasp the message I hope to convey.

REFERENCES

Bannerji, H. (2000). *The dark side of the nation: Essays on multiculturalism, nationalism and gender.* Toronto: Canadian Scholars' Press.

Canadian Health Network. (2007). How being Black and female affects your health. Retrieved 20 January 2007 from www.canadianhealthnetwork.ca.

Carson, T. & Johnson, I. (2000). The difficulty with difference in teacher education: Toward a pedagogy of compassion. *The Alberta Journal of Educational Research, 46*(1), 75–83.

Kumar, S. (2002). You are therefore I am: A declaration of dependence. Totnes, UK: Green Books.

Mohanty, C.T. (1995). Under Western eyes: Feminist scholarship and colonial discourses. In B. Ashcroft, G. Griffiths, & H. Tiffin (Eds.), *The post-colonial studies reader* (259–263). London: Routledge.

Palmer, P. (2000). A vision of education as transformation. In V.H. Kazanjian & P.L. Laurence (Eds.), *Education as transformation: Religious pluralism, spirituality, and a new vision for higher education in America* (17–22). New York: Peter Lang.

Walcott, R. (1994). The need for a politics of difference. *Orbit, 25*(2), 13–14.

Wane, N.N. (2002a). African women and spirituality: Harmonizing the balance of life. In N.N. Wane, K. Deliovsky, & E. Lawson (Eds.), *Back to the drawing board: African Canadian feminisms* (275–278). Toronto. Sumach Press.

Wane, N.N. (2002b). African women's technologies: Applauding the self, reclaiming indigenous space. *Colonial Journal of Education, 1*(1), 45–66.

Wane, N.N. (2002c). Black Canadian feminist thought: Drawing on the experiences of my sisters. In N.N. Wane, K. Deliovsky, & E. Lawson (Eds.), *Back to the drawing board: African Canadian feminisms* (29–53). Toronto. Sumach Press.

Wane, N.N., & Neegan, E. (2007). African women's Indigenous spirituality: Bringing it all home. In N. Massaquoi & N. Wane (Eds.), *Theorizing empowerment: Canadian perspectives on black feminist thought* (27–46). Toronto: Inanna.

Watson, J. (2003). Preparing spirituality for citizenship. *International Journal of Children's Spirituality, 8*(1), 9–24.

CHAPTER 14

CHRONICALLY DOING THE IMPOSSIBLE, ADEQUATELY AND CREATIVELY

Si Transken

"A Sensational Sensuous Poem"

if health were wealth
spread like clean air in Eden then
companies would have changed their paradigm,
banks wouldn't control the world,
authentic complex democracy would exist,
neither employment nor unemployment would make us sick,
we'd live long enough to profoundly know love in multiplicity,
other currencies would find equality with money,
the words *patriarchy* & *duplicity* would be archaic
& attendance at the academy would be free for everybody.

— S. Transken

MY ACADEMIC JOURNEY

I have been a university student non-stop since 1984 (*and* an employee somewhere doing something non-stop since 1975). I have completed a BA (sociology), an Hon.BSW (social work), an MA (equity studies), a PhD (equity studies), course work for a second MA (First Nations studies/creative writing), certificates, diplomas and continuing education courses. Since 1998 I have been teaching social work/sociology for two different universities.[1] I've taught in seven different geographies (northern rural communities as large as 120,000 to communities as small as 4,000) and now I also teach courses on the Internet! Yes, there are patterns and problems in academia: I have always felt that I'm being asked to do the impossible — and do it too quickly with too few resources. Yet somehow I have accomplished an education, a career and an understanding of the world that I share with the wider community. Throughout this chapter, I'll explore connections around creativity and teaching/learning that have had profound meaning for me in my attempts to go around/over/under/ straight through/away from those problems.

CLASS, GENDER, ABUSE, NORTHERN ISOLATION

No one in my northern Ontario mining family had completed even a high school diploma. I was the first to have such ambitions. I remain the only one from my family (perhaps my whole childhood neighbourhood) to complete a degree. The Ontario Institute for Studies in Education (OISE) initiated and enriched a marvelous cluster of revelations for me while I did my MA and PhD (from 1990 to 1998).[2] One of those life-changing insights was to note the profound significance of class. As I read critical scholarship, my whiteness and potential access to privilege became more apparent to me as class, gender and an assortment of other oppressions became more visible. I also learned that disciplinary and genre boundaries were MANmade — and that these boundaries could be pushed, made permeable and played with.

While completing my MA and PhD in Sociology and Equity Studies at OISE, the feminist anti-racist scholars around me affirmed my right to feel and express anger while discussing the unfortunate human realities of oppression. I have had a lot of anger to write about/with/through and OISE made my feminism sparkle in a fiercely excited and often joyful bright fuchsia-red! As a white anglophone Canadian-born working-class woman I could become a conduit for knowledge from the street (or the bush, the trailer park) to the university and back again — creativity is a necessary adhesive to be that "conduit."

As I continued my studies, I learned that I could boldly integrate poetry and storytelling into my "academic" writing. In a *Women and Health* course, Dr. Roxana Ng encouraged us to talk about our relationships with

our own bodies. This was the first academic setting in which I unam-
biguously disclosed that I was an incest survivor. A scholarly paper which
I wrote during the course included one of my poems, which was later
published by the Canadian Research Institute for the Advancement of
Women (Transken, 1995):

"Reclaimed Territory"

then (1970s) looking over the terrain of that body
its anemic whiteness, whiteness like the veal calf
the sunblocked asparagus
both cut down in their sweetest moments for consumption
by a casual enemy or whiteness like the geisha girl
or whiteness like in "white slave"

now (1990s) sometimes i tenderly
drape a thin cloak of cool lotion over this sullen terrain
this stroking is a declaration of resistance
understood only by my self, touching my self *for my self*
a self not cut down, a self that's not a girl and not a slave
a self that's white like a stormy winter mountain.

Writing this poem, deeply feeling the support from my teachers at OISE,
and realizing how intellectually and spiritually wholesome it felt to publish such a declaration, I continued to value that creatively integrative
style of writing, thinking, teaching, doing, being. I came to embrace creative multi-disciplinary and multi-genre scholarship which defies the conventions of academia.

GROWING AND STUMBLING AS AN ACADEMIC ACTIVIST

During my years as an academic I have had to face diminishment or
dismissal by many "scholars," but with enough support and affirmation
(from women like my OISE comrades) I *have managed* to become a tenured associate professor, have received $333,319 in grants as a primary
researcher and have been involved in many other grants as a supporter/
activist. I have a small bundle of rewards, and numerous acknowledge-
ments and blurbs to put on my C.V. I've been nominated five times for a
teaching excellence award. The poetry and stories that I write are applied
in the classroom (I've taught more than ninety groups of students now!).

I use this creative classed gendered material in guest lectures, as well as protests and fundraisers. I've presented at over sixty scholarly conferences and more than a hundred community events.

I know how to be a cheerleader — aware that a creative writing/performance is more likely to be quoted in the newspapers. If *how I say* what I say is interesting or innovative enough, we may make the news — our issues will be aired ... I learn how to be noticed. As Banks (1998) has written, academic research does not fully engage such an audience, as it "lacks the traditional qualities of good storytelling, qualities like plot development ... [c]haracter ..." (12). Hence, I put myself on stage and perform my part. However, as one who does not conform and refuses to "do" academia as expected, I inhabit an awkward position in the ivory tower:

"Inside Me Inside the Ivory Tower"

i have stumble-entered under scammed conditions.
fraudulent & underskilled at this impostoring
i endure the forwardness i'm headed in
because backwardness is undoable.
there are many potential affronts to my authenticity,
declaration of my inadequacy,
questioning of my credibility;
i throw brash-toned humor & unstructured responses
at the thick chaos i perceive here;
there's nothing more i can offer.
my few tools fail in their mission but not miserably enough
to evict me permanently enough
from these fear-peppered places.
as the only clumsy jester here they allow me to remain
for contrast; my disjointedness highlights
their polish & multi-generational beige belongingness.
i am an exception proving proving proving the righteousness of their rules;
i am the grain of sand that their line is finely drawn on.

As someone who waitressed in loud bawdy strip joints and greasy spoons for fifteen years while also pursuing higher educational opportunities, I have a particular sense of humour. I don't pronounce things the way the Queen of England does. My body language is not constrained and tight. Some of these attributes rupture students' and academic peers' expectations of what a "normal, real" professor is. Yet I maintain my tenacity, determined to remain comfortable with being uncomfortable.

I define myself as a "feminist organic intellectual," interested in combining grassroots wisdom with academia, seeking ways to integrate and disseminate the knowledge from all the spheres of our lives (Smith, 2006). Social work does have a tradition of bringing our whole imaginative/intellectual/physical selves to the work we do (see Addams, 1910; Baines, 2003). As Turner (1999), a social work scholar, has written, "linking the creativity of all members of society holds great potential for attaining the changes needed to achieve a just and equitable society" (97).

Turner is also highlighting the fact that we benefit as scholars by staying connected to our roots as practitioners. I work one or two shifts a week at a women's shelter — and this feminist clinical work, or praxis, integrates and informs my other spheres of learning/teaching. Hall (1996) refers to this as the job of the "organic intellectual," whose job it is "to know more than the traditional intellectuals do: really know, not just pretend to know, not just to have the facility of knowledge, but to know deeply and profoundly" (268).

DOING THE IMPOSSIBLE, ADEQUATELY AND CREATIVELY

In reflecting on what is lovely, insane, diabolical, ambiguous, contradictory and/or practical on this teaching/learning terrain — the contradictions and outrageous expectations of academia — I have written poetry as a means of healing from my experiences. I create "performance texts" (Denzin, 2003), "using the words and stories that individuals tell ... that imagine new worlds, worlds where humans can become who they wish to be, free of prejudice, repression, and discrimination" (105). Most importantly, these kinds of writings help me have fun, connect with comrades, make money for causes and teach students in a way that is accessible to them. Also, I get to piss people off, and there's not a lot they can do about it. After all, a creative piece of writing is — well, is just a creative piece of writing, eh?

I am located in such a way (as a feminist socialist social worker with a code of ethics that espouses equality) that I must *talk* about equality and co-operation, and simultaneously *behave* in ways that promote or maintain inequality and intensive competition. As someone who has mopped floors in public places and as the daughter of someone who worked as a cleaning woman, I'm usually conscious of my privileges and how they have been accomplished by someone's labour and attentiveness. I'm also conscious of how the space itself shapes our potentials for engagement — chairs are bolted down, there is only one pathway through the room, the teacher's podium is front and centre.

"The First Moment of the First Day Back at School"

scent of industrial cleaner watered down
foregrounds
the display & way of this non-/estranged room
wetted washed wiped surfaces – repaired &
left quietly for the contemplative summer are here for us now.
we've reopened this class space. shining flourescent simmer
soaks our frontal lobes, husky hearts.
effervescent hope hits the spines of our binders.
all is unfrail, new. now this is where we will ambiguously
ambitiously change. where we will mostly forget the how & where
of these undeniable transformations.
we will remember to conform
our fleshed messy selves to the needs
of bolted tidy rows.

Students have told me that they won't let themselves be late for other professor's classes or with other professor's assignments but they know they can get away with it with "someone like me." Students have told me they've handed in work of lesser quality in my classes because they "thought I'd be more understanding" (and yet they still want a high mark on that lesser quality work). I have to subtly or overtly remind students that I too am a "serious scholar" — but in a different way. I've taken to giving out my C.V. in the first class of the semester to all the students. I often feel I need to prove my right to be in academia — and the people I come in contact with also seem to need that reminder. I am grateful that I will not live a life of poverty — but I sometimes curse that spontaneous gratitude. It interferes with my ability to insist on the same respect, raises, perks and recognitions that some of my white, male, middle-class/privileged peers expect and demand. Of course, most students and peers aren't conscious that they may be imperceptibly "demoting" me because of classed and gendered assumptions.

"Lecturer (i.e. a person who is far from being a tenure-tracked assistant professor or a tenured assistant professor or a tenured associate professor or a tenured full professor ...)"

at the edge of this terrain of glimpsed privilege i'm impelled to bow. no. i am *not* trapped trying to make food last till the next government cheque – the food for my five kids anchored with me in a cranky-bush-road mobile home. no, cheeky & clever, i slithered past that cramped brain-crushing destiny. *here* five books always wait to feed me on this so-subtle-cranky trail through the ivy tangles in this ivory tower. one leaf, page, concept, bow taken or taking at a time. i am a tourist-refugee awaiting my next uncharitable cheque for my teaching assignments.

One of my worst moments with this gratitude/entitlement ambiguity occurred when I accidentally discovered that a male peer who had not yet started his PhD, had half as many publications as me, and one-fifth of my teaching experience was earning almost the same yearly wage as I was. That hurt.

RELATIONSHIPS

There is also a sense of joy in belonging to something as large as the whole world, acting as a bridge between/among grassroots interests and academia's resources. Yet this joy is tempered by the realities of working in a male-dominated system, in which I am often denigrated. My memories include being invited onto a thesis committee only because the student was a female and the others on the committee were male. I recall being later reprimanded in front of the student after offering a suggestion and was reminded that I was just there for "optics" and was therefore not expected to participate beyond rubber-stamping her text and showing up at her defense to sign the confirmation. I captured this memory in the following poem:

"Contrasts & Challenges"

appetites & apparitions around mentoring
prove excess for both of us;
frail, damaged, you skulk
the edges of relationship possibilities.

in contrast, i tumble, hulk, lunge
defeat is not possible
in the stupid language my heart sings -
only detours, efforts at damage control.

we now close our doors to each other
avoiding eye contact, cleverly
planning de-synchronized
schedules & associations.

you, motivated in fear;
i, in tender manners, i refuse
to collude in cowardly conspiracies
or attempts to crush spirit.

while i spoke of playfulness
your curdled tone slipped past my lips –
tried to poison my tongue –
but in innocent resilience
i chew & spit flowers at your feet.

It is not only male academics who are bemused by my behaviour.
Some secretaries, administrative people and non-feminist women academics also perceive me as a big, loud oddity.

"How an Educated Cranky-Bitch Feminist Feels on a Bad
Day after Too Many Meetings with Mainstream Mindless
Handmaidens"

i am a hairy fuchsia elephant
possibly from a future galaxy
wearing golden military boots.
my rage is glorious, magnificent, glimmering but
scraggly grey chickens   peck, peck, scatter, peck
peck at my huge boots & their noise irritates me.
the edges of this town are visible only from my eye level &
position.
i see no other fuchsia elephants; i never forget
i could crush these chickens or kick them but that is
outside of my nature & futile because
there is an infinite supply of them anyway.

every which way chickens populate
& dominate this sullen terrain
& i ask - which way to where the herds
of shimmering fuchsia elephants graze?
remember: elephants have excellent memories,
are led by the oldest female,
are loyal only to their own,
live a long time & may be on the verge of extinction. sadly
some fuchsia elephants survive only by submitting
to the depleting demands of the circus circuit.
fuchsia elephants certainly cannot blend into the chicken crowd.

LOOKING AHEAD

In a couple of years I will be fifty. I am still recovering from debts incurred by being a student for so long. I have no savings, am always maxed out on my credit cards and have never been on a non-working "vacation." I don't own a car, despite having taught full-time for the last decade. Being an academic *costs* me more than I'd ever imagined (social work registration fees, books, computers and other technology, travel costs, professional association fees, teaching resources, wages to students to assist me with my work). I expect I will continue to have this extra work/income until I am fifty. At that point I hope to have only one job — and to be able to actually save for a retirement. I wonder if, when I am fifty-plus, I will be able to have a few more slow sweet Saturdays?

"A Slow Sweet Saturday"

the last stack of marking's submitted;
the semester's last meeting's concluded;
the last student defended her thesis yesterday by 4:00;
everyone under the sun's been thanked ...
this morning i woke at 10ish
ate a slow interesting breakfast
napped
dressed in snuggly rags
walked in the sun to the gym
where i stretched it enough to feel
my muscles-veins-bones-mind flow again
walked in the sun to my favorite coffee spot
read newspapers slowly

ate two muffins slowly
drank two coffees slowly
walked in the sun

slowly
changed into a thin
curvey black dress, midnight-sun rhinestones
woke my re-youthed soul
went to a poetry reading
for a significant cause
where i was thanked by the sons & daughters
of many goddesses

& the last hours of this first day
of summer semester
are slowly preparing me
for a beautiful dream tonight ...
& thankfully tomorrow, being Sunday,
might last longer, be even slower still
& sweeter

Some days I know that I am one of the luckiest people in the whole world. I love my jobs and I know that this path is the one I was meant to be on. I feel fortunate to have found a medium (creative writing/performing) that acts as an adhesive among all the parts and portions of my life. OISE helped me feel that I had a "national culture" as a member of the working poor/as an abused woman/as a female trying to claim and share knowledge in a patriarchal, capitalist world. Graveline (1998), a First Nations feminist scholar and activist social worker, says this about knowledge and "national culture":

> Cultural knowledge is an essential component of cultural resistance. Language and, in particular, the practice of a "national culture" are central to resisting cultural hegemony. Slogans, pamphlets, newspapers, stories, poetry and drama organize and sustain communal memory. (41)

I'm honoured and delighted that I can participate in making and disseminating "feminist white bush trash academic social justice activism" and "cultural products and artifacts." Baines (2003), another feminist social worker/social justice activist and scholar, says this:

The challenge for left-of-centre social workers and others concerned with justice-directed social work practice is to develop, teach, and practice social work in a way that reflects race, class, and gender as a dynamic, contestatory but seamless whole that simultaneously resonates with the actual, depoliticizing, backlash conditions in which social workers and their clients work and struggle.(46)

I continue to pass that formula on to my students and the social justice activists I connect with in the community. I do the best I can every day to find the fuchsia elephants and the wannabe fuchsia elephants and celebrate our existence — in spite of the barriers and challenges.

NOTES

1 The vast majority of the courses I've taught have been in social work, and in this essay I am mostly speaking to my experiences as a social work professor and activist/practitioner. In the last two years I have also been teaching some women's studies overload courses.

2 I especially want to thank Dr. Sandra Acker, Dr. Margrit Eichler, Dr. Roxana Ng and Dr. Lana Stermac for the support they gave me as committee members, supervisors and courageous role models. In the decade since I graduated from OISE I have had the privilege of attending conferences and reading emails from these academics and have continued to feel connected to them and their intellectual concerns.

REFERENCES

Addams, J. (1910). *Twenty years at Hull House*. New York: Macmillan.

Baines, D. (2003). Race, class, and gender in the everyday talk of social workers: The ways we limit the possibilities for radical practice. In W. Shera (Ed.), *Emerging perspectives in anti-oppressive practice* (43–64). Toronto: Canadian Scholars' Press.

Banks, A. (1998). The struggle over facts and fiction. In A. Banks & S. Banks (Eds.), *Fiction and social research: By fire or ice* (167–178). London: AltaMira Press.

Denzin, N. (2003). *Performance ethnography: Critical pedagogy and the politics of culture*. Thousand Oaks, CA: Sage.

Graveline, F.J. (1998). *Circle works: Transforming Eurocentric consciousness*. Halifax: Fernwood.

Hall, S. (1996). Cultural studies and its theoretical legacies. In D. Morley and K.H. Chen (Eds.), *Stuart Hall: Critical dialogues in cultural studies* (262–275). London: Routledge.

Smith, D. (2006). *Institutional ethnography: A sociology for people*. Oxford, UK: AltaMira Press.

Transken, S. (1995). Reclaiming body territory. *Feminist Perspectives, 25,* 1–35.

Turner, L.M. (1999). Creativity: An overview and framework for the social work practitioner. *Canadian Social Work, 1*(1), 91–97.

CONTRIBUTORS' NOTES

SANDRA ACKER, Professor in the Department of Sociology and Equity Studies in Education, University of Toronto, is a sociologist of education with interests in gender and education, teachers' work and higher education. She has worked in the United States, Britain and Canada. Her book publications include *Gendered Education* and *The Realities of Teachers' Work: Never a Dull Moment;* her book chapters include "Women Working in Academe" (with Michelle Webber) in *The SAGE Handbook of Gender and Education;* and recent journal articles include "Sleepless in Academia" (with C. Armenti) and "Women 'Learning to Labour' in the 'Male Emporium'" (with J-A. Dillabough), both in *Gender and Education*. She is currently conducting research on university tenure practices, doctoral student experiences and women academics in leadership positions.

CYNDY BASKIN is of Mi'kmaq and Irish descent. She is originally from New Brunswick and has been living in Toronto for many years. She is currently an Associate Professor in the School of Social Work at Ryerson University. Her teaching and research interests involve working with Aboriginal communities, especially on how Aboriginal world views can inform social work education, Indigenous knowledges, spirituality in social work practice, anti-racist inclusive schooling, anti-oppressive theories and practices, and decolonizing research methodologies. Cyndy is a mom, a step-grandmother and an active member of Toronto's Aboriginal community. Her research interests focus on projects with Indigenous peoples and communities in areas such as structural determinants of health, child welfare, the racialization of poverty, education, food security and youth wellness. Her work has been published as both book chapters and in peer reviewed journals, including *Critical Social Work; Social Work Review; Australian Journal of Education; Journal of Ethics in Mental Health; Native Social Work;* and *Journal of Native Education*.

SUSAN FERGUSON is a graduate student in the Department of Sociology and Equity Studies in Education and is also a member of the Graduate Collaborative Program in Women and Gender Studies, University of Toronto. Working at the intersections of disability studies, feminist theory and anti-racism,

Susan's research interests include the cultural work of pain narratives, decolonizing methodologies and the politics of health and healing. Susan is committed to bringing embodied pedagogical practices into her teaching, scholarship and community work and is currently developing an embodied writing praxis through her thesis research.

JACQUELINE LIMOGES is a nursing faculty member in the collaborative B.Sc.N. program at Georgian College in Barrie, Ontario. Her research focuses on exploring power relations and circulating discourses in nursing education and nurses' work. Her PhD thesis showed how political and ideological texts and discourses, such as professionalism, caring and managerialism, have supported class and gender inequities for decades. Her current project uses discourse analysis to reveal how high-fidelity patient-simulated learning contributes to nursing education. Previous projects have explored how faculty and nursing students learn to engage therapeutically with patients. These research projects show how historical and contemporary discourses construct, subjugate and regulate nurses, their work and their resistance.

MARIA ATHINA (TINA) MARTIMIANAKIS is a PhD candidate in the Department of Theory and Policy Studies at the Ontario Institute for Studies in Education, University of Toronto, and a Fellow of the Department of Psychiatry and the Wilson Centre for Research in Education. Tina's area of research is the politics and sociology of knowledge production with a particular emphasis on faculty relations. She is studying the impact of socio-economic priorities on institutional restructuring with a focus on power relations that manifest systemically and are reproduced within and between disciplines. She is researching interdisciplinarity as a process of knowledge production and exploring the impact of related governance arrangements on faculty experiences. In the context of health professional education, Tina is also studying how medical researchers who are not doctors interface with clinical teachers and exploring ways to use faculty development for improving the integration of science into clinical teaching.

WAYNE MARTINO is an Associate Professor in the Faculty of Education at the University of Western Ontario. His research focuses on addressing issues of gender justice, masculinities and anti-oppressive education. His book publications include *So What's a Boy? Addressing issues of masculinity and schooling* (with Maria Pallotta-Chiarolli); *"Being Normal Is the Only Way To Be": Adolescent Perspectives on Gender and School* (with Maria Pallotta-Chiarolli) and *Gendered Outcasts and Sexual Outlaws: Sexual Oppression and Gender Hierarchies in Queer Men's Lives* (with Chris Kendall). His most recent publications are *Boys and Schooling: Beyond Structural Reform* (with Martin Mills and Bob Lingard) and

The Problem with Boys' Education: Beyond the Backlash. He is currently working on a SSHRC funded research project (with Goli Rezai-Rashti) entitled "The Influence of Male Elementary School Teachers as Role Models."

KIMINE MAYUZUMI is a PhD candidate in the Department of Sociology and Equity Studies in Education, University of Toronto. She is also part of the graduate collaborative program in Women and Gender Studies at University of Toronto. Her research interests are in women in higher education, transnational feminist theory and Indigenous knowledges. She is currently working on her dissertation on Asian women faculty in the Canadian academy. Her journal articles include "The Tea Ceremony as a Decolonizing Epistemology: Healing and Japanese Women," *Journal of Transformative Education;* "Transforming Diversity in Canadian Higher Education: A Dialogue of Japanese Women Graduate Students," *Teaching in Higher Education;* and "'In-between' Asia and the West: Asian Women Faculty in the Transnational Context," *Race, Ethnicity and Education.*

DONNA A. MURRAY is an instructor at Ryerson University in the Communication and Design Department and also teaches a variety of Ontario Management Development Programs at the Sheridan Institute of Technology and Advanced Learning. Her recent area of research has focused on First Nations female educators in terms of their experiences as students and/or members of faculty in higher education. She has an ongoing interest in gender, race and equity issues that impact educational equality for all women in higher education.

LINDA MUZZIN is an Associate Professor in the Higher Education program at the Ontario Institute for Studies in Education, University of Toronto, where she teaches courses on professional education, faculty, social science and feminist theory and research methods. Her research has focused on professionals and professional education, including physicians, pharmacists, and more recently, scientists and professors. In 2005, she co-edited a collection on feminist science, environmental and social issues and Indigenous knowledges entitled *Teaching as Activism: Equity Meets Environmentalism.* Her most recent book chapter is "How Fares Equity in This Era of Academic Capitalism? The Role of Contingent Faculty" in *The Exchange University.* She is co-researcher (with Diane Meaghan) on a national study of equity and faculty in community colleges.

ANN-KRISTINE PEARSON has been a Graduate Student Liaison Officer for the Department of Sociology and Equity Studies in Education, University of Toronto, for seventeen years. A mother, grandmother and actress in her "other" life, she has a BA in English Literature, French Literature and Language and an MA in Drama from the University of Toronto.

RIYAD A. SHAHJAHAN is a Postdoctoral Fellow and Lecturer in the Social Justice Concentration, Department of Educational Leadership and Policy Studies at Iowa State University. His areas of research interests are in equity and diversity, spirituality and higher education, Indigenous knowledges and anti-colonial thought. He currently teaches courses on qualitative methodology, anti-colonial thought, social justice theory and critical pedagogy. His most recent journal publications include "In the Belly of Paradox: Teaching Equity in an [In]equitable Space," *International Journal of Progressive Education;* "Mapping the Field of Anti-colonial Discourse to Understand Issues of Indigenous Knowledges: Decolonizing Praxis," *McGill Journal of Education;* and "Spirituality in the Academy: Reclaiming from the Margins and Evoking a Transformative Way of Knowing the World," *International Journal of Qualitative Studies in Education.* He is currently helping Iowa State University develop a social justice program in higher education.

TANYA TITCHKOSKY is Assistant Professor in the Department of Sociology and Equity Studies in Education, University of Toronto. Tanya's teaching and research in disability studies is committed to an interpretive sociological approach, informed by feminist, queer, and critical race theory. Her most recent book, *Reading and Writing Disability Differently: The Textured Life of Embodiment* (2007), as well as her first book, *Disability, Self and Society* (2003), attempt to make social theory engage our bodies, minds, emotions and senses in new ways as well as resist the devaluing of difference. Tanya has recently published "To Pee or Not to Pee? Ordinary Talk about Extraordinary Exclusions in a University Environment" in the *Canadian Journal of Sociology.* This article is part of a larger book-length project entitled *Disability and the Question of Access.* Tanya's work is supported by a standard SSHRC grant, "Organizing Disablement: The University and Disability Experience."

SI TRANSKEN is the Acting Chair of the School of Social Work at University of Northern British Columbia. She's been teaching for over ten years and has been a social justice activist for almost thirty. Her doctorate is in Equity Studies from the Ontario Institute for Studies in Education, University of Toronto. Si's poetry and scholarly writing have been published in *Canadian Woman's Studies; Cultural Studies <—> Creative Methodology; The Capilano Review; Atlantis;* and *Rural Social Work Journal.* She is also the editor and a contributor to *This Ain't Your Patriarchs' Poetry Book; Homeless Clowns & Social Work with Victims of Abuse; Making Noise: In/Visible Dis/Abilities* and *Northern Women's Caring.* Although she's known as a cranky bitch feminist, her hiss isn't as bad as her bite.

ANNE WAGNER is an Assistant Professor in the Department of Sociology and cross-appointed to Child and Family Studies at Nipissing University. Her teaching and research interests include gender, race and (higher) education, critical pedagogies and violence against women. Her recent publications include articles in *Race, Ethnicity and Education; Gender and Education;* and *Journal of Thought: A Journal of Critical Reflection on Educational Issues.*

NJOKI NATHANI WANE is Associate Professor in the Department of Sociology and Equity Studies at the Ontario Institute for Studies in Education, University of Toronto. Her areas of interest are African and Black feminisms, Indigenous knowledges, African women and development, Black women and mothering, and anti-racist/anti-colonial studies. Her most recent publications include the co-edited volumes *Back to the Drawing Board: African-Canadian Feminisms, Equity in Schools and Society* and *Theorizing Empowerment: Canadian Perspectives on Black Feminist Thought.*

MICHELLE WEBBER is an Associate Professor at Brock University (St. Catharines, Ontario) in the Sociology Department. Her research focuses on higher education, the regulation of academic work and gender. Her published journal articles include "'I'm Not a Militant Feminist': Feminist Identities and Feminist Hesitations in the Contemporary Academy," *Atlantis;* "Transgressive Pedagogies? Exploring the Difficult Realities of Enacting Feminist Pedagogies in Undergraduate Classrooms in a Canadian University," *Studies in Higher Education;* "'Don't Be So Feminist': Exploring Student Resistance to Feminist Approaches in a Canadian University," *Women's Studies International Forum.*

PATRICE A. WHITE is an elementary school teacher with the York Region District School Board. She completed her undergraduate degrees and a Master of Education at York University, where she focused on the use of elder methodology (specifically storytelling) as a means of preserving, passing on and developing cultural memory and imagination. Patrice is currently completing her Doctor of Education at Ontario Institute of Studies in Education, University of Toronto. Her current research focuses on the social reproduction of teachers and the conditions that may lead to a marginalization of and identity crisis among teachers' children. While Patrice has been a presenter at two international conferences, "Hot Seat" in this volume is her first published chapter. Along with teaching, Patrice is an aspiring children's book illustrator who would like to continue to publish academic articles while maintaining a very active role in her school board's action research initiatives.